Accounting Ethics

26

Foundations of Business Ethics

Series editors: W. Michael Hoffman and Robert. E. Frederick

Written by an assembly of the most distinguished figures in business ethics, the Foundations of Business Ethics series aims to explain and assess the fundamental issues that motivate interest in each of the main subjects of contemporary research. In addition to a general introduction to business ethics, individual volumes cover key ethical issues in management, marketing, finance, accounting, and computing. The volumes, which are complementary yet complete in themselves, allow instructors maximum flexibility in the design and presentation of course materials without sacrificing either depth of coverage or the discipline-based focus of many business courses. The volumes can be used separately or in combination with anthologies and case studies, depending on the needs and interests of the instructors and students.

1   John R. Boatright: *Ethics in Finance*

2   Ronald F. Duska and Brenda Shay Duska: *Accounting Ethics*

3   Richard T. De George: *The Ethics of Information Technology and Business*

4   Patricia H. Werhane and Tara J. Radin with Norman E. Bowie: *Employment and Employee Rights*

5   Norman E. Bowie and Patricia H. Werhane: *Management Ethics*

Accounting Ethics

Ronald F. Duska PhD
Charles Lamont Post Chair of Ethics and the Professions
The American College

and

Brenda Shay Duska, CPA, MT
Vice-President of Finance and Administration
Rosemont College

Blackwell
Publishing

© 2003 by Ronald F. Duska and Brenda Shay Duska

BLACKWELL PUBLISHING
350 Main Street, Malden, MA 02148-5020, USA
108 Cowley Road, Oxford OX4 1JF, UK
550 Swanston Street, Carlton, Victoria 3053, Australia

First published 2003 by Blackwell Publishing Ltd
Reprinted 2003, 2004

Library of Congress Cataloging-in-Publication Data

Duska, Ronald F., 1937–
    Accounting ethics / Ronald F. Duska and Brenda Shay Duska.
        p. cm. – (Foundations of business ethics ; 2)
    ISBN 0-631-21650-2 (hardcover : alk. paper) – ISBN 0-631-21651-0 (pbk. : alk. paper)
        1. Accountants – Professional ethics. 2. Accounting – Moral and ethical aspects. I. Duska, Brenda Shay. II. Title. III. Series.
    HF5625.15 .D87 2003
    174'.9657 – dc21

                                                                                        2002004856

A catalogue record for this title is available from the British Library.

Set in 10.5/12.5 Plantin
by SetSystems Ltd, Saffron Walden, Essex
Printed and bound in the United Kingdom
by MPG Books Ltd, Bodmin, Cornwall

The publisher's policy is to use permanent paper from mills that operate a sustainable forestry policy, and which has been manufactured from pulp processed using acid-free and elementary chlorine-free practices. Furthermore, the publisher ensures that the text paper and cover board used have met acceptable environmental accreditation standards.

For further information on
Blackwell Publishing, visit our website:
http://www.blackwellpublishing.com

To:
Elizabeth Catherine Duska
and
Catherine Shay

A daughter and mother who put up with tax seasons and manuscript deadlines, and whose Irish eyes and smiles bring joy and love to our lives without ever holding us to account for the cost to them of our writing this book.

Contents

Preface

The manuscript for this book had been sent to Blackwell in early November of 2001, just before the Enron collapse had begun to dominate the front pages of newspapers and lead stories of television news shows across America. Yet most of the problems that came to light with an accounting profession in crisis had been documented in the text. The types of problems that the Enron bankruptcy brought to the fore were nothing new. They had been talked about for years, especially in a particularly prescient book by Abraham Briloff, *The Truth About Corporate Accounting*, published in 1980 by Harper and Row. Dr. Briloff was at the time the Emanuel Saxe Distinguished Professor of Accountancy at the Baruch College of the City University of New York.

Briloff's critique of the accounting profession helped us gain a focus on the important and salient issues in the ethics of accounting. Following Briloff's lead, our manuscript detailed the chief ethical difficulties facing the accounting profession, and included the words "The Accounting Profession in Crisis" in the title of chapter 10, a phrase not horribly original, but extraordinarily apt given the high profile case of Enron and Arthur Andersen.

Subsequent to the breaking story of the Enron scandal, we asked the publishers for some time to revise the manuscript to take into account the difficulties in accounting practices that helped contribute to Enron's demise. Consequently there are references in the text to this most recent, but regrettably not the last, case of accounting irregularities. After Enron came WorldCom and the Sarbanes Oxley legislation.

To keep the book as current as possible and to aid the reader in sorting out the facts of Enron's collapse and Andersen's role in that collapse, we are appending a chronology of stories run in the *Wall Street Journal* and provided in the *Journal*'s online edition, beginning

October 2001 and continuing up to August 2002. The articles are available from the *Wall Street Journal* Archives. Enron and Andersen would make a fruitful case study for most of the problems in accounting ethics. We are also appending a short chronology of the WorldCom collapse as well as a portion of the SEC complaint against the company, which clearly specifies WorldCom's unacceptable practice of capitalizing expenses. Other scandals are likely to occur, but one must write a finish to one's work at some point. The hope, however, is that the scandals of the future will be lesser ones and that the accounting firms will have learned from the Enrons and WorldComs of the world.

Acknowledgments

When Mike Hoffman and Bob Frederick first suggested a book on accounting ethics the names of all the people more qualified came to mind. However, what better challenge for a business ethicist than to tackle the field his wife dealt with in her day-to-day work, and who better to work with than an accountant with integrity who has no time for cutting corners? Against the advice of those who counseled against spouses writing a book together, we plunged in where angels fear to tread. It has been a fruitful opportunity for both of us to learn more and more about the other's enterprises. So we are grateful to both Mike and Bob for the opportunity, and trust the endeavor has provided worthwhile fruit.

We would also like to thank Beth Remmes for her constant attention, not to mention gentle prodding, which helped us get on with the work when the tedium got the better of us, and Paul Stringer for his thorough, tireless, and penetrating help in editing the manuscript after its initial completion, always performed with remarkable insight, a relaxing style and a wonderful sense of humor. Thanks also to our colleagues and friends Patricia Werhane, Norman Bowie, Tom Dunfee, and Jim Mitchell for their input and encouragement during the preparation of this book. They should not in any way be held accountable for the shortcomings of this book. Gratitude is also called for toward the American College, Sam Weese, its president, and Gary Stone and Walt Woerheide, who enabled time for the completion of this text. Thanks are also due to Charlene McNulty who assisted in the production of the manuscript. Finally, we are grateful to Jack Del Pizzo, CPA, of Del Pizzo & Associates, PC, for his insights, encouragement, and general knowledge of accounting practices, which he was happy to share during the writing of this book.

Enron, Arthur Andersen, and the Financial Markets: A Chronology of Wall Street Journal Articles

OCTOBER 2001

Oct. 16: Enron takes $1.01 billion charge related to write-downs of investments. Of this, $35 million is attributed to partnerships until recently run by CFO Andrew Fastow.
• Enron discloses it shrank shareholder equity by $1.2 billion, as a result of several transactions including ones undertaken with Mr. Fastow's investment vehicle.

Oct. 19: The *Wall Street Journal* reports that general partners of Fastow partnerships realized more than $7 million last year in management fees and about $4 million in capital increases on an investment of nearly $3 million in the partnerships, set up principally to do business with Enron.

Oct. 23: Enron's treasurer acknowledges the company may have to issue additional shares to cover potential shortfalls in investment vehicles it created, although he says the company believes it can repay about $3.3 billion in notes that were sold by those investment vehicles without having to resort to issuing more stock.

Oct. 24: Enron replaces Andrew Fastow as chief financial officer with Jeffrey McMahon, the 40-year-old head of the company's industrial-markets division.

Oct. 25: Enron draws down about $3 billion, the bulk of its available bank credit lines. The Fitch rating agency puts Enron on review for a possible downgrade, while another, Standard & Poor's, changes Enron's credit outlook to "negative" from "stable." A noninvestment-grade rating would throw the company into default on obligations involving billions of dollars of borrowings.

Oct. 29: Moody's Investors Service lowers its ratings by one notch on Enron's senior unsecured debt and kept the company under review for a possible further downgrade.

Oct. 31: The SEC elevates to a formal investigation its inquiry into Enron's financial dealings.

▲ NOVEMBER 2001 ▲

Nov. 1: Enron says it has secured commitments for $1 billion in financing from units of J.P. Morgan and Citigroup.

Nov. 5: Enron has held talks with private-equity firms and power-trading companies for a capital infusion of at least $2 billion as it faces an escalating fiscal crisis.

Nov. 8: Enron reduces its previously reported net income dating back to 1997 by $586 million, or 20%, mostly due to *improperly accounting* for its dealings with the partnerships run by some company officers.

Nov. 20: Enron warns that continuing credit worries, a decline in the value of some of its assets and reduced trading activity could hurt its fourth-quarter earnings.

Nov. 28: Standard & Poor's lowers Enron's credit rating to "junk" status.
• Energy trading is sent reeling as EnronOnline is shut down.
• Mutual funds may get hit by Enron's meltdown.

Nov. 30: The *Wall Street Journal* reports that the Securities and Exchange Commission is investigating the actions of Arthur Andersen, Enron's auditor.
• Federal prosecutors in New York and Texas want to monitor the SEC's investigation into possible accounting fraud at Enron.

▲ DECEMBER 2001 ▲

Dec. 2: Enron files for protection from creditors in a New York bankruptcy court, the biggest such filing in U.S. history.

Dec. 3: Enron secures almost $1.5 billion in debtor-in-possession financing and presses negotiations for an additional lifeline for its energy-trading operations.

Dec. 4: The collapse of talks between Enron and Dynegy has raised a potential conflict in the negotiations involving Lehman Bros.
• Enron's highly questionable financial engineering, misstated earnings and persistent efforts to keep investors in the dark were behind its collapse.

Dec. 5: Enron's bonds climb as "vulture" investors scooped up Enron's bonds and bank loans, sensing a bargain.
• Dynegy, seeking to reassure investors about its financial health, says its short-term borrowings of nearly $1 billion over the past week aren't related to its failed attempt to acquire Enron.

Dec. 6: Bankruptcy court proceedings start to take shape; U.S. Bankruptcy Judge Arthur Gonzalez, who will hear the Enron case, is known as a stickler for detail.

Dec. 9: Citigroup and UBS work to finalize separate bids to take over Enron's trading operations, the first step toward a potential bankruptcy-court auction for the flagship business.

Dec. 12: Enron unveils a one-year plan to restructure its way out of trouble, including a reorganization around its core businesses.

Dec. 13: Questions arise about Enron's outside auditor, Arthur Andersen, which did double-duty work for the company.

Dec. 14: Moody's Investors Service downgrades its credit ratings of Calpine and Dynegy unit Dynegy Holdings. Following Enron's collapse, Moody's stressed the risks posed by high leverage and reduced access to capital markets.

Dec. 17: Volumes surge at several major online-trading firms amid heavy trading in Enron shares as the company lurched toward bankruptcy.

Dec. 18: Credit agencies crack down on power companies, warning them to slash debt, after falling asleep when California's deregulated energy market imploded and reacting slowly to Enron's demise.

Dec. 20: Citigroup is close to cementing a bid for most of Enron's flagship energy-trading operations.

Dec. 30: Enron asks the judge overseeing its bankruptcy case to approve the sale of assets worth several hundred million dollars by the end of the year.

Dec. 31: J.P. Morgan Chase files a motion to quash demands from nine insurance companies for information about $2 billion in Enron-related surety bonds, a sign that the interests of various creditors of the now-bankrupt energy trader have begun to collide.
- U.K. companies saddled with losses from Enron's collapse have seen their credit ratings downgraded.

JANUARY 2002

Jan. 2: Internal Enron documents show top management and directors viewed controversial partnerships as integral to maintaining its rapid growth in recent years.

Jan. 7: To shore up investor confidence in financial reporting following the collapse of Enron, the Big Five accounting firms ask the SEC to quickly issue guidance to improve disclosure in corporate annual reports.

Jan. 10: Arthur Andersen discloses that individuals at the accounting firm disposed of "a significant but undetermined number" of documents related to its work for Enron.
- Chief Executive Joseph Berardino gave what now appears to be inaccurate information in testimony to Congress in December 2001.
- Enron and its creditors negotiate to coax the highest possible offer for parts of the company's once-powerful wholesale trading unit.

Jan. 14: Some of the world's leading banks and brokerage firms come under scrutiny for providing Enron with help in creating the intricate – and, in crucial ways, misleading – financial structure.
- Jeffrey Skilling, who resigned as chief executive of Enron in mid-August, made a speculative stock-market bet against an Enron rival, selling short a large chunk of shares of AES Corp., an energy producer.

• Enron's collapse, and the failure of auditors to detect questionable bookkeeping, puts the spotlight on the accounting industry's peculiar self-policing system.

• Joseph Berardino, who has been at the helm of Arthur Andersen for a year, faces a period that is even more threatening to its future than the breakup of the company.

• A House committee seeks information about an Arthur Andersen memo, which committee aides believe advised the firm's Enron audit team to abide by an Andersen policy to destroy electronic and paper documents relating to audits.

Jan. 15: A newly discovered letter written by an Enron employee last summer warned the company's chairman about its accounting practices and prompted an internal investigation.

• Enron pleas for federal assistance to stave off collapse.

Jan. 16: An August 2001 letter from an Enron executive raises serious questions about the company's business and accounting practices, highlighting a growing struggle that had been going on inside the company for more than a year.

• A venerable and politically connected law firm advised Enron officials not to worry about the company employee's warnings of questionable accounting.

• Arthur Andersen fires a partner it charged with directing the destruction of thousands of e-mails and paper documents related to its Enron audit, declaring that he acted after learning that federal regulators were probing the energy giant's finances.

• The New York Stock Exchange suspends trading in Enron and moves to delist the energy company's shares from the Big Board.

• Investigators look into the practice of "locking down" employee retirement-savings plans to make administrative changes. A lockdown by Enron prevented employees from moving out of Enron stock as its price continued to plummet.

• Citigroup's October decision to change its Enron debt from unsecured to secured is now sparking an outcry.

Jan. 18: The SEC says it didn't do a thorough review of Enron's annual reports for at least three years prior to its collapse.

• SEC Chairman Harvey Pitt proposes a new body that would have broad-reaching power over discipline and quality control of accounting firms.

• Enron's board fires longtime auditor Arthur Andersen, but

Andersen said the relationship ended when Enron's business failed and it went into bankruptcy.
• The recent wave of disclosures about the big accounting firm's role at Enron has made some Andersen partners anxious about their careers.

Jan. 21: Some question whether ties between Enron and Arthur Andersen were too cozy.
• Investigators sift through the complex financial structures of Enron's partnerships, which hid hundreds of millions of dollars of losses and debt from public view.
• New York law firm Weil, Gotshal & Manges is Enron's main bankruptcy counsel, but Arthur Andersen, another Weil Gotshal client, is rapidly turning into one of Enron's biggest adversaries.
• Accenture, which insists it has no connection to Arthur Andersen's problems, may have legal exposure to its parent's role in the collapse of energy trader Enron.
• The SEC comes under heat in Congress for a 1993 decision freeing units of Enron from complying with a utility holding company law that would have given regulators stronger oversight of the company's operations.

Jan. 23: The Arthur Andersen executive fired for destroying Enron documents has told a House committee through counsel that he may invoke his Fifth Amendment right against potential self-incrimination to avoid testifying at a hearing.
• The complexity of corporate accounting – and how it has changed – has become painfully clear in the collapse of Enron. A special package explores how financial statements from General Electric, AIG, Williams, IBM, and Coca-Cola can often be difficult for investors to interpret.
• With Enron in the spotlight, the long look back at accounting mishaps looks more disconcerting.
• The accounting industry's Public Oversight Board, which oversees auditors' "peer review" method of self-regulation, unexpectedly voted itself out of existence to protest SEC Chairman Harvey Pitt's plans to devise replacement body to monitor the industry.
• In Texas, the State Board of Public Accountancy has opened an inquiry to determine whether "possible misdeeds, omissions or malfeasance" took place in Enron's accounting practices, and other state boards may follow suit.

Jan. 24: Kenneth L. Lay resigned as chairman and chief executive

of Enron, less than 24 hours after the court-appointed creditors committee requested his removal.
• Enron's chief auditor at Arthur Andersen warned the energy-trading giant against putting "misleading" information in a news release about third-quarter earnings last October.

Jan. 25: Arthur Andersen analysts determined during the fall that there was significantly "heightened risk of financial-statement fraud" at Enron, a newly released document shows.
• Off-balance-sheet partnerships – those sometimes debt-laden entities through which companies can do business while keeping financial obligations off their books – are getting more scrutiny from individual investors.
• A number of institutional investors – with Enron's rapid collapse in mind – are calling for companies to adopt "conflict of interest policies" that would prevent their accounting firm from providing anything beyond auditing services.
• Accounting failures that helped precipitate the collapse of Enron have made reform of accounting-industry oversight the biggest issue immediately facing the Securities and Exchange Commission. But President Bush's plan for a Securities and Exchange Commission dominated by commissioners with close ties to the accounting industry is raising concerns in Congress.
• Outraged lawmakers are pointing fingers about bad accounting, but they shoulder some of the blame: Congress, including some of Enron's most vocal critics there, routinely opposed significant new accounting rules over the past decade.

Jan. 28: Police investigators in Sugar Land, Texas, said they are continuing their investigation into the death of former Enron Vice Chairman J. Clifford Baxter. Mr. Baxter had been engaged in the difficult task of trying to sell off assets as the company's finances started to take a turn for the worse.

Jan. 29: Enron's collapse has Congress taking its finger off the deregulation button, as members suddenly queue up to push for new controls on the financial community.
• When Harvey Pitt became Securities and Exchange Commission chairman in August, the SEC staff stopped work on a lengthy report detailing what it concluded were severe shortcomings in how the accounting industry regulates itself.
• Delta Air Lines is struggling with whether to end its long-time

ties to Arthur Andersen and has begun a search for a new independent auditor.

Jan. 30: The smoldering corporate accounting scandal, which started with Enron and quickly spread to Arthur Andersen, reached a wide group of U.S. companies and seriously singed their stock prices. Accounting problems surfaced at companies ranging from banking to oil, prompting fears of new mini-Enrons and spurring a sell-off of shares at the slightest whiff of such trouble.
• Global Crossing's accounting practices are drawing more interest in the wake of Enron's accounting scandal, and concerns about how telecom companies report their results continue to mount. Arthur Andersen, which audited Enron's books, also audited Global Crossing and a number of other emerging telecom carriers.
• Enron named Stephen Cooper, a principal at New York restructuring firm Zolfo Cooper, as acting chief executive officer, succeeding Kenneth Lay, who resigned from the embattled energy concern last week.

Jan. 31: Enron's acting chief executive Stephen Cooper said he believes that the troubled energy company is salvageable, and he pledged to move "at light speed" to get it out of bankruptcy court.
• Four employees who were important figures in Bank of America's relationship with Enron, which triggered huge losses for the bank when Enron collapsed, have left the company.

FEBRUARY 2002

Feb. 1: Amid finger-pointing at top management and the company's outside auditors at Arthur Andersen, Enron's audit committee is under harsh scrutiny from a slew of civil, criminal and congressional investigations of the company's board of directors.
• Citigroup lent money to Enron in October, when the energy company's finances were sliding. At the same time, the Wall Street giant pitched Enron bonds to clients as a solid investment. Now, at least one institutional investor who bought the bonds is hopping mad has taken a complaint to court.
• More details are emerging about how the company got into such a mess. On Nov. 5, 1997, the top echelon of Enron assembled for a meeting where its now-infamous outside partnership arrangements

took a turn from the straightforward and mundane to the deceptive and possibly illegal.
• Earlier this week, Linda P. Lay, the wife of former Enron Chairman Kenneth L. Lay, told a national television audience that nearly everything the couple owns is for sale as they struggle with a personal financial crisis. But few of the couple's vast real-estate holdings are on the market, according to Multiple Listing Service records.

Feb. 4: Enron's rise and fall mirrors the collapse of Middle West Utilities seven decades ago.
• Goldman Sachs invented a security in 1993 that offered Enron and other companies an irresistible combination. The security was designed in such a way that it could be called debt or equity, as needed. For the tax man, it resembled a loan, so that interest payments could be deducted from taxable income. For shareholders and rating agencies, who look askance at overleveraged companies, it resembled equity.
• Looking to bolster its damaged image, Arthur Andersen said it has retained former Federal Reserve Board Chairman Paul Volcker to lead an outside panel that will guide Andersen in making "fundamental change" in the accounting firm's audit practice.

Feb. 5: Lawmakers say they will issue a subpoena to compel Kenneth Lay, former chairman of Enron, to appear before committees investigating the collapse of the Houston energy trading giant. Mr. Lay also announced his resignation from the Enron board.
• Enron's board is expected to put the company's two top accounting officers on administrative leave this week in reaction to an internal report that says neither did his job adequately, sources close to the matter say.
• Legal liability in the Enron debacle could depend, in part, on who knew about an innocuous-looking, two-page memorandum dated Dec. 30, 1997, involving one of the now-controversial outside partnerships run by company executives.

Feb. 6: Enron executives tried to get one of the company's in-house lawyers fired in 2000 after their boss expressed unhappiness with the way the lawyer was negotiating with a partnership in which the boss had an interest, congressional investigators said.
• With the accounting profession facing a credibility crisis, a wide array of critics – from members of Congress to small investors to

officials of the big accounting firms – have begun calling for a major overhaul of the system.
• After first pulling down stock prices, Enron accounting worries are now unnerving the bond market, as well.

Feb. 7: The gold market has begun to confirm what analysts have been whispering for weeks: The "Enron effect" is rivaling, or even surpassing, September's terrorist attacks in its ability to scare the public into more conservative investments.
• Within two months of assuming his job as general counsel at Enron's global-finance unit in October 2000, Jordan Mintz began raising questions about procedures used in approving executive-run partnerships.
• Enron's quest to avoid taxes by using offshore tax havens took the company to some unlikely places, including Holland, which embraces its citizens with a cradle-to-grave welfare state and takes half their salaries in taxes to pay for it.
• Kenneth Lay, the former chairman of Enron, is cutting back on his commitments of time to nonprofit organizations, some of which are worried he will cut back on his financial commitments, as well.

Feb. 8: A company run by one of Enron's outside directors and biggest shareholders indirectly supplied money used to fund a 1997 partnership that eventually helped lead to Enron's collapse.
• The official unsecured creditors committee of Enron rebuffed a recommendation by the company's advisers to immediately file suit against Arthur Andersen, former Enron Chief Financial Officer Andrew Fastow, and other individuals whose relationships with Enron have come under attack.

Feb. 11: Mr. Cooper, the restructuring specialist hired as Enron's acting chief executive, said he believes it possible to salvage a smaller but stable company from the turmoil now swirling around the energy concern.

Feb. 12: An internal Enron document indicates for the first time that Mr. Lay had a direct role approving deals with at least one of the company's controversial executive-run partnerships.
• The possibility of criminal charges against senior Enron executives is already being raised by lawmakers investigating the company's collapse. Mr. Lay, Enron's just-departed chairman, has announced he will invoke his Fifth Amendment right against self-incrimination at a Senate hearing Tuesday.

Feb. 13: Enron announced the planned resignations of six board members, including four who served on its highly criticized audit committee. Simultaneously, Enron dropped its request to employ its longtime outside counsel, Vinson & Elkins, as special counsel to the bankruptcy proceedings.

• Remarks by Mr. Lay to a special internal investigative committee in January indicate that on at least two occasions he may have deliberately misled the public in order to keep the energy giant's problems from becoming known.

Feb. 14: Ms. Watkins, who warned Enron's chief executive in August that the company might be swamped by an accounting scandal, later urged him to contain the damage by restating earnings by pleading ignorance, a strategy he eventually employed, newly released documents show.

• Enron's interest in expanding its political influence extended to a little-known group that sets international accounting standards.

Feb. 15: When numerous Enron directors finish leaving the board-room, Raymond S. Troubh may be the only director left. Earlier in the week, the Enron board picked Mr. Troubh to run a restructuring committee that is overseeing efforts to reorganize the company following its Dec. 2 bankruptcy filing.

• Enron executive Sherron Watkins told a House subcommittee that the collapsed energy trading company's corporate culture was "arrogant" and "intimidating," and discouraged employees from blowing the whistle on partnerships used to conceal debt and enrich executives.

Feb. 19: For years, Enron disclosed little information about the outside partnerships that would eventually contribute to the company's collapse. But an allusion to one of the most controversial and secretive of those partnerships in Enron's 1999 annual report could be a liability-filled time bomb for former top officials.

• Between February and October of last year, Mr. Lay sold $70.1 million of stock back to the company, conducting transactions even as the Houston energy giant's shares were in free fall and he was exhorting employees to stand by the company.

Feb. 20: Top former Enron executives were personally involved in stage-managing a fake trading room to impress analysts, an episode employees jokingly referred to as "The Sting." Former employees said secretaries and other staff who in 1998 once posed as busy energy traders in an unused trading room were part of a more elaborate charade.

• Amid heightened investor awareness about what executives and directors are doing with their own company shares, hedging maneuvers often are off the radar screens of shareholders. Yet experts say that hedging strategies designed to limit an individual's downside risk in stock are becoming increasingly common.

• In an internal company interview last August, former Enron CFO Andrew Fastow strongly defended his role in controversial outside partnerships, saying they were good for the company and blaming criticism about them on a rival's efforts to get his job.

Feb. 21: Arthur Andersen has begun the arduous task of trying to negotiate a universal settlement with Enron's angry shareholders, creditors, and employees, extending an offer of between $700 million and $800 million in a meeting with Enron's creditors committee.

Feb. 22: The Federal Reserve Bank of New York is examining J.P. Morgan Chase's accounting for commodity-related trades with Enron.

Feb. 25: Thirty-three states are asking a bankruptcy court to block Enron executives from securing millions of dollars from the company for their legal defense.

Feb. 26: The cozy relationship between Enron and its former auditor Arthur Andersen developed more than a decade ago. Arthur Andersen came to view the energy company as a key building block in its effort to expand a nascent business of providing internal-auditing services along with its traditional external-auditing function.

Feb. 27: Investors in an Enron-backed community-development fund run by Mark Lay, Mr. Lay's son, are raising concerns over potential fund mismanagement last year, and asking that their money be returned.

• There are two new members of the team studying the practices at Arthur Andersen.

Feb. 28: Facing scrutiny from the Internal Revenue Service, Enron is considering using a temporary government amnesty program to seek relief from potential tax-shelter penalties.

• The nation's accounting standards board is speeding up its timetable slightly on enacting new, stricter rules governing when companies are allowed to keep affiliates and their debt off their financial statements.

▲ MARCH 2002 ▲

March 1: The SEC is pushing plaintiffs to agree to a broad settlement of all their claims against Arthur Andersen related to its role in the Enron scandal. But it is unlikely that will happen anytime soon.
• A federal judge will allow Enron's creditors committee extensive latitude in probing document destruction at Arthur Andersen, and in determining whether a law firm held any responsibility for the auditor's actions.

March 4: Merck & Co. sacked its auditor, Arthur Andersen, in a harsh blow to the accounting concern already reeling from client defections amid questions about its role in Enron's collapse.
• Arthur Andersen agreed to pay $217 million to settle all pending litigation related to its audits of the Baptist Foundation of Arizona, whose 1999 collapse led to the largest Chapter 11 bankruptcy filing by a nonprofit organization in US history and cost investors nearly $600 million.
• The major accounting firms and their trade group have made a break with Arthur Andersen to aid the industry's fight against mounting legislative proposals to revamp the auditing business.
• For several years, Enron lobbied unsuccessfully to be allowed to postpone paying U.S. taxes on some overseas profit, including income from its derivatives deals, according to newly disclosed documents.

March 6: It may be only weeks before the Securities and Exchange Commission rolls out proposals that stand to dramatically change corporate America's disclosure practices. A plan to accelerate quarterly and yearly filings was likely be the first out of the gate.

March 7: Senate investigators signed an agreement with Enron's lawyers to open up the company's tax returns, but the company left itself some loopholes.
• Freddie Mac sacked Arthur Andersen as its auditor in yet another sign that the accounting firm's client base is continuing to erode.

March 8: Federal prosecutors warned Arthur Andersen they may seek to indict the firm for alleged obstruction of justice related to its accounting work for Enron, people close to the case said.
• Delta Air Lines, ending a 53-year relationship with Arthur Ander-

sen LLP, is dropping the embattled accounting firm as its auditor, awarding that business instead to Deloitte & Touche.

March 11: Arthur Andersen pursues high-stakes rescue plans on two fronts: trying to interest another accounting firm in buying some or all of Arthur Andersen, and negotiating with federal prosecutors threatening to indict the firm.

March 12: FedEx will drop Arthur Andersen as its auditor, in another blow to the struggling accounting firm in the wake of questions about its role in Enron's collapse.
• In the latest sign of the speed with which events are forcing change at Arthur Andersen, Mr. Volcker rushed to announce a list of actions for the embattled accounting firm.
• Arthur Andersen, which has offered $750 million to settle Enron-related lawsuits, has as much as $160 million of insurance from outside insurance companies that it could tap to help it pay any settlement related to its audits of collapsed Enron.
• The cover of Arthur Andersen's 2000 "highlights report" speaks volumes about how the accounting firm has evolved. Nowhere in the flashy report is there an image of an accountant poring over a ledger.

March 13: Arthur Andersen worked unsuccessfully to forge a settlement with the Justice Department, racing against a deadline to resolve possible criminal charges.
• As federal prosecutors threaten possible obstruction-of-justice charges against Arthur Andersen, two of the firm's employees said they believed they were following company policy when they destroyed Enron-related documents in Houston last fall.
• Still pending against Arthur Andersen is a lawsuit filed last year in US District Court in Phoenix by Boston Chicken's bankruptcy trustee, alleging that Arthur Andersen helped Boston Chicken create "a facade of corporate solvency" by hiding its franchisees' losses.

March 14: Since the crisis involving the collapse of Enron began, every strategy Arthur Andersen has tried to calm its clients, salvage its reputation and stay out of trouble with the government has had far from impressive results. Now, its problems appear to be growing by the day.
• Arthur Andersen's hopes for a merger dimmed considerably as the company faces a criminal indictment.
• Long before Arthur Andersen's document-shredding became headline news, accountants, the pinstriped paragons of rectitude and

respectability, found themselves coming under pressure from many directions to alter their centuries-old practices as their environment changed.

• Arthur Andersen's for-sale sign has represented a rare shot for accounting rivals to snap up valuable assets on the cheap. But no price may be cheap enough. Several Big Five accounting firms have been exploring potential deals with Arthur Andersen, despite the huge liability that the firm potentially faces from its relationship with collapsed Enron.

• The accounting industry's trade group told lawmakers to resist a rush to regulate and strongly objected to proposals to ban auditors from marketing consulting services and force public companies to rotate auditors periodically.

March 15: The Justice Department unsealed a criminal obstruction-of-justice indictment against Arthur Andersen that the Big Five accounting firm likened to the "death penalty" and said would be vigorously contested.

• In the 212-year history of the US financial markets, no major financial-services firm has ever survived a criminal indictment. Now, Arthur Andersen will either make history – or be history.

March 18: Nearly three years ago, a top Enron risk-management official began warning top executives of the improprieties of some of the company's off-balance-sheet partnerships.

March 19: After eight straight days of frantic negotiations, a team was preparing to announce a merger with Deloitte & Touche Tohmatsu that they hoped would rescue Arthur Andersen from collapse. But Deloitte announced the deal was dead because the legal risks were simply too great.

• Wyeth, which changed its name from American Home Products last week, said it has dropped the accounting firm as its auditor. That makes at least seven companies – including other prominent clients such as SaraLee – that have dumped Arthur Andersen since it was indicted on a charge of obstruction of justice.

• International partners of Arthur Andersen spent the weekend nervously considering their next steps, amid concerns that an indictment against their big US affiliate could have repercussions abroad.

• KPMG is moving closer to a deal to buy Arthur Andersen Worldwide's non-US business, the companies said in a joint statement.

• Thirteen Asia-Pacific affiliates of Arthur Andersen will back a

global merger with rival KPMG, executives from both companies said.
• New Jersey Attorney General David Samson wants Atlantic City casinos to stop doing business with Arthur Andersen because of the company's federal indictment.

March 20: The Securities and Exchange Commission announced plans to complete an outside review of Big Five accounting firms and ensure continuing oversight of the industry after March 31, when the current oversight board disbands.
• Adding to the chorus calling for reform of the accounting industry, an influential professional group of finance executives is throwing its weight behind some stiff measures for cleaning up auditing practices.
• With Arthur Andersen Worldwide's future uncertain, and efforts to sell parts of its business facing legal and regulatory problems, the accounting firm's US arm recently reduced by half the amount of money it is offering to reach a universal settlement with Enron's shareholders, unsecured creditors and employees.
• Managers of 13 Arthur Andersen accounting affiliates in Asia jointly endorsed a merger with KPMG, a potential marriage that would make Arthur Andersen's name disappear from the region.
• Talks between KPMG and Arthur Andersen Worldwide about a merger face legal and regulatory questions as well as other tough hurdles.
• Harrah's Entertainment is looking to replace Arthur Andersen as its auditor, and MGM Mirage is similarly weighing its options in the wake of a move by New Jersey's attorney general to block the embattled accounting company from auditing Atlantic City casinos.
• Arthur Andersen employees from the District of Columbia area are planning to rally at the Capitol Building, as part of a larger effort to have the indictment overturned.

March 21: Winning an early trial date, Arthur Andersen gained a potential edge in its battle with the Justice Department to avoid a criminal conviction that the firm says could amount to a corporate death penalty.
• Arthur Andersen's travails are a serious blow to all 85,000 of its employees around the world, but they pose an unusual trauma for its 4,700 partners, most of whom had nothing to do with Enron.

March 22: Arthur Andersen Worldwide, which has taken decades to build one of the world's largest accounting networks, began to

crack as partners in Hong Kong, China, and Russia agreed to merge with rival firms.
• The Securities and Exchange Commission is looking at Arthur Andersen's role as auditor for three telecommunications companies whose accounting methods are under review by the agency.
• A U.K. accounting regulatory body is demanding more information about any shredding at the British unit of Arthur Andersen in light of the firm's acknowledgment that it destroyed what it says were unimportant Enron accounting documents.

March 25: As federal investigators, creditors and angry shareholders scramble to piece together what happened at the failed energy giant, the odd tale of New Power raises serious questions of whether this IPO was used by Enron executives to falsely bolster the company's earnings.
• Arthur Andersen's former lead auditor on the Enron account met with federal prosecutors last week to discuss cooperating with the government's criminal case against Arthur Andersen.
• As bad news mounts, Mr. Volcker offered to take control and oust the accounting firm's top management – a bold but precarious plan dependent upon, among other things, the Justice Department dropping its plan to prosecute the firm on a criminal charge.
• Arthur Andersen's China offices broke ranks in the interest of clients, veterans said.

March 26: Arthur Andersen's once-flourishing energy-sector auditing practice took a further blow, as Calpine ended its auditing relationship with the firm, while Mirant said it is evaluating alternatives even amid plans to stick with the auditor this year.
• KPMG reaffirmed its desire to merge with nine Arthur Andersen units in Asia.
• Arthur Andersen asked a federal judge to throw out subpoenas to Arthur Andersen employees scheduled to appear next month before a federal grand jury, saying the government was improperly attempting to gather evidence for the firm's May 6 trial on obstruction charges related to the Enron debacle.

March 27: Arthur Andersen's audits of Waste Management continue to soil the accounting firm.
• Mr. Berardino, the embattled chief executive officer of Arthur Andersen, announced his resignation. His resignation may have soothed angry partners who believe he handled the fall-out from the collapse of Enron as badly as the firm handled Enron's audits. But

his decision doesn't solve Arthur Andersen's bigger challenge: finding a way out of its mounting problems.

March 28: The Securities and Exchange Commission was concerned enough about International Business Machines' financial disclosure practices two years ago that it asked the company to consider amending its 1999 annual report.
• Arthur Andersen's top executives are scrambling to unite an increasingly fractious group of partners.
• New Jersey gambling regulators ordered Arthur Andersen to stop doing business with the state's casinos, citing the accounting firm's federal indictment this month.
• For Joseph Berardino, any hope of saving Arthur Andersen's global empire died early this month.
• A complaint has been filed in the U.S. against Arthur Andersen's U.S., Singapore, and Indonesia operations.

March 29: Two senior Arthur Andersen partners will temporarily lead the struggling accounting firm's efforts to implement reforms under a long-shot rescue plan.
• Despite long odds, Arthur Andersen partners are vowing to tough it out, hoping to keep the once-venerable accounting partnership alive.
• Citigroup, along with Bank of America and Barclays Bank, arranged with a bank syndicate a $700 million credit line for Arthur Andersen on Oct. 31, the day Enron disclosed that federal regulators were investigating the Houston firm's accounting practices.
• Ernst & Young said it will integrate the Australian operations of accounting giant Arthur Andersen Australia into its own local business.
• The accounting practices of retailers may face tighter regulation in the wake of the Enron scandal, particularly for their use of so-called special-purpose entities.

▲ APRIL 2002 ▲

April 1: An Arthur Andersen auditor who was removed from an oversight role involving Enron after raising questions about aggressive accounting is talking to federal investigators, lawyers close to the case said, and his testimony could be used in the obstruction case against Arthur Andersen.

• The Bermuda insurance company that Arthur Andersen said it intended to use to pay $217 million to settle an Arizona fraud case was rendered technically insolvent because the accounting firm failed to make a $100 million premium payment.

April 2: Ernst & Young's stepped up efforts to acquire the Asian affiliates of Arthur Andersen could pre-empt rival firm KPMG International's plans to acquire Arthur Andersen's non-U.S. businesses.

• Among the life-threatening issues facing Arthur Andersen, one looming especially large for its partners is how effectively the firm's limited liability partnership shields them from potentially ruinous personal liability.

April 3: Accounting firms Arthur Andersen Singapore and Ernst & Young said they would merge their operations – a deal that is likely to lead to similar mergers in other countries.

• Any hope that Arthur Andersen Worldwide had of selling off its European and Asian businesses in bigger, more valuable chunks all but disappeared as Arthur Andersen's much-coveted Spanish practice agreed to merge with Deloitte Touche Tohmatsu.

• The German partners of Arthur Andersen and KPMG are making substantial progress in talks about merging their operations.

• Arthur Andersen Worldwide's Japan affiliate will have a tough time trying to join KPMG International's global network, despite an agreement last week to do so.

April 4: The Department of Justice is willing to consider a deal to settle its criminal obstruction case against Arthur Andersen, as long as the firm somehow admits it "illegally shredded documents."

• Occidental Petroleum announced on March 22 that it was abandoning Arthur Andersen and since has switched to KPMG International. Yet, like many of the nearly 100 other clients of Arthur Andersen that have switched auditors, replacing the once-venerable firm has been far less stressful so far than Occidental thought it would be.

• CNN anchor Lou Dobbs defended his commentaries criticizing the Justice Department's indictment of Arthur Andersen after questions were raised whether he should have disclosed ties to the accounting firm.

April 5: Andersen Worldwide tapped Aldo Cardoso, managing partner for France, as its acting chief executive, and the new CEO said he will fight to keep the breakup of the accounting firm's global empire from descending into chaos.

• Lawyers for Arthur Andersen, seeking to salvage at least some portion of the beleaguered accounting company, plan to meet with Justice Department officials in Washington to discuss settling the criminal-obstruction case against the firm.

• Under siege from lawsuits and criminal charges related to its botched audits of Enron, Arthur Andersen took the first steps toward breaking its US operations into pieces, agreeing to tentative pacts with two Big Five rivals.

• Two investment bankers at Credit Suisse First Boston who helped design some of the financing vehicles used by Enron served as directors of one of those entities, underscoring Wall Street's major role in helping create the complex financial structure of the former Houston energy giant.

• With Arthur Andersen looking as if it may not have especially deep pockets for Enron creditors and shareholders to recover their losses, aggrieved parties are taking aim at another potential target: Enron's bankers.

April 8: In an intensified effort to recoup billions of dollars for investors in bankrupt Enron, an amended class-action lawsuit alleges that nine major banks and securities firms and two national law firms participated in a scheme with Enron's top executives to defraud shareholders and creditors.

April 9: Enron called it "snowballing," a recognition that project costs needed to be watched and controlled or they could run over the company. But an amended class-action lawsuit is claiming it is a method of avoiding write-offs that would otherwise bring the company's earnings below Wall Street's expectations.

• The Arthur Andersen partner fired by the firm for shredding Enron audit documents has agreed to plead guilty and cooperate with federal prosecutors, strengthening the government's hand in its criminal case against the firm.

• Arthur Andersen will cut roughly 7,000 jobs, or 27% of its 26,000 U.S. employees, in a move that will hit audit and administrative staff the hardest.

• San Francisco leveraged-buyout firm Fox Paine & Co. signed a memorandum of intent to acquire Andersen's entire tax unit in a management-led buyout for between $800 million and $900 million, challenging the bid for a portion of the unit made by rival accounting firm Deloitte & Touche.

April 10: The Arthur Andersen partner in charge of the Enron account pleaded guilty in federal court in Houston to obstruction of justice, turning the tables on his former employer and handing prosecutors a potent weapon in their criminal case against the firm.
• Andersen Worldwide's unit in the United Kingdom agreed to join Deloitte & Touche, as the troubled accounting firm's initial plans to fold its non-U.S. units into KPMG continue to unravel.
• The latest buyout offer for Arthur Andersen's tax unit could make it more difficult for the accounting firm to quickly settle civil claims by Enron's shareholders, creditors and employees, according to a person involved in the talks.
• Three remaining high-profile clients announced plans to defect from Arthur Andersen and one of its largest clients says it is talking to other auditors. The client losses made for one of the accounting firm's worst days since its indictment on March 14, with International Paper, Oracle and Walgreen dropping Andersen and Halliburton announcing its intent to consider alternatives.
• Ernst & Young has signed at least a half-dozen pacts with individual Andersen partnerships. It announced plans with Andersen to merge their Poland operations, and more deals are expected.

April 11: In the months before Enron filed for bankruptcy-court protection late last year, the company had been quietly trading tens of millions of dollars in stocks through an internal hedge fund – among the riskiest forms of financial trading.
• KPMG Germany expects to sign a memorandum of understanding "within the next days" on merging its operations with the German arm of Andersen.
• Qwest Communications International said it dismissed its auditor, Arthur Andersen, from performing non-auditing services like consulting.

April 12: In the months before the collapse of Enron, facing three other high-profile botched audits, top executives at Arthur Andersen were trying to reduce the risks.
• Fighting to survive, Arthur Andersen is prepared to settle a criminal case with the government in which it would publicly admit for the first time that some of its partners and lower-level employees obstructed justice in destroying tons of documents involving Enron.
• Scoring its first major victory in the battle for Andersen World-

wide's Asian accounting operations, Deloitte Touche Tohmatsu signed a deal to merge its Taiwan arm with the larger Taiwan affiliate of Andersen.
• In the months before the collapse of Enron, facing three other high-profile botched audits, top executives at Arthur Andersen were trying to reduce the risks.
• In his first address to the company's demoralized employees, Enron's acting chief executive officer, Stephen F. Cooper, laid out plans for restructuring as a smaller firm and for digging out from under a mountain of claims that he estimated at between $60 billion and $100 billion.

April 15: Congressional investigators turn up the heat on J.P. Morgan Chase over its ties to collapsed Enron.
• A trove of tape transcripts reveals just how close they were, showing how effusively people at Enron and Arthur Andersen spoke of their intertwined operations.
• John Hancock Financial Services joined the raft of investors suing Arthur Andersen and former Enron executives and directors over losses tied to Enron's collapse, as litigation over the matter continues to spread.
• Federal regulators interceded into Enron's restructuring for a second time, objecting to a company plan to earmark as much as $140 million for employee retention and bonuses.

April 16: Arthur Andersen drew closer toward settlements with the Justice Department, as well as shareholders, creditors and others who lost billions of dollars in the Enron debacle.

April 17: Arthur Andersen scrambled to settle its Enron-related legal woes, but two disputes, involving the energy trader's creditors and a new complaint by a state attorney general, threatened to snag a possible deal.

April 18: Arthur Andersen scrambled to settle a criminal case with the government as the accounting firm's plans for resolving its civil litigation troubles showed signs of unraveling.
• Andersen officially lost its biggest remaining auditing client, when Halliburton announced it was switching to KPMG, and another big client, Marriott International, appeared poised to jump ship as well.

April 19: Arthur Andersen broke off settlement talks with the Justice Department aimed at resolving its criminal indictment, a move that

placed the firm's future in doubt and complicated the government's broader investigation of Enron.
• Andersen's plan to settle its tug of war with the Justice Department fell apart.
• Rupert Murdoch's News Corp. and Fox Entertainment Group have dropped Arthur Andersen as their external auditor and brought Ernst & Young on board to handle the audit of the 2001–2002 accounts.
• Pricewaterhouse-Coopers and Andersen said their Hong Kong and China audit and tax practices have signed an agreement to start operating as a combined firm July 1.
• Andersen Worldwide in the United Kingdom will announce plans to lay off up to 1,500 people across its business units.

April 22: Mr. Volcker looks likely to step aside in his role to rebuild Andersen, deepening the crisis within the accounting firm.
• Andersen's negotiations with the Justice Department to settle criminal charges against have collapsed, but the firm continued talks regarding a civil settlement with the Securities and Exchange Commission.
• Enron's president and chief operating officer, Jeffrey McMahon – one of the few top executives to survive the company's collapse – is resigning June 1 amid heightened government scrutiny of his role in questionable Enron-related deals.

April 23: In a bid to restore credibility to its post-bankruptcy finances, Enron said it could post a write-down of the value of its assets by about $14 billion and raised further questions about the auditing work done by Arthur Andersen.
• Congress is moving to impose tough new penalties to address future securities and accounting-law violations similar to those that allegedly surfaced in the collapse of Enron.
• Arthur Andersen is going to new lengths to cut fat. The embattled accounting firm has banned partners from having company-paid lunch meetings, as well as free morning doughnuts. Partners no longer will be able to fly first class on flights longer than three hours.
• In the latest rupture of its world-wide network, the Italian practice of global accounting group Arthur Andersen agreed to merge with rival Deloitte & Touche Italia.

April 24: The breakdown of Arthur Andersen's talks with the Justice Department, coupled with the exodus of partners and clients, has renewed concern that the embattled accounting firm will write its

own last chapter by seeking Chapter 11 bankruptcy protection. For a service partnership like Andersen, such a move would be tantamount to closing its doors.
• Andersen's failure to reach a settlement with the Justice Department has put the criminal case back in a Houston courtroom.

April 25: Arthur Andersen made a last-ditch effort to revive negotiations with the government to settle a criminal-obstruction charge, even as the firm's plans to resolve its civil-litigation troubles appear to have crumbled.
• The Andersen attorney at the center of the firm's document-destruction imbroglio has been told she is under criminal investigation as part of the Justice Department's probe into the collapse of Enron, according to a sworn statement by a government prosecutor filed under seal here with a federal court.

April 26: In building its criminal case against Arthur Andersen, the Justice Department has sought evidence from at least two Andersen employees who refused to destroy documents related to Enron, despite receiving instructions from colleagues to do so.
• Nancy Temple, an attorney at Arthur Andersen, has become a focus of the government's investigation into rampant shredding of Enron audit documents by Andersen employees.
• The same attributes that underpinned former Enron Chairman Kenneth Lay's success – tireless ambition, stubborn optimism, and sometimes easy trust – helped bring about his downfall. (Read excerpts from an interview with Mr. Lay on the web site.)

April 29: The federal judge presiding over Arthur Andersen's criminal obstruction-of-justice proceedings rejected a request by Andersen attorneys to postpone the firm's trial, scheduled to begin May 6.
• In one week, Arthur Andersen will be fighting for its life in a Houston courtroom, trying to persuade a jury not to convict it on a criminal charge stemming from its audit work for Enron. But Andersen first faces another court battle in Phoenix.

April 30: While employees still spend a portion of their time servicing Arthur Andersen's remaining clients, during the past two weeks, work inside the firm has in many places slowed to a crawl.
• KPMG Consulting is close to a deal to acquire Arthur Andersen's US consulting arm and parts of the overseas consulting business for more than $250 million, accelerating the break-up of the beleaguered accounting firm.

• A group of retired partners of Arthur Andersen asked a federal judge for a restraining order to prevent the accounting firm from selling off its assets at what it believes are cheap prices.
• The Baptist Foundation of Arizona Liquidation Trust is suing the wrong people.

🔺 MAY 2002 🔺

May 1: Investors applauded a potential deal for KPMG Consulting to buy Arthur Andersen's U.S. consulting arm and possibly parts of its overseas consulting business, but obstacles to the deal appeared high.
• The business world now wonders whether Andersen can survive, but similar questions swirled more than half a century ago when company founder Arthur Andersen passed away.
• Investors in the failed Baptist Foundation of Arizona invested hundreds of millions of dollars based on "gold standard" reputation of Andersen, but auditors were turning a blind eye to allegations that the foundation was engaged in fraud, attorneys told jurors in a civil trial against Andersen.

May 2: Enron plans to reorganize as a small company under a new name, returning to its roots of a decade ago, before the aggressive strategy that led to its spectacular expansion and then collapse.
• The mediator appointed to help broker a settlement in the class-action litigation between Arthur Andersen and the various parties suing the firm over its audits for Enron declared the talks officially dead.
• Andersen did little to investigate allegations of fraud at the Baptist Foundation of Arizona that would have normally "panicked" a good auditor, a witness testified in the civil trial against Andersen.

May 3: The trial against Arthur Andersen, set to get under way, legally looks to be an open-and-shut case, some specialists say. (Read Andersen's response to the federal indictment on the web site. View some key documents relating to Arthur Andersen's obstruction-of-justice indictment in March.)
• In its civil trial in Arizona, Arthur Andersen testified it did alert the board of the Baptist Foundation of Arizona to a problem about a lack of collateral to back up receivable notes on its balance sheet.

May 6: Documents show Enron officials were aware, at least a year ago and long before the energy concern filed for bankruptcy protection in December, that the company's portfolio of foreign assets had lost as much as half of the $6.15 billion value shown on its books at the time.

• Enron's chief executive told unsecured creditors that the collapsed company aims to recover $15 billion to $20 billion through the bankruptcy-court process, roughly 40%, at best, of the $50 billion or more Enron is believed to owe creditors.

• Paul A. Volcker, a former Federal Reserve chairman who had been tapped to reform Arthur Andersen, formally acknowledged that his role was over.

• Rival accounting firm KPMG recently laid off some of its own staff, despite making initial job offers to a number of Andersen personnel.

May 7: Federal prosecutors will present evidence that senior partners and lawyers at Arthur Andersen knew about the alleged effort to cover up the accounting firm's role in flawed Enron audits.

• In a turnabout, Andersen agreed to pay $217 million to settle civil litigation over its audits for the Baptist Foundation of Arizona, the second-largest settlement ever agreed to by a major accounting firm.

• Running out of flanks to protect, Arthur Andersen faces legal skirmishes on several fronts.

• Enron's energy traders manipulated California's power system to increase profits during the height of the state's 2000--2001 energy crisis, documents released by federal regulators show.

May 8: A major setback hit Arthur Andersen one day into its criminal trial, as the federal judge presiding over the case ruled that the government could introduce the firm's past misconduct as evidence that Andersen had ample motive for obstructing justice by destroying documents related to its audits of Enron.

• Several directors' professed ignorance of Enron's questionable accounting practices is contradicted by documents showing that a senior Arthur Andersen auditor warned them about the maneuvers more than three years ago.

• Federal energy regulators significantly widened their investigation into California's troubled energy market, after regulators released a trio of explosive Enron memos that outlined how the energy trader profitably manipulated the state's deregulated markets.

May 9: Enron and at least two other power sellers combined to profit by using false information to resell extra power during California shortages in 2000, according to internal Enron memos.
• An Arthur Andersen partner warned colleagues in August 2001 of "'smoking guns' that you can't extinguish" relating to the accounting firm's controversial audits for Enron.
• KPMG Consulting signed a letter of intent to acquire nearly all of Andersen Worldwide SC's business-consulting operation for a total price that could exceed $400 million in cash and stock.

May 10: In trial proceedings, Andersen's lead lawyer, Rusty Hardin, unequivocally signaled that the firm's defense strategy will be to convince jurors there was nothing improper about destroying Enron-related documents last fall in the weeks before the firm received a Nov. 8 subpoena from the Securities and Exchange Commission.
• A marketing video for Arthur Andersen featured testimonials from Vice President Dick Cheney and prominent chief executives.

May 14: Mr. Duncan told jurors that he ordered subordinates to follow Andersen's "document-retention policy," knowing the instruction would direct them to destroy – not save – documents related to the firm's audits of Enron.

May 15: The Federal Energy Regulatory Commission investigated Enron's online energy-trading system last year but found no cause for concern, according to Sen. Joseph Lieberman.
• Blasting the ethics of the accounting profession, Arthur Levitt, the former chairman of the Securities and Exchange Commission, warned that the remaining Big Four auditing firms and their allies in Congress are trying to block effective reform of the U.S. accounting system.
• Mr. Duncan told jurors he launched the accounting firm's massive campaign to destroy documents in October because he feared potential lawsuits and regulatory inquiries over Andersen's audits for Enron. (The web site outlines how Mr. Duncan, a bright star at Arthur Andersen, burned out along with Enron. Read Mr. Duncan's e-mail exchange with the Andersen standards group.)

May 16: Mr. Duncan testified that he knew he could face a stiff prison sentence and possible accounting-fraud charges related to Enron's collapse if he didn't cooperate with the government in its prosecution of the accounting firm.

May 20: The government's star witness in the criminal trial of

Arthur Andersen lost some of his shine, as Andersen lawyers extracted statements from former Andersen auditor David Duncan that he couldn't recall much at all about the Enron-related documents he destroyed last fall.

May 21: The Securities and Exchange Commission charged Ernst & Young with violating SEC rules by entering into lucrative business deals with a software company that it also audited.
• The chairman of the Senate Banking Committee has put off action on a sweeping overhaul of accounting practices, hoping to buy time to develop a consensus on the Enron-inspired package.
• A top Arthur Andersen auditor who was identified by government witness David Duncan as one of the people who helped shape his instructions to destroy Enron-related documents invoked his Fifth Amendment right against self-incrimination to avoid testifying in the accounting firm's criminal trial here.
• Long before Enron came along, Andersen was making a name for itself because of its document-handling prowess.

May 22: An Arthur Andersen auditor testified that her boss held a private meeting with her last fall to discuss "getting rid of documents" and explained that if he ever raised the subject with her it would take the form of "being in compliance" with the firm's document-retention policy.
• Twenty-five former Andersen partners have created a new consulting firm in Chicago that already has 75 clients and plans to expand internationally.
• As Enron structured ever-more-complex deals, Enron's lawyers at Vinson & Elkins sometimes objected, saying the deals posed conflicts of interest or weren't in Enron's best interests, but the firm didn't blow the whistle.

May 24: In a much-anticipated decision in Enron's bankruptcy case, Judge Arthur Gonzalez Thursday denied a motion to disqualify the lead law firm for Enron creditors' committee.
• Prosecutors asked the judge overseeing Arthur Andersen's document-shredding trial to let the jury consider three Andersen employees' refusal to testify as evidence that the firm obstructed justice.
• The Texas state accounting board moved to revoke Arthur Andersen's accounting license in Texas because of its role in Enron Corp.'s collapse.

May 28: The government rested its case in the criminal trial of

Arthur Andersen, which began presenting its defense by immediately trying to discredit the credibility of prosecutors.

May 30: Arthur Andersen used witnesses off the government's own list to counter an allegation in the government's March indictment that Andersen personnel in the firm's Portland, Oregon, office were instructed to destroy documents related to Enron.
• Wrapping up the corporate equivalent of a giant yard sale, Deloitte & Touche, Ernst & Young and KPMG are looking to hire 200 partners each from the beleaguered Andersen.

May 31: Arthur Andersen tried to counter government allegations at its criminal trial that a coordinated effort to destroy Enron-related documents spread overseas last fall. But the attempt partly backfired when a London-based partner testified that a call from the firm's Houston office triggered widespread shredding in the United Kingdom.
• Enron continues to revamp its board, naming a veteran electric-utility executive and a private investor who specializes in risk management as members.

▲ JUNE 2002 ▲

June 3: Arthur Andersen's 1,700 partners could be held personally liable for major chunks of the firm's debts, Enron creditors asserted in a bankruptcy-court filing.
• Teary testimony from Shannon D. Adlong, former assistant to the firm's lead auditor on Enron, came at a crucial point ahead of the last weekend before the jury is likely to deliberate as Andersen's criminal trial is drawing to a close.
• An Arthur Andersen partner and former top federal regulator said that he heard a shredder running when he came to Houston last October to look into problematic Enron accounting, and advised the firm's top Enron auditor against destroying documents.
• Reacting to a spate of recent corporate scandals, the New York Stock Exchange this week will consider tough new governance rules for its listed companies.

June 4: Texas energy regulators are seeking to fine a unit of Enron more than $7 million for violating the state's wholesale power market rules last summer, according to documents released by the Public Utility Commission.

xlii ENRON/ANDERSEN: A CHRONOLOGY

June 5: The defense rested in Arthur Andersen's criminal trial.

June 6: In its summation in the criminal trial against Arthur Andersen, the government portrayed a firm whose top lawyers and partners anticipated weeks before Enron's meltdown that they would face scrutiny from securities regulators and scrambled to destroy any Enron documents they could.
• A federal bankruptcy judge blocked an effort by Enron creditors to force Arthur Andersen to disclose details about its finances and potential liquidation.

June 10: Andersen's descent from conscience of the accounting industry to accused felon didn't happen overnight, but stemmed from a series of management miscues and compromises over the decades.

June 11: Hundreds of clients have dumped Andersen as their auditor in recent months, fearing the firm's role in the Enron scandal could taint them, or that Andersen soon might not be around to audit their books, or both. But it's questionable whether investors have rewarded them for it.

June 12: CMS Energy said former auditor Andersen formally ended its relationship with the company and won't give an opinion on the energy firm's restated financial results.
• New Power Holdings, which was launched by Enron in an ill-fated bid to revolutionize the retail energy business, has filed for Chapter 11 bankruptcy protection.

June 13: The jury in the Arthur Andersen criminal trial said it was deadlocked, prompting the federal judge who is hearing the case to order jurors to redouble their efforts to reach a verdict and resume deliberations.
• (A recap of the proceedings in Andersen's criminal trial on a single felony count of obstruction of justice, which opened in U.S. District Court in Houston on May 6 with jury selection, can be read on the web site.)

June 14: The judge in the Arthur Andersen trial ruled that jurors don't have to agree on who committed the crime as long as each juror believes someone did.

June 15: A federal jury convicted Arthur Andersen of a single felony count of obstructing an official government proceeding. The conviction, decided after ten days of deliberations, bars Andersen from auditing the financial statements of companies registered with the Securities and Exchange Commission.

June 16: Former Andersen partners hired by rival auditing firms are working side by side with their ex-colleagues to tie up loose ends with clients not following them to their new firms. At some offices around the world, Andersen signs are being replaced with those of rival acquirers.

June 17: The guilty verdict against Arthur Andersen recharged federal prosecutors' pursuit of the people responsible for Enron's collapse last fall, increasing pressure on reluctant witnesses to cooperate.

• Jurors said they focused on the mounds of shredded documents – and a single e-mail written by Ms. Temple. To jurors, the e-mail showed that the attorney had at least attempted to get former Andersen auditor David Duncan to edit one of his file memos at a crucial point last October "to protect ourselves" from SEC regulatory scrutiny.

• Arthur Andersen could pay up to $30 million in legal fees after trying to defend itself on a number of issues related to its botched audits of Enron. Besides the expense of a major trial, Andersen has been coping with myriad other lawsuits and probes, including actions by Enron shareholders and employees.

• The Securities and Exchange Commission and the Justice Department could still go after Arthur Andersen, its partners and staff members involved in the Enron audits for securities fraud, violating professional standards and engaging in improper or unprofessional behavior.

June 18: The Senate Banking Committee approved legislation creating an oversight board to set bookkeeping standards, limit firms' consulting work and discipline wayward auditors.

• Securities and Exchange Commission Chairman Harvey Pitt plans to introduce his blueprint for a strong oversight board with at least six independent members – plus three accounting professionals, who wouldn't be allowed to vote on disciplinary matters.

June 20: Congressional Democrats are assailing a Securities and Exchange Commission proposal for a new auditor-oversight board for not going far enough. The SEC proposed creating a private, nine-member Public Accountability Board that would have the power to discipline auditors, examine accounting firms' auditing procedures and draw up new standards.

• The Arthur Andersen Community Learning Center was designed to demonstrate that Arthur Andersen's competence and conscience stretched far deeper than corporate books. Now, this tiny high school may well wind up being the last holder of the Arthur Andersen corporate name.

• The scope and scale of the corporate transgressions of the late 1990s exceed anything the U.S. has witnessed since the years preceding the Great Depression. And the victims are the shareholders the executives were supposed to be serving.

June 21: Dynegy said it halted energy trading on its Dynegydirect online system only hours after it replaced its top financial officer and announced it was laying off 16% of the staff of its trading operations.

• Eleven insurance companies file legal documents stating J.P. Morgan Chase conspired to make Enron look healthier than it was as part of an effort to cover J.P. Morgan's exposure to the energy company.

June 24: Stocks continue to plummet on investors' fears about corporate profits after the collapse of Enron.

June 25: Arthur Andersen asked a federal judge to reverse this month's jury verdict that it criminally obstructed an investigation into its onetime client Enron, saying the verdict was "insupportable," and the company should at least be granted a new trial.

June 27: WorldCom's disclosure of roughly $3.8 billion in improper accounting underscored how potential fraud on a huge scale can still be executed in a simple way.

▲ JULY 2002 ▲

July 1: Accounting rule-makers could announce proposals for new rules intended to make it tougher for companies to keep debt-laden partnerships off their books. But the revised approach is not likely to be as tough as envisioned several months ago.

July 2: The office of Manhattan District Attorney Robert Morgenthau has been making inquiries into financing arrangements that J.P. Morgan Chase and Citigroup pursued with Enron.

July 21: Citigroup arranged a financing technique for Enron that enabled the energy trader to appear rich in cash rather than saddled with debt.

July 23: Citigroup and J.P. Morgan Chase, already facing scrutiny for devising allegedly deceptive transactions for Enron, marketed similarly structured deals to a slew of other companies.

July 24: Citigroup and J.P. Morgan Chase made more than $200 million in fees for transactions that helped Enron and other energy companies boost their cash flow and hide debt.

July 25: The Senate's Permanent Subcommittee on Investigations has sent letters to the chief executives of Citigroup and J.P. Morgan, demanding that they provide sworn affidavits testifying to the nature of offshore entities that were used to help Enron hide its finances.
• Citigroup's reputation is increasingly at risk because of its association with high-profile corporate scandals. The company reported a quarterly profit of more than $4 billion last week but so far its shares have fallen 18% since the announcement.

July 29: One of the Merrill Lynch point men for Enron work was placed on administrative leave by the firm after learning he could face criminal liability as part of a Justice Department probe.

July 30: Congressional investigators are exploring Merrill Lynch's role in raising funds for LJM2, the $386.6 million Enron-related partnership that engaged in several transactions that helped Enron hide debt and appear financially stronger.

July 31: It was only after stock-research analyst John Olson left Merrill Lynch in August 1998 that Merrill eventually did win tens of millions of dollars in Enron banking business and upgrade the company's stock. "There was a clear preference for positive recommendations regarding Enron, and I wasn't going to give them that," Mr. Olson said.

▲ AUGUST 2002 ▲

Aug. 1: The Federal Energy Regulatory Commission began investigating whether Enron may have improperly used two pipeline subsidiaries to secure a $1 billion loan from bankers.

Aug. 5: Federal prosecutors are investigating whether Enron bribed foreign government officials to win contracts for its far-flung operations abroad, underscoring the sweep of the U.S. government's probe into Enron's collapse.

Aug. 6: The Justice Department and SEC are examining whether Enron committed accounting fraud when it borrowed $1 billion in a last-ditch attempt to stave off bankruptcy late last year. Investigators are looking at the transactions to determine whether Enron improperly used two of its publicly regulated pipeline subsidiaries to secure the loans and then transferred the money to Enron's accounts with no plans to repay the companies.

Aug. 12: Investigators sifting through the collapse of Enron have shifted their focus to the role of the financiers. The result: three of the country's biggest financial firms are facing uncomfortable questions from Congress, the SEC and the Justice Department about financing they provided to Enron that may have been used to deceive investors.

Aug. 13: The Federal Energy Regulatory Commission said Enron, Avista and El Paso Electric could face sanctions if they are found to have violated agency rules or federal law. A preliminary probe found evidence the companies may have manipulated prices during California's energy crisis.

• As Jeffrey Skilling reached the first anniversary of his surprise resignation as Enron chief executive, he faces the possibility of a criminal indictment for alleged crimes at the collapsed energy trader.

Aug. 15: Dynegy agreed to pay $25 million to settle Enron's claim that its one-time rival breached a contract when it walked away from a proposed merger, accelerating Enron's collapse.

Aug. 16: Arthur Andersen lost its license to practice in Texas, the home state of its former client Enron. The board that regulates the Texas accounting profession voted unanimously to revoke the firm's license because of the company's obstruction of justice conviction.

Aug. 21: Michael Kopper, a former Enron financial executive, will plead guilty to two felony charges and cooperate fully with government investigators. Mr. Kopper will surrender $12 million in illegally obtained assets and plead guilty to money laundering and conspiracy to commit wire fraud.

Aug. 22: Prosecutors sought an order to seize $23.6 million of assets from former Enron CFO Andrew Fastow and several of his friends and family members on the grounds that they obtained the money illegally.

• Michael Kopper is the government's new star witness in its Enron investigation, but the former executive appears to be far less obliging in the legal entanglement stemming from his role in running LJM2, a partnership that helped Enron hide debt from investors.

Aug. 23: Federal prosecutors investigating Enron moved quickly to try to freeze bank accounts of former Enron Chief Financial Officer Andrew Fastow and members of his family to keep them from withdrawing money.

• When Michael Kopper negotiated last year to get bought out of Chewco, he demanded an additional $2.6 million to cover taxes on the $10 million payment he would receive from Enron.

And then there was WorldCom

WorldCom, the nation's second-largest long-distance carrier, went from being one of the biggest stock market stars of the past decade to the brink of bankruptcy. The firm had already been hobbled by an industry-wide meltdown, which was exacerbated by a Securities and Exchange Commission probe and $30 billion in debt. After this week's events . . . the company unveiled what may be *the biggest accounting fraud in history.*

Wall Street Journal web page

▲ SEC Complaint Against WorldCom ▲

On June 26, 2002, the Securities and Exchange Commission ("the Commission") filed the following complaint against WorldCom.

1. From at least the first quarter of 2001 through the first quarter of 2002, defendant WorldCom Inc. ("WorldCom") defrauded investors. In a scheme directed and approved by its senior management, WorldCom disguised its true operating performance by using undisclosed and improper accounting that materially overstated its income before income taxes and minority interests by approximately $3.055 billion in 2001 and $797 million during the first quarter of 2002.

2. By improperly transferring certain costs to its capital accounts, WorldCom falsely portrayed itself as a profitable business during 2001 and the first quarter of 2002. WorldCom's transfer of its costs to its capital accounts violated the established standards of generally accepted accounting principles ("GAAP"). WorldCom's improper transfer of certain costs to its capital accounts was not disclosed to investors in a timely fashion, and misled investors about WorldCom's reported earnings. This improper accounting action was intended to manipulate WorldCom's earnings in the year ending

2001 and in the first quarter of 2002 to keep them in line with estimates by Wall Street analysts.

3. By engaging in this conduct, WorldCom violated the anti-fraud and reporting provisions of the federal securities laws and, unless restrained and enjoined by this Court, will continue to do so. The Commission requests, among other things, that WorldCom be enjoined from further violations of the federal securities laws as alleged herein, and that it pay a monetary penalty.

The fraudulent scheme

4. WorldCom is a major global communications provider, operating in more than 65 countries. WorldCom provides data transmission and Internet services for businesses, and, through its MCI unit, provides telecommunications services for businesses and consumers. WorldCom became an important player in the telecommunications industry in the 1990s. However, as the economy cooled in 2001, WorldCom's earnings and profits similarly declined, making it difficult to keep WorldCom's earnings in line with expectations by industry analysts.

5. Starting at least in 2001, WorldCom engaged in an improper accounting scheme intended to manipulate its earnings to keep them in line with Wall Street's expectations, and to support WorldCom's stock price. One of WorldCom's major operating expenses was its so-called "line costs." In general, "line costs" represent fees WorldCom paid to third party telecommunication network providers for the right to access the third parties' networks. Under GAAP, these fees must be expensed and may not be capitalized. Nevertheless, beginning at least as early as the first quarter of 2001, WorldCom's senior management improperly directed the transfer of line costs to WorldCom's capital accounts in amounts sufficient to keep WorldCom's earnings in line with the analysts' consensus on WorldCom's earnings. Thus, in this manner, WorldCom materially understated its expenses, and materially overstated its earnings, thereby defrauding investors.

6. As a result of this improper accounting scheme, WorldCom materially underreported its expenses and materially overstated its earnings in its filings with the Commission, specifically, on its Form 10-K for the fiscal year ending on December 31, 2001, and on its Form 10-Q for the quarter ending on March 31, 2002.

7. In particular, WorldCom reported on its Consolidated Statement of Operations contained in its 2001 Form 10-K that its line costs for 2001 totaled $14.739 billion, and that its earnings before income taxes and minority interests totaled $2.393 billion, whereas, in truth and in fact, WorldCom's line costs for that period totaled approximately $17.794 billion, and it suffered a **loss** of approximately $662 million.

8. Further, WorldCom reported on its Consolidated Statement of Operations contained in its Form 10-Q for the first quarter of 2002 that its line costs for that quarter totaled $3.479 billion, and that its income before income taxes and minority interests totaled $240 million, whereas, in truth and in fact, WorldCom's line costs for that period totaled approximately $4.276 billion and it suffered a **loss** of approximately $557 million.

9. Worldcom's disclosures in its 2001 Form 10-K and in its Form 10-Q for the first quarter of 2002 failed to include material facts necessary to make the statements made in light of the circumstances in which they were made not misleading. In particular, these filings failed to disclose the company's accounting treatment of its line costs, that such treatment had changed from prior periods, and that the company's line costs were actually increasing substantially as a percentage of its revenues."

▲ Chronology ▲

The following is a chronology of recent events:

Feb. 8, 2002: WorldCom cuts 2002 revenue and earnings projections and announces second-quarter charge of $15 billion to $20 billion to write down some acquired operations.
• CEO Bernard Ebbers owes his company $366 million to cover loans he took out to buy his own shares.

Feb. 15, 2002: WorldCom suspends three star employees and freezes the commissions of at least 12 salespeople over an order-booking scandal in three of its branch offices.

March 12, 2002: The SEC launches inquiries into WorldCom's accounting practices, on the heels of Enron scandals and Global Crossing' s bankruptcy filing.

April 3, 2002: WorldCom plans to lay off as much as 10% of its 75,000 workforce.

April 22, 2002: WorldCom slashes at least $1 billion from its revenue projections for 2002.

April 24, 2002: WorldCom debt is downgraded by Moody's and Fitch.

April 30, 2002: Bernard J. Ebbers resigns as chief executive of WorldCom.

May 9, 2002: Moody's and Fitch each slash WorldCom's debt three notches, to "junk" status, pushing shares to a new low.

May 21, 2002: WorldCom eliminates its MCI Group tracking stock, hoping to save money that would have gone to dividends.

June 5, 2002: WorldCom announces plans to cut up to 20% of its workforce in a restructuring that would involve selling its wireless unit.

June 20, 2002: WorldCom says it will defer interest payments on some preferred securities of MCI Group, to conserve cash.

June 24, 2002: WorldCom shares fall below $1 after analyst Jack Grubman issues a negative report about the telecom's finances.

June 26, 2002: WorldCom unveils massive corporate fraud, with $3.8 billion in expenses that were improperly booked as capital expenditures.

June 27, 2002: SEC files a civil suit alleging WorldCom engaged in a fraudulent scheme to pad earnings by $3.8 billion.

June 28, 2002: House launches probe into WorldCom accounting scandal with flurry of subpoenas.

July 9, 2002: Congressmen blast WorldCom executives for accounting misdeeds and telecom analyst Jack Grubman for not catching it.

July 12, 2002: WorldCom's lenders unsuccessfully try to freeze $2.65 billion of the troubled telecom's funds.

July 17, 2002: California pension funds sue WorldCom, some of its former executives and a host of major banks, alleging fraud in connection with a major bond offering last year by the telecom company.

July 22, 2002: WorldCom files for Chapter 11 bankruptcy court protection.

Introduction

Rosemarie is the new controller for a small construction company, Acme builders. She is new on her job and grateful that the CEO, Peter, has allowed her to go on flex-time to help her take care of her young daughter, who is in day care. Rosemarie is concerned about the collectibility of receivables from Fergus Motel, for whom Acme has done extensive work. Rosemarie thinks that the allowance for these receivables must be adjusted. Upon expressing her concern to Peter, she is told that he thinks adjusting for them might put the approval of a much-needed loan in jeopardy. Rosemarie thinks she should account for them, but it seems clear that when Peter said, "Well . . . do what you think is right," he was really saying that he expected her to look out for the company and fudge the figures. Should she be a team player and go along with what Peter obviously wants, but didn't specifically ask for?

John is a fairly young accountant working at a local CPA firm. John is wrestling with a problem. He is trying to decide whether to cover up a mistake made in not attaching an irrevocable election to a client's recently submitted tax return. If he does not report the mistake he can relieve a significant portion of the tax burden of an important client. John thinks taxes are unfair anyway, and that his obligation to his client is to look out for the best interest of the client and save him from paying as much tax as possible. John also knows that keeping the client is important for the financial health of the company. Do you think most accountants would cover such a mistake? Would they be justified in covering such a mistake?

Leo is a senior accountant who has been assigned to the audit of a closely held corporation, CHC. Leo discovers that CHC's income has been materially misstated, probably due to what appears to be a cutoff error, but possibly has been misstated deliberately. Leo takes the information to Adele, the audit manager. The work on the audit has already taken significantly longer than was projected in the budget, and investigating the misstatement would involve too much time. Besides, there are no tax implications due to the mistake, and the managing partner, who is also negotiating a consulting contract with CHC, is pressuring Leo to get the files to him as soon as possible. Adele tells Leo not to mention the adjustment in the working papers, because she sees no tax implications. No harm, no foul. Should Leo follow Adele's "advice," or does he have a responsibility beyond that to work for the benefit of the client?[1]

Situations such as those portrayed in these scenarios happen every day in the world of accountants. They raise ethical concerns that are typical of those that face accountants, whether they are management accountants, tax accountants, auditors, valuation specialists or accountants performing any number of other accounting activities.

Such situations existed long before the now infamous Enron bankruptcy case, in which their auditors and consultants from the accounting firm of Arthur Andersen came under criticism for not appropriately carrying out their responsibilities as accountants. In one instance Arthur Andersen, functioning in the role of outside auditor, failed to detect and/or disclose financial transactions wherein Enron shifted assets to a special purpose entity, which allowed the value of the company to appear significantly more than it was. While defenders of Arthur Andersen declared such activity was within the law and generally accepted accounting principles, critics claimed that accountants are obliged to do more.

Whatever the outcome of the Enron/Andersen case, it is important to remember that it does not present new ethical difficulties. It simply brings to light ethical questions that have been simmering for well over a quarter of a century. Because it involved billions of dollars and affected so many people's lives, it brought to light in a dramatic fashion the ethical difficulties accountants face. The Enron/Andersen case, and each of the scenarios above, raise the ethical question, what is the appropriate behavior for accountants? What are accountants supposed to do? That is the major question for any book on accounting ethics.

Ethics is an overarching human concern which covers all areas of human life, but in this book we will examine how it is applicable and relevant to this one corner of human activity, accounting. Accounting as a human activity has an ethical dimension, for ethics is involved in all human activity. Human activity is precisely the kind of thing for which people can be held responsible, for it is activity that is done deliberately, and which individuals can control. It is also activity that helps or harms, either oneself or others, or which is deemed to be either just or unjust, right or wrong. But to understand fully the ethical dimensions of accounting we will need to examine where and how the activity of accounting fits into the larger scheme of human activities.

We will examine in what way accounting is both an essential practice and a vital profession in the economically developed world of today. It is an essential practice because the current economic system could not exist without it. Business and the market, as we know it, would grind to a halt if there were no way to account for the existence and disposition of the wealth and goods of the world. For financial markets to function efficiently it is necessary to have transactions based on accurate portraits of the financial worth of any entity being traded. Those portraits are painted by accountants. Power relationships, property rights, ownership claims, valuations, receivables, and debts are all mental social constructs that define who owns what and owes what to whom. All of these constructs are identified and tracked by accountants and bookkeepers.

Because of this essential role in tracking the indeterminately large nexus of complicated financial relationships in the economic world of today accounting developed into a service profession. We will examine the nature of the accounting profession from the perspective of the general ethical responsibilities that accrue to professionals, as well as from the perspective of the specific responsibilities that arise from being a professional accountant.

To cover all the areas and activities engaged in by accountants that have an ethical dimension would require an inordinately large book. This book will concentrate on what we see as major areas of concern for the ethics of accounting.

Determining, examining, and evaluating the purposes of activities or practices is one of the major tasks of ethics. This approach to ethics is a functional one and involves an evaluation of a function or purpose. For example, if we take a functional approach to a knife we see that a knife has a basic purpose or function – to cut. It is considered a good knife, with respect to its basic function, if it cuts well, and if it is a dull knife which does not cut sharply, it is not a very good knife. But we can also analyze whether the function itself is a worthwhile activity. Whether cutting is worth while depends on what is being cut and why – i.e. the purpose for which the activity is carried on.

Every activity is either done for its own sake, in which case it is called *intrinsically worth while*, or it is done for the sake of something else, in which case it is *instrumentally worth while*. Cutting is an instrumental activity for the sake of something else, and it is judged as worth while or not depending on the purpose for which it is done. A good knife can be used to cut up food; conversely it can be used to kill human beings.

Accounting, being a practice and an activity, is done for some purpose. Thus, we can determine whether an accountant is acting well if he or she is fulfilling their purpose, to render accurate portraits of a financial entity. But we can ask the larger question: why is this activity of creating financial portraits being carried out? What is this practice to accomplish? So, accounting as an instrumental activity can also be judged on the basis of the purpose for which it is used. It is important in this context to remember that the clever accountant can hide assets as well as disclose them.

Providing accurate financial pictures of business activities, which is the primary activity of an accountant, is an instrumental activity, because it provides a necessary service for those who need that information to engage in financial decision making. While instrumental activities can be viewed as noble activities when they provide great benefits to human beings, they can also be instrumental in bringing about great harm. Accounting and the skills of the accountant can be utilized to do great harm to society if the purposes for which the information is used are harmful, or illegal. For example, an accountant for organized crime or an accountant for the Nazis are providing a useful service for their clients, but their clients corrupt that service by putting it to use for evil purposes or ends.

Hence we judge the purpose of accounting – which is to provide information on economic affairs – as a laudable purpose. Having done that, though, we need to judge the skilled accountant from the perspective of the use to which his or her accounting skills are put. If it is a noble purpose – to keep a worthwhile business functioning well – it will be lauded. If it is a malicious purpose – to cheat the public out of legitimate tax burdens – it will be condemned.

With those goals in mind the book will start by briefly examining the history, nature, and purpose of accounting. Accounting is the invention of human beings, and this is the result of human conventions. That being the case, it will be helpful to examine the history of how accounting came to be. Financial activities are necessary for survival in our present world, and because accounting helps facilitate these activities it is usually a beneficial activity. Still, accounting can be misused to benefit some at the expense of others, to deceive and to defraud others. At such times the accounting might be done well, but the practice and skills of the accountant are denigrated by their unethical use.

After examining the nature of accounting, we will turn our attention to the question, what is ethics? We will examine current ethical theories to show how they can be applied to accounting today. In that discussion we will examine both the ethics of purpose as well as the ethics of relationships. We will devote a section of the book to a discussion of this question, detailing not only what we have alluded to above as the ethics of purpose but also another aspect of ethics, the ethics of relationships. Ethics is about pursuing the good but it is also about fidelity to ethically acceptable relationships.

A crucial relationship is that of a professional toward his or her clients. Since accounting is a skill demanding expertise, and since accountants have clients who depend on that expertise, accounting can be included among the professions. We will try to show why the fact that accounting is a profession invests accounting with an ethical dimension. We will look at the characteristics of professionalism, and the notion of agency that is involved in any profession. We will show that being a professional puts obligations upon the accountant to look out for the best interests of various constituencies, from the client to the company to the general public.

Accountants, as professionals, have developed various codes of ethics, the rules accountants themselves lay down if one is to be an accepted member of a profession. We will examine the American Institute of Certified Public Accountants' code of ethics since it is the most extensive code and probably representative of most other codes. We will attempt to show the ethics and ethical standards that code puts forward.

After those considerations we will examine specific ethical issues involved in what seem to be the four major functions of the accountant today.

(1) Auditing – What are the ethical issues involved in auditing? Here we will pay particular attention to the conflict of interest problems that arise for public auditors. The question of the responsibility of auditors, and to what extent they need to avoid conflicts of interest, has now become a commonplace question in the daily news as a result of the Enron/Andersen situation. Public policy debates will rage about what sorts of limits should be put on auditors in order to assure they perform their function well. We will look at the nature and purpose of auditing and see what responsibilities that function entails.

(2) Management accounting – External auditors, of course, function as the watchdogs who examine the financial statements prepared by internal accountants and internal auditors. What are the responsibilities and limits of one doing internal audits or preparing financial statements for companies to be used by management, and perhaps to be used by external constituencies? Is the management accountant's primary responsibility to the company or to the general public?

(3) Tax accounting – What are the responsibilities faced by the tax accountant? How aggressive are they to be in being an advocate of their clients in the face of legitimate government tax requirements?

(4) Consulting – Consulting is the newest growth area for accounting firms. How does this work, which rests on their knowledge of financial situations, complement or conflict with the audit function? Should accounting firms consult for firms that they audit? Does this consulting function jeopardize their independence as auditors?

After examining these major functions of the accountant, we will look at the responsibilities of the accountant to the broader world. Do accountants have a responsibility to concern themselves with the legitimacy and ethics of companies they work for? Are *generally accepted accounting principles* (GAAP) ethically neutral principles? What are the responsibilities of accountants to blow the whistle? What are accountants' roles and responsibilities likely to be in the future? What are the ethical problems that will arise in the expansion of accounting firms into multinational firms? What are the implications of multidisciplinary practices in estate and financial planning?

Finally, in the light of what currently appears to be a crisis for the business, we will look at the social responsibilities of accounting firms, examining how the changing world of the financial services and increased competition have changed the nature of the accounting profession and the companies where accountants find their home.

▲ NOTES ▲

1. These scenarios are adapted from Arthur Andersen and Co.'s Business Ethics Program: Minicase Indexes, 1992.

chapter one

The Nature of Accounting and the Chief Ethical Difficulty: True Disclosure

The problems encountered in the Enron/Arthur Andersen case in 2001–2002 were not unique within the accounting industry. Consider the following article from the *Washington Post* in October of 1999.

After directors of **Rite Aid** Corp. ousted the chief executive last week and announced that earnings going back to 1997 would be "restated" to wipe out $500 million in pretax profits, one stock analyst said it might take some time before investors get a true picture of the drugstore chain's finances.

Rite Aid's announcement raised an important question for investors: If the public has yet to see a true picture, what good were the two years' worth of audited financial statements that the company issued earlier?

There's been no suggestion that the **Rite Aid** write-down resulted from any impropriety by its auditor, KPMG LLP, which declined to comment, citing client confidentiality. However, regulators have been troubled for some time about the quality of corporate financial statements. And investors should be, too.

In recent years, companies such as Waste Management Inc., Cendant Corp. and Sunbeam Corp. have disclosed that the picture painted by their earlier financial statements was not accurate. More than a year ago, Securities and Exchange Commission Chairman Arthur Levitt Jr. called attention to what he dubbed a "numbers game" in which companies manipulate accounting data to produce desired results.

These results range from "making one's numbers" – meeting Wall Street projections – to smoothing out quarterly results to produce a steady run of increases.

"This process has evolved over the years into what can best be characterized as a game among market participants," Levitt said in a speech last year.

Many investors agree. Richard P. Howard, manager of the T. Rowe Price Capital Appreciation Fund, said there is immense pressure on company managers to match or outperform market expectations.

"Top managers are almost more managers of their stock than they are managers of their own companies," he said.

But if outside auditors are doing their jobs and making sure that the numbers presented to the public present a true picture of the company within the rules of generally accepted accounting principles, how can companies play games with their books?

The answer, in the view of some experts, is that auditors don't do their jobs properly. In most cases, when a fraud is exposed or when a company makes a large restatement of its earnings, it is management that has done something wrong, but "I would consider it also an audit failure," said Howard Schilit, a former American University professor, who now runs the Center for Financial Research and Analysis Inc., a Rockville firm that analyzes corporate financial statements and has issued several prescient warnings about companies about to tumble.

Schilit said accounting problems typically arise when a previously healthy company starts having business problems.

"The starting point is always the same – a business that is starting to struggle. At that point, management has two choices – come clean and get hammered" in the stock market, as happened to Unisys Corp. earlier this month, or "don't play fair."

Those that don't are a minority, but they "are the ones that become the giant accounting frauds," said Schilit, who has been dubbed "the accounting sleuth."

Outright fraud, of course, can be difficult to detect if management is clever enough, and especially if it is able to enlist vendors and customers in the scheme.

For example, said Alan Anderson of the American Institute of Certified Public Accountants, auditors are supposed to verify that a company's receivables exist and are likely to be paid. In the aftermath of some frauds, auditors' records contained letters from customers verifying the receivables and saying they intended to pay – when in fact the sales were bogus.

SEC officials noted that the agency brings about 500 enforcement cases a year, of which about 100 involve financial or reporting fraud, a rate of about one-half of 1 percent of public companies.

Far more common is what is called aggressive accounting, experts say. Auditing, though it requires a great deal of number crunching and tire kicking, also typically involves many judgment calls, and those calls leave room for pressure by management, critics say.

This pressure can be effective because of the internal dynamics of the accounting firm. In many firms, consulting has become the major income source, while the auditing market is very competitive and prices are down. Thus, audit partners may be struggling to keep revenue up and reluctant to risk losing an engagement by angering management.

"The auditor is being paid by the person they are evaluating," noted Stephen Loeb, professor of accounting at the University of Maryland, and partners in accounting firms "don't have tenure."

The judgments involved cover a wide range of subjects. Recently controversy has arisen over some Internet companies' practice of bartering advertising on their sites for advertising on the other firms' sites. The companies are assigning value to these transactions and booking it as revenue. Plainly such transactions do have value, but how much? That is where judgment can come into play.[1]

This article highlights a number of ethical problems faced by the accounting profession today. The general public has become familiar with these problems recently because of the Enron/Arthur Andersen case, in which the corporate auditors of Enron, Arthur Andersen, either failed to notice or ignored transactions by Enron that distorted the financial picture of the company.

What has become abundantly clear in the Enron/Andersen debacle is that financial statements should be accurate and usable in a market system that relies on accurate information to make rational decisions. But pictures are not always accurate. They are distorted to produce desired results, like "meeting one's numbers" or "smoothing out quarterly reports." We need to examine why and to what extent such distortions constitute unethical procedures. To do that though it is necessary to give an overview of what accounting is, so as to better appreciate its nature and purpose, for it is only in the light of that purpose that we can adequately evaluate accounting behavior in ethical terms.

Accounting is a technique and its practice is an art or craft originally developed to help people keep track of their economic transactions. Accounting gives people a financial picture of their affairs. Its original and still fundamental purpose is to provide information about the economic affairs of a person or organization. Originally only the person needed the information. Then the government needed the information. As the economy got more and more complex and regulated, the number of those who needed the information, and the number of users of economic statements, increased.

The extent to which the information has become important to the user increases the ethical factors governing the development and disbursement of the information. Some people have a right to the information, others do not.

The accountant provides information that can be used in a number of ways. An organization's managers use it to help them plan and control the organization's operations. Owners, managers, and/or legislative bodies use it to help them appraise an organization's performance and make decisions about an organization's future. Owners, managers, lenders, suppliers, employees, and others use it to help in deciding how much time and/or money to devote to the organization. Finally, government uses it to determine how much tax organizations must pay.[2] Hence, the accountant's role is to furnish various entities who have a legitimate right to know about an organization's affairs with useful information about those economic affairs. What is owed to those various entities, and the accountant has an obligation to provide, is a true picture of those affairs. As the article asks about Rite Aid's situation, "If the public has yet to see a *true picture* [of the economic affairs of Rite Aid] what good were the two years' worth of audited financial statements that the company issued . . .?"

So, accountants issue financial statements that need to be used by various constituencies, from company management, to tax agencies, to potential investors. Those statements, which are expected to give a true, reliable, and useful picture of the financial affairs of an organization, are made within the guidelines developed by the profession itself. The accounting practice rests on what the Financial Accounting Standards Board of the Financial Accounting Foundation calls a conceptual framework.

> The conceptual framework is a coherent system of interrelated objectives and fundamentals that is expected to lead to consistent standards and that prescribes the nature, function, and limits of financial accounting and reporting. It is expected *to serve the public interest* [authors' italics] by providing structure and direction to financial accounting and reporting to facilitate the provision of evenhanded financial and related information that helps promote the efficient allocation of scarce resources in the economy and society, including assisting capital and other markets to function efficiently.[3]

Of course, as we see in the Rite Aid example, stock analysts and investors are expecting to get a "true picture" of a company. However, the very notion of "true" presents some problems in this context, for there are any number of ways of looking at the economic status of an organization, and in reality several pictures of a company can be developed. Quite often the picture developed by an accountant serves the interest of the party who hires the accountant more than other parties who need to know the picture of the organization. Depending on the techniques used, a corporate accountant can make an organization look better or worse. For loan purposes, it can be made to look better. For tax purposes, it can be made to look worse. But we will return to the issue of the true picture later. For now we ask: what kinds of pictures are there, and what kinds of financial statements do accountants produce?

There generally are four components of financial statements: the balance sheet, the income statement, the statement of changes in retained earnings, and the statement of changes in cash flow.

The balance sheet has three elements: *assets*, which are the tangible and intangible items owned by the company; *liabilities*, which are the organization's debts, involving money or services owed to others; and *owners' equity*, which are funds provided by the organization's owners and the accumulated income or loss generated over years. The total assets, of course, equal the total liabilities plus the owners' equity. Owners' equity equals the total assets minus the total liability (net assets).

Developing such statements is where the art and craft of accounting comes in, for it takes skill, judgment, technique, and the application of principles to determine what counts as assets and liabilities. Sometimes the assets and liabilities are clear, but at other times they are dependent on the accountant's judgment, which for better or worse can be influenced by the pressures of the situation. There are, of course, *generally accepted accounting principles* (GAAP) which detail various acceptable ways to account for assets and liabilities, as well as other sets of principles such as *generally accepted auditing standards* (GAAS). However, as with all general principles, there are times when the principles used don't fit the situation and individual judgment is required.

For example, in the article quoted above, T. Rowe Price's manager, Richard P. Howard, says that many accountants' way of looking at companies is out of sync with modern markets, which focus on a company's earnings rather than its asset value.

One of the problems that accountants have is that they're still working on the theory that the balance sheet [the statement of assets and liabilities] is sacrosanct. So they err on the side of writing down assets. They think that they're being conservative, but that's wrong.

Howard points out that writing down assets – reducing their value on the company's books – actually results in aggressive statements of profit.

> For example, if you write down the value of a plant, you take a one-time hit, but in future years the depreciation that would be assigned to the plant, and that would be subtracted from earnings, is reduced or gone, so earnings are higher. And as equity is reduced, the same amount of income produces higher return on equity.[4]

Assets and liabilities can be classified as either current or non-current – the non-current being non-current receivables and fixed assets such as land, buildings, and long-term investments. Current assets include cash, amounts receivable, inventories, and other assets expected to be consumed or readily converted into cash in the next operating cycle – production, sale, and collection. Hence, the owners' equity is divided between common or preferred stock, paid-in capital, and retained earnings, where common stock is the set dollar per share, paid-in capital is the premium paid for the stock (shares), and the amount of retained earnings equals the amounts earned/lost in the past and dividends distributed to owners. But what is "expected" to be consumed or converted into cash? Such items can be manipulated or at the least reported in any number of ways to determine what the owners' equity is.

Beside the balance sheet, there are: (1) *income statements*, where net income (profit) will occur when revenues exceed expenses, and a net loss will occur when expenses exceed revenues; (2) *statements of changes in retained earnings* – assets minus liabilities equal paid-in capital and retained earnings; and (3) *statement of changes in cash flow* that serve to identify existing relations and reveal operations that do or do not generate enough funds to cover an organization's dividends and capital investment requirement.

Since, as we noted, preparation of such statements allows great leeway in what to take account of and what not, as well as where to put things in presenting the statements, there is quite a bit of room for painting quite different pictures of an organization's financial affairs. It takes little imagination to envision a manager who, for fear of jeopardizing his job and wanting to impress his board, puts pressure on the managerial accountant to "cook the books" so that retained earnings look much more substantial than they are. But "cooking the books" and "creative accounting," as the names suggest, have an unethical element to them and are activities which need to be examined under the ethics of truth telling and disclosure. More recently "aggressive accounting" and "pro-forma accounting" seem to be euphemisms, at least in some cases, for being less than candid in presenting pictures of companies' financial situations.

But the ethics of truth telling and disclosure is a complicated issue for the accountant. *Why and to what extent is the accountant ethically obliged to disclose a true picture? Is there such a thing as a true picture?* To get at the principles that ought to be utilized in answering the first question – "Why is an accountant obliged to disclose a true picture?" – we will reflect for a moment on three things: first, how accounting is involved in exchange which involves selling; second, how exchange and selling is a market transaction; and third, what lack of disclosure in market transactions has in common with lying.

Accounting is developing information that is going to be used. If the use of the information is benign and the information is truthful, no ethical problems arise. But if the information persuades people to act in one way or other, and their action either benefits or harms the persons giving or getting the information, such information-giving takes on ethical importance. Depending on the use, giving out information can be very much like selling. The CEO is selling the board or the stockholders on the soundness of a company's financial situation. His bonus might be tied to how rosy a picture he is painting. The worth of his stock options rest on the financial picture. The CEO is selling the IRS a different picture of the company, and still a different one to potential investors and or lenders. Since accounting involves presenting the product to be sold, it enters into and influences market transactions.

In the ideal market transaction two people decide to exchange goods because they hope the exchange will make both better off. In a market exchange, nothing new has been produced, but both people are better off because of the trade. Ideally there is perfect information about the worth of what is being given and gotten in return. Such a trade, freely entered into with full information, should maximize satisfaction on both sides. That is the genius of the market, and the defense of our free-market system – freedom of exchange that leads to the overall improvement of the traders' lot.

However, if one of the parties is misled into believing a product is not what it is because it is misrepresented, the effect of both sides being better off is undermined. Deception usually leads to the deceived party getting something different and less valuable than they expected. The deceived party most likely would not have *freely* entered into the exchange had that party known the full truth about the product. If the true picture of the company had been available, the bank would not have made the loan, the public offering of stock would not have been so successful, the bonus for the CEO would not have been so large.

So, the conditions for an ideal market transaction include the freedom or autonomy of the participants, and full knowledge of the pertinent details of the product, which are required if we are to have what is often called *informed consent*. One's consent cannot be presumed if one is either forced into an exchange or lacks adequate knowledge of the product one is bargaining for. One could even say that a choice based on inadequate information is not a choice at all.

It is important to note that lying is not identical to saying something false. For example, sometimes people simply make a mistake and misspeak. In that case they say something false, but their action can hardly be characterized as lying. Telling a lie involves more than simply getting things wrong and not telling the truth. The essence of lying is found in its purpose, which is to alter another's behavior. Lying involves deliberately misrepresenting something to another person to get that person to act in a certain way, a way the liar finds desirable. We can, therefore, characterize lying as an attempt by one person, usually by means of speech, to present untruths (although one can lie also with gestures or looks), to get another person to act in a way they would probably not act if they knew the truth. So, misrepresentation or lying can be defined as a deceptive activity meant to evoke a certain response that would not have occurred if the truth were told. Simply put, we lie and deceive others to get our way. If the officials at Enron misrepresented the financial health of the company to their employees, in an effort to get them to hold on to their stock, to keep the value up so they could cash their own stock options at an inflated price, they did so knowing that if the employees had known, they probably would have sold their shares, thereby deflating the value of the stock even more.

If we apply this notion of lying to an activity where we paint a false picture of an organization's affairs in order to change a prospective investor's view of the financial health of the company, we see that we misrepresent the state of the organization in order to get him, the investor, to do what we think he wouldn't do if he had a true picture. Viewed from this perspective, a deceptive sale is an activity whose goal is to get the buyer to do what the seller thinks they probably won't do if they know the truth. From an economic point of view, as we have seen, such behavior violates the ideal market principle of free exchange based on perfect information, but more importantly from a moral point of view, in getting the buyer to act in a different way than they would in an ideal market, the seller takes away the buyer's *real* choice. In this situation, by lying the deceivers thereby use the buyer for their own ends. Such use, as we will see in the next chapter, is unjust and immoral, and is often called exploitation and/or manipulation.

Quite often we hear it said that we shouldn't lie because, if we do, people will not trust us. That is true, but it is a somewhat self-centered reason for not lying. From a moral perspective, the primary reason for not lying is that it subordinates another to your wishes, without their consent, for your benefit, without concern for theirs. It violates the rule, a version of the golden rule which says, "Don't do to others what you wouldn't have done to you." You want to know what you are getting when you buy something; so does everyone else.

Does failure to disclose fit into these considerations? Some would say, "not disclosing isn't lying, it's just not telling," but that misses the point. Any action of deliberately withholding information, or coloring information to get others to act contrary to the way they would if they had true information, has the same deceptive structure and consequence as the overt lie. It doesn't allow an informed choice.

But, the question occurs, "How much must the accountant disclose? Must he or she disclose everything?" It is an accepted principle in effective salesmanship (not to be confused with ethical salesmanship) not to say anything negative about the product one is selling and certainly not to disclose shortcomings unnecessarily. Managers selling the worth of their company to a bank where they hope to obtain a loan are in much the same situation. How many of the warts in the company need to be exposed to the bank? What is the obligation of the accountant in such a situation? There are pictures and pictures. Is the obligation in business more stringent than the one applied to private affairs? For example, if a person is selling their home, is it necessary to point out all the little defects that only the person living in the home knows about? There are, after all, laws that require some things to be disclosed. Is one ethically obliged to go beyond the law? If you do, you might succeed in discouraging every prospect from buying the home. People who go on job interviews need to sell themselves. Should they point out the flaws they have to their prospective employers? I know of no job counselor who would suggest that.

So, the questions arise, how much does one need to disclose and to what extent can failure to disclose be construed as market misconduct? Certainly some failure to disclose is wrong, but how much must we disclose? The above characterization of lying should help us decide. Whenever people are tempted not to disclose something, they should ask themselves why they are not disclosing. If you are withholding information because you fear the person won't act as you wish them to if they knew the whole story, you are manipulating.

One might object, saying there are times when one doesn't benefit from not disclosing, as in some social situations. For example, when your friends ask how you are, you don't have to disclose that you feel miserable. They probably don't want to hear it. Or when your friend asks if they look OK, you don't have to say, "You look terrible, like you just crawled out of bed." That kind of social non-disclosure is acceptable because in those cases one is not trying to change the behavior of another to personally benefit from it. Hence, if one fudges on the truth for some reason other than manipulating the behavior of the person lied to, that kind of lying may not be wrong. It is what we call a "white lie."

Nevertheless, a caveat is in order. In such social situations there may be a great deal of paternalism involved, and a great many assumptions being made about what the other wants or needs. It is not clear it is a totally harmless activity.

To return to our main point, it is the case that in some situations it might be hard to decide how much to disclose. One ought to at least meet the disclosure requirements of governing authorities.

What sort of disclosure and auditing requirements do accountants face? The Securities and Exchange Commission (SEC) oversees financial statements of corporations. The financial statements are prepared by the company's own accountants. Outside accountants audit the financial statements. In the United States, Certified Public Accountants do the audits. In the United Kingdom and its affiliates, Chartered Accountants perform the audit function. In all those places, the auditors certify that the companies' financial statements are *complete* in all material aspects and the figures have been arrived at through the *use of acceptable measurement principles*.

The most common set of measurement principles are "generally accepted accounting principles" (GAAP), which are supervised by the Financial Accounting Standards Board (FASB). The principles as supervised by the FASB can be overridden by the SEC, which, however, generally doesn't happen, and were being watchdogged by the Independence Standards Board until its dissolution in Summer 2001. In the United States, much of this is now under review, given some of the shortcomings of the regulatory system that came to light during the Enron/Andersen investigations.

As we saw there and in other situations, even in following GAAP, problems of disclosure arise. Take for example the problem of determining and disclosing asset value. Asset measurement provides a problem because it can be based on what assets cost or on what assets could be sold for now. They can be manipulated in other ways, too. For example, according to a 1994 report by Howard M. Schilit in *Business Week*, Heiling-Meyers Co.'s books showed the company included installment sales in revenues before sales were final. Now such a practice is perfectly legal and in accordance with GAAP, but according to Schilit "these accounting policies may distort the true financial condition" of the company.[5]

As another example of deceptive practices, Howard Schilit claimed that Kendall Square Research Corporation in a 1993 report was "booking sales for which no cash was coming in" or "claiming revenue from computer sales to universities that had not paid for the equipment."[6]

Finally, in the now infamous Enron case, Enron was selling assets to special purpose entities (SPEs), which were limited partnerships, most of which were under control of Enron. Only 3% of the SPE needed to be owned by people or organizations independent of Enron. This allowed Enron to show gains of $63 million, even though they still owned a majority share of the assets and liabilities, and they hadn't really been sold. Such exceptions for certain assets and liabilities that need not be counted were written into law in the late 1990s.

In addition, executives get rewarded with stock options, and while common sense indicates these are liabilities for the company since they are compensation for the executives, they are not accounted for in the statements. Yet in the Enron situation they made up at least $500 million dollars' worth of equity.

So, what is asset value? Asset value means value to the owners or what the company would be willing to pay the owners, which can be determined by what the company expects to be able to do with the asset. The value depends on three factors:

1. The amount of anticipated future cash flows
2. Their timing
3. The interest rate

Or the asset value could be determined by the amount the company could obtain by selling its assets. This determination, however, is rarely used because continued ownership of an asset implies that its present value to the owner is greater than its market value, which is its apparent value to outsiders. (In such a formulation, however, we enter into values beyond monetary, even including possible ethical values.)

Besides asset value, there is asset cost – most assets are measured at cost because it is difficult to verify forecasts upon which a generalized value system would have to be based. The historical cost of an asset equals the sum of all the expenditures the company made to acquire it. This obviously is sometimes difficult to determine.

Consequently with so much leeway in establishing the value of the assets of an organization, the delivery of the financial and economic picture can be skewed in any number of ways. Thus it is important from an ethical standpoint to determine: (1) who the financial picture is being created for and for what purpose; (2) who has the right to the picture and for what purpose; and (3) what is to be done when different pictures benefit different parties at the expense of other parties entitled to the pictures. For example, should the picture developed for the IRS show less assets and earnings than a picture developed for a prospective financier? Should those two pictures be different from the picture developed for the consumption of the board or the stockholders? Further, should the 10-K form reflect merely the quantitative picture of the company or should it emphasize the red flags and tendencies that will affect an organization's operations in the next business cycle?

Finally, to fill out the picture of the financial statement, where it comes from, and its elements, we need to mention some of the chief concepts and techniques utilized by accountants.

1. *Net income* – Income equals by definition a change in the company's wealth, during a period of time, from all sources other than the injection or withdrawal of investment funds.
2. *A transactions approach* – This recognizes as income only those increases in wealth (that can be substantiated) from data pertaining to actual transactions that have taken place with persons outside the company. This obviously doesn't recognize the wealth that is gained by service companies who hire a dynamic new worker who will produce salable commodities, for example.[7]
3. *Recognition of income* – This involves revenue estimates and expense estimates. The accountant needs to estimate the percentage of gross sales, recognizing that for some goods payment will never be received. Expense estimates are based on historical cost of resources consumed. Thus, net income equals the difference between value received from the use of resources plus the cost of the resources consumed in the process.
4. *Historical cost less depreciation* – To determine the value of assets it is necessary to depreciate some items. There are several depreciation formulas, including (but not limited to) the modified accelerated cost recovery system, the accelerated cost recovery system, straightline method, the double declining balance method, and the sum of the year's digits method. Which of these one uses will certainly affect the picture of the financial affairs of the company.
5. *Examples of formulas* – To determine the cost of goods sold one can use one of several measurement principles.
   (1) FIFO (first in, first out). In FIFO, the cost of goods sold is equal to the total cost of various batches of goods available, beginning with the oldest batch in the starting inventory.
   (2) LIFO (last in, first out).
   (3) Average cost.

Once again, when we look at the multiple procedures that are acceptable for portraying the financial affairs of an organization, it becomes clear that there are ample opportunities for presenting a picture of the organization that meets acceptable methods of accounting, but with clever manipulation that picture can be distorted.

While the major purpose of the accountant is to present a picture of the financial affairs of an organization, accountants play many other roles. These include the following:

Auditing: The most important role is the function of the independent accountant (auditor). The task of the auditor is to check whether the organization's estimates were based on formulas that seem reasonable in the light of whatever evidence is available and that those formulas are being applied consistently from year to year. The role of the auditor is not to determine whether the formulas are justifiable – that, at least in the United States, is the job of the Financial Accounting Standards Board.

Managerial accounting: A second role for accountants is that of managerial accounting. Businesses need controllers and internal auditors – for example, they need in-house accountants whose role would be to give the most accurate picture of the economic state of the organization, so that it can flourish. The accountant's primary responsibility would be to the company, respecting the truth. But, to the extent that board, managers and shareholders are at cross-purposes, the accountant is conflicted. These conflicts create the grounds for many ethical problems.

Tax accounting: A third role for accountants is the determination of tax liabilities for clients, either individual or corporate.

Financial planning: More and more accountants are engaging in financial planning, a fourth kind of activity, which springs from their knowledge of tax law and financial investment markets. One could argue this is not a role of an accountant as such, but rather a role an accountant is well qualified to take on given some of his or her areas of expertise.

Consulting: Finally, there is the area of consulting. Since an accountant is so familiar with the financial workings of organizations they become quite valuable for companies as consultants in helping with money management, income distribution, and accounting and auditing functions. Here, too, we could argue that this is not strictly a role of an accountant, but a potential role an accountant can play based on the expertise he or she has.

In later chapters we will examine the first three of these roles – auditing, managerial or financial accounting, and tax accounting – and the consequent ethical responsibilities that they involve. We will look briefly at the role of consulting and the difficulties that ensure with respect to conflict of interest and independence, particularly for accountants or firms who are fulfilling both an auditing and consulting role for a client.

The performance of all these different functions, and in particular the adoption of roles such as consultant and financial planner, has caused the accounting profession to move from the more traditional profession of the auditor into the more entrepreneurial professions of the consultant and planner. Many claim that these moves have created a crisis for accountants. Once again, the Enron/Andersen case brought some of these difficulties to the forefront of the news. Consequently accounting is no longer viewed as the staid, reliable profession it once seemed. It is now viewed as a profession in crisis, whose credibility is in question. The face of accounting is changing, if not in accounting itself (which maintains the same functions of auditing, attesting, preparing taxes, and presenting the financials of a company), then at least in the make-up and orientation of the larger accounting companies, and sometimes even the smaller ones.

Rick Telberg, on a pessimistic note, long before the Enron/Andersen debacle, in *Accounting Today*, noted that:

> In fact we are probably past the time when independence mattered. CPA firms long ago became more like insurance companies – complete with their focus on assurances and risk-managed audits – than attestors. Auditors are backed by malpractice insurance in the same way that an insurance company is backed by a re-insurer, so they have become less like judges of financial statements than underwriters weighing probabilities.
>
> Some in the profession have even argued that auditors should function less like ultimate arbiters of fact and financial reality, and be allowed, instead, to function more like investment bankers, and provide only "due diligence". So that CPAs, who once valued fairness and truthfulness in financial reporting, would then promise little more than nods and winks, all beyond the reach of meaningful oversight.[8]

But the danger in that case is that if every auditor or attestor acted in that way, the audits and attestations would be worthless. There would still be a use for accountants as tax preparers, and financial reporters, but the audit function, the heart of the accounting profession, would be cut out of the practice, rendered virtually useless by its misuse.

One could, of course, write a book on accounting ethics that simply said the function of the accountant is to do what is required for a company to flourish monetarily, but that would not be ethics. Society needs audited reports. It needs truthful reports. If the delivery of such reports is not profitable, then accounting firms committed to maximizing their own profit will turn away from the audit function. That will leave a large accounting job still to be done. Someone will step into the gap and perform the service. That person will then be subject to the same ethical requirements as the professional auditor of today. The names may change, but the function will remain.

In summary, the accounting profession was developed to give a true and accurate picture of the financial affairs of organizations. That picture was important to a number of constituencies. The accuracy of the picture is crucial. The creation of inaccurate pictures used to exploit those with a legitimate right to know the accurate pictures is structurally equivalent to the unethical behavior of lying. That constitutes a distortion of the true function of the accountant. We will look in the final chapter to see the numerous ways the profession is in crisis today. Largely it is an ethical crisis. But before dealing specifically with some of the issues mentioned, it will be helpful if we can spell out what ethics involves. When applied to areas of accounting ethics, it is not the simple matter we learned it to be when applied to everyday life. Business, accounting, managing, and market exchanges are complex procedures and we need a sophisticated code of ethics to deal with them. Consequently at this point we turn to a deeper examination of what constitutes ethics.

◢ NOTES ◣

1. Albert B. Crenshaw, "In The Red Or In The Black?; Pictures Painted By Company Statements, Audits Questioned," *Washington Post*, October 24, 1999, Sunday, final edition, financial section, p. H02.
2. Cf. *Encyclopedia Britannica Micropaedia*, "Accounting."
3. "Proposed Statement of Financial Accounting Concepts; Using Cash Flow Information and Present Value in Accounting Measurements," Exposure Draft (Revised) From the Financial Accounting Standards Board of the Financial Accounting Foundation (FASB), March 13, 1999, Revision of Exposure Draft issued June 11, 1997.
4. Albert B. Crenshaw, "In The Red Or In The Black?; Pictures Painted By Company Statements, Audits Questioned," *Washington Post*, October 24, 1999, Sunday, final edition, financial section, p. H02.

5. Michael Schroeder in *Business Week*, September 5, 1994.
6. Michael Schroeder, ibid.
7. The problem of what counts as wealth is a perennial one for economists, dating back even before Adam Smith's argument with the monetarists.
8. Rick Telberg, *Accounting Today*, editorial, September 26, 1999.

chapter two

Ethical Behavior in Accounting: What is Ethics?

KPMG quit as the auditor of Rite Aid Corporation, because they could not rely on the financial information the drugstore chain was reporting. Rite Aid's CFO resigned after the firm decided to restate three years of earnings downward by $500 million.[1] A Class action suit was filed in March of 1999 that alleged Rite Aid and some of its officers and directors had committed securities fraud by, inter alia, improperly reporting artificially inflated net income in violation of GAAP, and by failing to disclose other adverse information relating to its business practices and performance. The auditors failed to uncover such fraud.

In May of 1999 the SEC initiated litigation against the management of W. R. Grace for putting out numbers with the goal of misleading capital market participants. Specifically the SEC alleged that "Grace's managers tucked some of the division's unanticipated earnings away in a cookie jar for later. They then dipped into the jar for 1995's fourth quarter to get reported earnings closer to their target."[2] The SEC also alleges that "the auditors [Price-Waterhouse] knew about the initial false bookings but chose to let them slide because of their immateriality."[3]

In January 2000 the *New York Times* reported that the SEC found that partners and employees at Pricewaterhouse-Coopers routinely violated rules forbidding their ownership of stock in companies they were auditing. The investigation found 8,064 violations at the firm, resulting in the dismissal of five partners.[4]

SEC scrutiny of auditing practices came "after a series of high-profile corporate accounting frauds that auditors missed at companies including Cendant, Sunbeam, and Livent. Public shareholders lost hundreds of millions of dollars in these cases, and confidence in accountants was shaken."[5]

Last but not least, December 2, 2001. "Enron files the largest bankruptcy petition in U.S. history amid revelations of off-balance-sheet partnerships headed by company execs and other accounting irregularities. Six weeks earlier, Enron had restated earnings back to 1997, loping off almost $600 million in profits. . . . As the tawdry chapters in the Enron fiasco unfold like some dreadful penny novel, with explosive revelations of hidden partnerships, shredded documents, and shocking conflicts of interest, it's clear that the fall of Houston-based Enron is in a class by itself.

Everything about this debacle is huge: a $50 billion bankruptcy, $32 billion lost in market cap, and employee retirement accounts drained of more than $1 billion. The lapses and conflicts on the part of Enron's auditor Arthur Andersen are equally glaring. Andersen had been Enron's outside auditor since the 1980s, but in the mid-1990s the firm was given another assignment: to conduct Enron's internal audits as well.

For working both sides of the street, Andersen was rewarded richly. In 2000, the firm earned $25 million in audit fees from Enron, and another $27 million in consulting fees and other work. Sure it's possible that Andersen's auditors blocked all of those connections from their minds and managed still to render an objective opinion, but even former insiders wonder how . . .

As shocking as Enron is, it's only the latest in a dizzying succession of accounting meltdowns, from Waste Management to Cendant. Lynn E. Turner, former chief accountant for the SEC . . . calculates that in the past half-dozen years investors have lost close to $200 billion in earnings restatements and lost market capitalization following audit failures. And the pace seems to be accelerating. Between 1997 and 2000, the number of restatements doubled, from 116 to 233.[6]

Stories like these about "unethical" behavior by accountants abound. This is not to say that all accountants or accounting firms act unethically. By and large most act honorably. But stories such as the above are an indication that there is a need for ethical sensitivity and ethical behavior in the accounting profession. The past quarter-century has seen an increased awareness of the importance of ethics and morals in general, and the application of ethical principles to business and, along with that, to accounting in particular. But just what is ethics, and how is it to be applied and recognized in business in general and accounting in particular?

This chapter will focus on the nature of ethics and morality and its various dimensions so that we can see its import when it is applied to accounting practices and the accounting profession.

The words "ethics" and "morals" have a number of meanings. *Webster's Collegiate Dictionary* gives four basic meanings of the word "ethics":

1. The discipline dealing with what is good and bad and with moral duty and obligation
2. A set of moral principles or values
3. A theory or system of moral values
4. The principles of conduct governing an individual or group

"Ethics," in all its forms, is concerned with right or wrong, good or bad. It is either a set of principles held by an individual or group or the "discipline" which studies those ethical principles. The task of that discipline is the analysis and evaluation of human actions and practices. For example, according to some people or groups, assisted suicide is ethically acceptable. The discipline of ethics would examine what "assisted suicide" means (analysis) and what reasons can be given in support of or against such a practice (evaluation).

ETHICS: THE INTELLECTUAL ENTERPRISE

Every person has an ethical set of beliefs or ethical principles. For example, most people have some belief about whether practices such as euthanasia, abortion, capital punishment, and adultery are good, bad, right or wrong, acceptable or unacceptable. Most people think cheating and stealing are wrong, promises ought to be kept, and so forth. Each of these opinions constitutes a moral belief. If you were to write down what you believe about each of those actions or practices, that would constitute part of your ethic. One purpose of this chapter will be to help you examine your ethical beliefs. To begin, we will look at the structure of an ethical belief. Every ethical belief contains two elements. It has what logicians call a subject and a predicate. A subject is what the belief is about. "Wrong," of course, is the ethical predicate. A predicate, is what is said about the subject. Hence for the person who believes that "assisted suicide is wrong," "assisted suicide" is the subject of the belief and "wrong" is the ethical predicate. In the judgment (judgment here means simply the expression of our beliefs) "cooking the books is wrong," "cooking the books" is an action or practice. The subject of an ethical belief is usually an action or practice, sometimes a system or institution.

Actions

Human actions are the primary subject matter of our ethical judgments. By human action we mean behavior or activity that is *deliberate*, i.e. an action about which a person deliberates and freely chooses to perform. People deliberate about those things over which they have control, and consequently are held responsible for those actions. We don't hold animals responsible for their actions, because there is no evidence that they do things "deliberately" in the same way that humans can and do.

However, not all deliberate human actions have ethical import. The action must have a certain gravitas. One can deliberately decide to wear a red rather than a blue tie, or decide to eat mashed potatoes with one's fingers. But these are not actions with ethical impact. There are rules about what kind of tie goes with what and whether to eat potatoes with one's fingers, but those are rules of fashion or etiquette, not ethical rules. The deliberate actions we designate as "ethical" or "unethical" are usually actions that benefit or harm other people or ourselves positively or negatively in some serious way. They either benefit or harm others or us.

Social practices, institutions, and systems

Human actions are not the only subject matter for ethics. Besides actions, ethics examines and evaluates social practices, organizations, institutions, and even social, political, and economic systems. Whereas actions are individual activities, such as John's stealing in a specific situation, a social practice is a class of individual actions. When we say "stealing is wrong," we are evaluating a social practice and not a specific action. Thus we say, John's individual act of stealing is an instance of the general practice of stealing. Insider trading is a general practice. John's action of using insider information to buy a specific stock is an individual action, which is an instance of the general practice of using inside information.

Ethics also evaluates organizations, institutions, or systems. For example, we can evaluate the practices of an organization such as the American Institute of Certified Public Accountants, a company such as one of the Big Five accounting firms, the entire accounting profession, or even a system such as our free enterprise economic system which stresses free market exchange and profit making.

Those who would say "capitalism is a corrupt system" are evaluating a system. The recent calls for reform in the accounting profession imply that the practices of the profession are inadequate and need to be improved. It is, implicitly at least, an ethical judgment. In short, ethics can examine and evaluate actions and practices or systems, at both the institutional and individual levels. That leads some ethicists to distinguish between individual ethics and social ethics, which need not concern us here.

▲ WHY STUDY ETHICS? ▲

Why should an accountant get involved in this study of ethics? Doesn't every accountant already have a set of moral beliefs that he or she already follows? Certainly, but even so, there are several reasons for studying ethics.

- First, some moral beliefs one holds may be inadequate because they are simple beliefs about complex issues. The study of ethics can help a person sort out these complex issues, by seeing what principles operate in those cases.
- Second, in some situations, because of conflicting ethical principles, it may be difficult to determine what to do. In this case, ethics can provide insights into how to adjudicate between conflicting principles and show why certain courses of action are more desirable than others.
- Third, individuals may hold some inadequate beliefs or cling to inadequate values. Subjecting those beliefs or values to ethical analysis may show their inadequacy. It could be that at one time you thought some things were wrong but now you think they are acceptable, or vice versa. In short, after consideration you changed your mind about some of your ethical beliefs. Similarly, managers had thought in the past that it was acceptable to fire someone for little or no justifiable reason but ethical reflection and examination seems to show now that that practice is questionable. Some would claim that while accounting firms operate within the letter of the law in attesting to the fact that companies followed generally accepted accounting principles, they had an ethical obligation to encourage more realistic financial pictures. In another case, some would claim that while managers have obligations to stockholders not to

retain unneeded employees, they still have some obligations to those who are fired. Another example is seen in the diminished use of the principle of *caveat emptor*. At one time, this principle, let the buyer beware, was acceptable. Now, it is generally believed that in a great number of cases, the manufacturer has the obligation to inform the buyer of potentially harmful defects: *caveat emptor* has become *caveat vendor* (let the seller beware). At one time accountants thought it unacceptable to advertise. Today it seems a justifiable practice. So ethical reflection can make us more knowledgeable and conscientious in moral matters.

- A fourth, and very important, reason to study ethics is to understand whether and why our opinions are worth holding on to. The philosopher Socrates is known for showing that the unexamined life is not worth living. As an accountant, what are your basic goals in life? Are they compatible with other values that you have? If you need to choose between keeping a job and violating your professional responsibilities, what should you do? When your responsibility to family conflicts with your responsibility to your job, how do you resolve this?

- A final reason for studying ethics is to learn to identify the basic ethical principles that can be applied to action. That should help develop the skill of determining what should be done and an understanding of why it should be done. When faced with trying to decide what to do in a difficult situation, it is often helpful to have a checklist of basic questions or considerations that need to be raised and applied to the situation to help determine what the outcome should be. Just as in engineering one learns the principles of construction so as to apply them to certain activities, and in accounting one learns the principles of accounting in order to apply them to specific situations, so one also needs to learn the principles of ethics that govern human behavior in order to apply them when faced with difficult ethical situations. In that way, we can at least be sure we have examined the issue adequately by employing all the ethical principles available. The study of ethics can make us aware of the number and types of principles that can be used in determining what should be done in a situation involving ethical matters. Because ethical issues grow ever more complex in an ever more complex world, it behooves one to have a grasp of the underlying structure of ethical reasoning to help navigate the ethical sea.

A caution is in order at this point. Just as some people excel at baseball or golf without knowing the principles of a good swing, some people can act ethically without knowing the principles of ethics, or without knowing why an action is ethically "right." But, just as most of us can improve our golf by learning the principles governing a sound swing, it follows that we should be able to improve the ethical decision-making dimension of our behavior by studying why certain actions and practices are correct. For example, well-meaning people are often led astray by their intuitions without understanding or applying the principles or concepts that justify those intuitions and without appreciating the complexity of the situation. If you feel your only responsibility as a business person is to make a profit, that simple, yet inadequate, view will blind you to other responsibilities such as those you have to employees, employers, clients, and to others in the community in which you do business. If you feel your responsibility, as a management accountant, is simply to do what is in the interest of the company, even though it gives a false picture of the financial affairs of the company, you are blind to other possible responsibilities you might have.

▲ BEING ETHICAL: HOW TO DETERMINE ▲ WHAT TO DO

Accountants have a number of ethical responsibilities, to themselves, their families, and their profession as well as to the clients and company for which they work. But what is the accountant's basic responsibility as an accountant? Let us suggest a quite simple answer to begin with. Accountants should do their job! That's the ethical thing to do. We will show why later. For now though, suffice it to say that accountants implicitly promise to do that when they enter the profession and take a job, and promises should be kept. If one's responsibility is to do one's job, that fills in a lot of content about specific responsibilities. The responsibilities of a job are spelled out in either the job description, the employees' handbook, the managerial guide book, the company's code of conduct, and/or finally in the profession's code of conduct or ethics. Thus, a professional code of ethics and/or a job description set the standards for what one should do. For example, the American Institute of Certified Public Accountants code of ethics quite clearly mandates certain types of behavior in its seven principles.

1. In carrying out their responsibilities as professionals, members should exercise sensitive professional and moral judgments in all their activities.
2. Members should accept the obligation to act in a way that will serve the public interest, honor the public trust, and demonstrate commitment to professionalism.
3. To maintain and broaden public confidence, members should perform all professional responsibilities with the highest sense of integrity.
4. A member should maintain objectivity and be free of conflicts of interest in discharging professional responsibilities.
5. A member in public practice should be independent in fact and appearance when providing auditing and other attestation services.
6. A member should observe the profession's technical and ethical standards, strive continually to improve competence and the quality of services, and discharge professional responsibility to the best of the member's ability.
7. A member in public practice should observe the Principles of the Code of Professional Conduct in determining the scope and nature of services to be provided.

There is a great deal of ethics in those principles. Later in the book we will examine the AICPA code more thoroughly, but we will at this point address the notion of exercising sensitive moral judgment, as expressed in the first principle: "*In carrying out their responsibilities as professionals, members should exercise sensitive professional and moral judgments in all their activities.*" What is involved in sensitive judgment?

Sensitive ethical judgment would be attuned to the different factors that go into the making of ethical judgments. So it will be helpful to illustrate how moral judgments are constructed and what they are based on. If we can determine that, we can then discover ways of justifying our moral beliefs – ways to focus in on trying to get the right or most adequate answer possible about what to do in particularly difficult situations. Ethics gives us a powerful tool to employ in adjudicating ethical conflicts and resolving ethical issues.

Right now, you have a set of moral beliefs, one of which is that "People should do their jobs." But why is that the right thing for them to do? Why should people do their jobs, and should people do their jobs under any and every circumstance, even when it is not beneficial to them? For example, if we look at the second principle, it states that *"Members should accept the obligation to act in a way that will serve the public interest, honor the public trust, and demonstrate commitment to professionalism."* Does that mean that the accountant needs to place his or her family's interests below those of the public? If the accountant has an obligation to a client and one to his or her child or spouse, does he or she necessarily have to place the public's interest first? Further, what should one do when the interests of the company, say the need for more business, conflicts with the needs of the client or the public?

Thus, even if we agree that one ought to do one's job, there are times when it is problematic. There are times when there are conflicts within the job, and between the job, one's profession and one's personal life. What does one do in those cases? What standard does one turn to to adjudicate those conflicts? How can we tell what standards are acceptable, what actions are acceptable, what practices are acceptable?

How can the study of ethics help in answering some of those questions? Recall that ethics involves the analysis and evaluation of moral beliefs or judgments. Let us expand on that definition. We said that *analysis* of a moral belief or judgment might involve determining what is meant by one of the words in the belief. For example, the third principle states that *". . . a member should perform all professional responsibilities with the highest sense of integrity."* But exactly what is meant by "integrity"? The code suggests asking oneself, "Am I doing what a person of integrity would do?" But how are we to know what integrity demands? Hence, *analysis* of a moral belief involves determining what exactly the belief is asserting, i.e. whether the action under scrutiny is an action that a person of integrity would perform.

After analysis, we can move to evaluation, a determination of whether the belief is correct. Many people think that moral beliefs are subjective. They think just holding a moral belief is sufficient to make it correct. They say something to the effect of, "Well that's your opinion, so I guess it's true for you." But such an attitude has no room for *evaluating* beliefs. It just accepts anyone's belief as correct. But if just holding a belief makes it correct, then Hitler's belief that the Jews should be annihilated, and the slave owners' belief that slavery was justified, and infant sacrificers' beliefs that infant sacrifice is acceptable would make those pernicious beliefs correct. That just won't do.

But how are we to *evaluate* beliefs? How are we to tell whether a moral belief is correct or not, what a person of integrity would do, or whether our judgment is sensitive enough? Moral judgments are not like factual judgments, which express beliefs about the way things are, and consequently moral beliefs don't get verified or justified in the way factual beliefs do. For example, a factual belief might be something like the earth is a sphere. How do we justify that? Well, through observation and scientific theorizing. Some beliefs, like "it's raining," are verified by simply going out of doors and looking. Other beliefs, such as "light rays bend when they travel around the sun," are verified by speculating and using a hypothetical deductive method. But we can't justify or verify moral beliefs in the same way as we do factual beliefs. Moral beliefs have to do with values and values can't be seen or touched, and they involve emotions and desires and subjective preferences among other things. That's why many people think each person's belief is "true for them." Everyone must judge, but sometimes those judgments are correct and sometimes incorrect. How are we to evaluate them? In a good number of cases we have a perfectly straightforward procedure for *evaluating* moral beliefs. That procedure is to ask whether there are any *good reasons* why a certain action is morally acceptable or any *good reasons* why it is not.

Let's consider an example. Go back to your youth and imagine you had a very important date. You wanted to show up for the engagement in a very classy car, and your father had a Jaguar. You went to your father and asked if you could borrow the Jaguar on Friday. He said, "Sure, no problem." Friday came and when you went to ask for the car, your father said, "No. You can't have the car." How would you respond? Possibly with disbelief. You would say one of two things: either, "But you promised," or ask, "Why not?" This is simply our way of indicating that if your father thinks (believes) he is not obliged to give you the car, either his belief is not justified (correct), or he needs to justify it.

Suppose he answers your "Why not?" with "I don't feel like it." You wouldn't accept that as a good reason. That's no reason, and you would probably respond that way, and remind him that he had promised you the car. Promises, after all, are made precisely because people might not always feel like doing what they promised to do. If everyone always felt like doing what they promised we wouldn't need promises. So your father's justification, that he won't give you the car because he doesn't feel like it, carries no weight. He, like everyone else, is expected to overcome his feelings and honor his commitments. Imagine if everyone did whatever he or she felt like. Human institutions would collapse. A spouse could wake up one morning and simply say, "I don't feel like being married today." At any rate, your father, if he believes he has no obligation to give you the car simply because he doesn't feel like it, has got it wrong. His belief is incorrect.

But there might be a way he is correct. Suppose you ask, "Why not?" and he says, "Because the brakes just failed on my way home and there was no time to get them fixed." This is a perfectly *good reason* for not giving you the car – for his not keeping his promise. Furthermore, his belief that he is not obliged under those circumstances to keep his promise, but rather is obliged not to keep it and that you are obliged to let him out of it is *justified*.

The point of the example above is to show how moral beliefs are evaluated as correct or incorrect. They can be justified if there are good reasons for accepting them. *Good reasons* function in justifying moral beliefs similar to the way *observations* function in justifying factual beliefs. Furthermore these good reasons are the basis of ethical principles and are at the core of ethical theory.

What counts as good reasons are a number of precepts from common morality that we learned growing up. Let's list them. Do good. Don't harm. Don't lie. Don't cheat. Don't steal. Be fair. Respect others. Treat others as you would be treated yourself. Follow your conscience. Keep your promises or your word. Thus, if a person falsifies an expense account, we would agree that what they did was wrong because it was lying or stealing, just as you agree that what your father did was wrong because he didn't keep his promise.

When we look at the kinds of reasons given to justify our moral beliefs, we find two kinds of reasons, those that justify doing something and those that are reasons for *not* doing something. However, it is much harder to recommend a positive course of action than to prohibit a course of action, because when doing something positive we have an indefinite number of options open to us. It is much clearer to prohibit an action, for if we know an action will harm another, we only need to avoid it. So quite often we are clear what we should not do (negative injunctions), while we are not quite clear what we should do (affirmative duties).

A very good reason for doing anything will be that the action is good for you; that it's in your interest or benefits you. Another good reason for doing something is that it is good for or benefits society.

Other good reasons for performing an action are that it is just or fair, or because it is something you promised to do, as long as what you promised to do will not bring harm to someone. There are also reasons for *not* doing things, and they are the more common rules of morality. We should not do something because doing so would be to harm or use others. So, we don't cheat or lie or steal. We should not do something that harms others or ourselves. We should not be unjust or unfair. We should not break promises.

Let's apply those reasons to our recommendation that one should do one's job. Why should we do our jobs? In the first place, doing one's job usually benefits that person, by giving them a salary and meaningful work, so it is good for them. In the second place, because the division of labor provides the most efficient way for society to operate, one's job is a necessary cog in the wheel of progress, and doing it will benefit society. Finally, in taking a job one makes at least an implicit promise to do it, and promises should be kept.

▲ QUESTIONS TO ASK TO JUSTIFY ANY ▲ ACTION: THE BASIS OF ETHICAL THEORY

To evaluate any proposed course of action we need to ask one or more of the following basic questions.

Is the action good for me?

Obviously, if one can perform an action which is good for or benefits oneself, that is a good reason for doing it. As we saw, a very important reason for working is that it provides one with the where-withal to live, and hopefully in a number of cases it allows one to engage in fulfilling activity. There is a great deal of emphasis nowadays on the importance of meaningful work. But what is meaningful work except work that is beneficial to the person? We have a need to be creative and productive, and meaningful work will help us fulfill that need. Hence, it is good for us.

On the other hand, if an action harms oneself, that is a good reason for not doing it. Quite often people equate ethical behavior with actions that are detrimental to oneself and are hesitant to defend actions that are beneficial to oneself. But that is a mistake. A healthy self-interest is a good thing. If you don't concern yourself with your benefit, who will?

However, several caveats are necessary here. What is of benefit to oneself is not necessarily what one wants or desires. Our wants and our desires are a mixed bag: "I want the piece of cake but it is not good for me because I'm on a diet." We need to be a little clearer about what we mean by *what is good*. For our purposes let us say, that which fulfills basic human needs is good, although there may be other things that are also good. When we look at human beings we see several levels of need corresponding to several dimensions of human nature. There are material needs that fulfill the bodily dimension of human beings: needs for food, shelter, and clothing, as well as needs for health, some minimum wealth, and early solid training. Beyond that, since human beings are social, there are needs for relating to other people, as in friendship. These are the needs of the social dimension of human beings. Finally, because human beings are potential producers, there is a need for projects and goals and actions with a point to them; in short, meaningful activity. These are the needs that fulfill the active dimension. These are roughly what human goods are, and an action that provides one or more of these is a good action. To provide these needs for oneself is an important *reason* for performing an action. In short, in some cases, we can justify our belief that an action is good simply by showing it is good for us.

Is the action good or harmful for society?

The second question to ask of any intended action is whether it is going to be good for society. When we are thinking ethically, we don't usually stop at considering the benefit of the action for ourselves, we go further and think of its benefits for everyone affected. It should also be remembered that not every action performed in the world will affect us. If I suppose that neither I nor anyone else I knew used Tylenol, then whether Johnson and Johnson pulled it from the shelf really wouldn't affect me, so it's neither good nor bad for me. But I can say that it was a good thing to do, because taking it from the shelves probably prevented harm to those who might have used it. Simply, if a good reason for doing an action is that it benefits me, then that's true for everyone, so the more people benefited, the better. Of course, when the action benefits society but does harm to me there is a problem. We will return to this shortly.

Is the action fair or just?

A third question to be asked involves a cluster of considerations, one of which is, "Is it fair?" When you were a child, your mother probably treated you to a piece of cake numerous times. But imagine a time when your mother was giving you a piece but she was giving a bigger piece to your brother or sister at the same time. Wouldn't you think (you might be afraid to say) she was being unfair? In all of us, there is a belief that equals should be treated equally. Thus, if there is no relevant difference between you and your sibling you think you should get roughly the same size piece of cake. However, if it were your sibling's birthday, then you are not equal in all relevant respects, and the birthday creates a good reason for the sibling to get a bigger piece. So, the principle of justice, which all of us recognize, is that the same (equals) should be treated the same (equally). Of course, there is often disagreement about who and what are equal, but unless there is some relevant difference, all persons should be treated equally.

This notion of fairness gives rise to another reason that is often raised for or against a course of action, namely, the fact that I am entitled to have something or have something done, or I am entitled to have one of my rights respected. This leads on to the next question.

Does the action violate anyone's rights?

To the extent that all humans are equal, they have rights. Rights mean that they are *entitled* to be treated in a certain way. And the principle of equal justice means we have a right to be treated equally. A word about rights (entitlements) – there are two kinds, negative rights and positive rights. Negative rights are rights to things no one has to provide for us, things we already have, which are to be respected and not taken away, such as a right to life, a right to liberty, and, as some would argue, a right to property. For example, we have a right to liberty, because if we are the equal of others, by what right would they restrict our liberty? Why would their liberty be more important than ours? How would they be superior? A parent can restrict a child's liberty, but their relationship is not one of equality. Such rights are extremely important in business, in market transactions, where deceptive advertising and coercive marketing practices are condemned because they violate the liberty of the customer, and where government regulations are often objected to because they violate the right of the business entrepreneur to do business. In fact the entire free-market system sees the right to liberty as essential.

Positive rights are the entitlements to have something provided. For example, a child has a positive right to be educated. Now, it can be argued that for every positive right there is a corresponding obligation, for if there is not someone with the capability and responsibility to provide something, it is futile to claim a right to receive, a right of recipience. Thus, in a society without healthcare services, it makes no sense to claim a right to adequate healthcare. But even in a society with adequate healthcare, we need to specify who has the obligation to provide such rights. In a society with not enough jobs, it makes no sense to claim a right to employment. Who is obligated to provide it? On the other hand, in our society, customers have a right to quality merchandise, and should not be subject to *caveat emptor* (let the buyer beware). Also, stock purchasers have a right to accurate information about the financial picture of a company.

At any rate, if an action treats people fairly and does not violate their rights, then there is at least no reason not to perform it. On the other hand, if an action treats someone unfairly, and/or violates their rights, that is a reason not to do it.

Have I made a commitment, implied or explicit?

Besides asking about the harm, fairness, and rights implications of an action, there is another question that covers the area of relationships. It is the question, "Do I have a commitment?" This question asks whether any promises (explicit or implicit, based on an ongoing relationship) to act in a certain way were made. If there were, those promises ought to be kept. Thus, if the question, "Did I promise to do this?" is answered "Yes," then there is yet another *good reason* for doing it.

There are commitments we agree on that go beyond those that are the result of explicit promises and contracts. If we reflect a bit, we realize that any lasting relationship rests on implied promises and expectations of guaranteed behavior in spite of the contingencies of the future. Customers expect to get the benefits promised in insurance ads, and do not expect to get cheated because of the small print. Human beings can't live constantly redirecting their world on a day-to-day basis. They need to make and depend upon long-term commitments. As a professor I commit myself to showing up at classes a certain number of times, at a certain time, for a certain length of time. My commitment penetrates the future, and binds me to a course of action, whatever I am feeling.

People are promise-makers. It is what distinguishes us from the rest of the animal kingdom. Our social structure could not function if that were not true. Thus, a very *good reason* for doing something is that you have promised or committed yourself. But there is a caveat here. There is the old example of the ethical question, "Should I return the gun I borrowed from my neighbor if he asks for it back in order to shoot someone? After all, I had promised to return it when he asked." Clearly in this case, the harm that would come from returning the gun and thereby keeping the promise outweighs the responsibility to keep that promise.

▲ USING THE REASONS ▲

Let's see how considerations of these reasons work. If I am thinking of producing some commodity, one that brings a profit to the company, a commission to me, benefits society, and doesn't in the process treat anyone unfairly, or violate some promise or commitment, there are none but *good reasons* for doing so; it should be done. However, if I am tempted to falsely declare profits in a financial statement developed for a merger, and I see that it is not beneficial to the company, its executives, or the general society, and that the action would be deceptive and hence unfair, as well as violating the relationship of trust that my corporation has with the community, there are nothing but *good reasons* for *not* performing the action. (I assume that executives of companies which declare assets that don't exist, of course, think the fraud won't be detected, and they will benefit from it. If they know they will get caught, that gives them a good reason not to do it.)

Thus we have a decision procedure for determining what to do and what not to do. Ask the questions of common morality. If there are good reasons for performing the action such that it benefits me, and society, and does not violate justice or a commitment, then do it. If, on the other hand, an action does not benefit society or me, is unfair and requires breaking a commitment, then don't do it. Let's look at two examples: first, getting an education; second, abusing cocaine.

Presumably getting an education is beneficial to oneself, because it is personally fulfilling in any number of ways. Secondly, it is presumed in this society that the more people who are educated, the better the society will be. Thus, if you get an education, not only will you benefit, but society will also benefit. If in getting the education you need you do not violate any commitments and no one is unfairly deprived because you are getting an education – that is, you are not using up someone else's spot, or you are not going to college while your younger sibling is staying home and working to help you through college – then the action has no unethical consequences. In this case we have a prima facie example of an action that should be done. It benefits the person, society, and is not unfair or does not violate someone else's rights. Not only should it be done, one would be hard-pressed to justify not getting an education under those circumstances. What reasons could a person give? As a matter of fact, your reading of this passage is an action that can be described as getting an education. Ask yourself why you are doing it. Presumably, you will answer that it will benefit you, by allowing you to learn, or pass a course, or some such. Secondly, this learning will make you a more productive – and, perhaps in this case, a more ethical – employee, and hence your company, society, and your family will all benefit. Suppose you are learning at no one's expense, and that studying is not interfering with your personal responsibilities, then you have very *good reasons* for getting an education. You are doing what you should and it is a justified action.

Of course, it is easy to imagine circumstances or situations that make getting an education problematic. Let's examine some of those. Suppose you just hate this subject. In that case you are torn between doing something you don't like that may be good for you, and giving in to your likes and dislikes, which may be bad for you, but may also be good for you. As already pointed out, we shouldn't confuse what benefits one with what one desires, wants, or likes. Nevertheless, sometimes getting what one wants can be beneficial and doing what one hates may be harmful. At times we need to defer pleasure or suffer pain for some long-run benefit, but there are times we need to pursue pleasure in life.

Similarly, suppose that we could show that taking a particular course does not benefit society. Then that is a reason not to do it. Finally, suppose you have other commitments, to family, friends, or significant others. If taking a course of study means less time with your loved ones or someone else to whom you have responsibilities,

THE ETHICS OF ACCOUNTING   41

then getting an education becomes problematic. Thus, circumstances are important. They can change the appraisal of an action. But, by and large, getting an education is what one should do.

Now consider the other example – abusing cocaine. Is abusing cocaine good for you? Certainly not. Is it good for society? It costs society in terms of lower productivity, higher medical costs, unreliability, etc. Is it fair or just? While the action of taking cocaine might not involve unfairness or injustice, it may lead to unfair or unjust practices, or actions such as not fulfilling one's commitments. (*Note:* here we talk of abusing cocaine, not simply of using it.) In this case, then, we have a proposed action that has *no good reasons* in support of it. We can see this is a prima facie case of something we should not do.

▲ ETHICAL DILEMMAS ▲

The questions we have asked are answered by providing the reasons which give us the principles that form the basis for what is often called "ethical theory." Basically what are called "ethical theories" are simply very general principles which are claimed to be the basic foundation for all ethical rules or judgments.

It is important to note that there would be no ethical theory necessary if all our cases were clear-cut. The examples show there are many situations where what needs to be done is perfectly clear. That's when an action fulfills all the considerations we have mentioned. It is also important to note that you don't have to take an ethics course to ask those questions. They are questions you and everyone else ask when faced with a decision. So, when you had to decide whether to take a particular course, you asked yourself those questions, not perhaps in those words, but with the purpose of investigating the costs, benefits, and fairness to you and others. We presume also that you answered them all yes, for you are taking the course, and don't question your right to do so. But suppose in making your decision you had some difficult questions.

Suppose taking a course of action would mean you could not keep a promise to your children to go on vacation this spring. So, it might benefit you, but it might not be fair to your children. In a situation like this, when there are reasons for doing something and reasons for not doing it, we are faced with an *ethical dilemma*. Because dilemmas exist, ethicists in looking for a way to resolve them appealed to what they considered the most basic ethical principles. These principles became identified as their theory of what the primary ethical principle was. Thus, those who appeal to fairness over harm, when they conflicted, fell into one camp, and those who appealed to benefits over fairness or rights, fell into an opposing camp. For example, drug testing may prevent harm, a good reason for doing it, but it may violate a right to privacy, a good reason for not doing it. Blowing the whistle on the accounting procedures of a firm may prevent harm as well as fulfill an accountant's responsibility to the general public, but it might violate a feeling of loyalty. For those who give precedence to harm considerations, there is reason to do it. For those who give precedence to rights considerations there is reason not to do it. So, to resolve dilemmas, ethical theories developed.

Ethical dilemmas occur when there is a conflict of reasons

An ethical dilemma is a problem that arises when a reason to act in a certain way is offset by a reason not to act that way. Ethical theories arise as the court of last resort to help resolve such dilemmas. Each rival ethical theory maintains that, when there is a conflict of reasons, there is an overriding reason that takes precedence over all other reasons. That reason is articulated in the principle that expenses the theory. Those who appeal to fairness and rights over consequences are called *deontologists*. Those who appeal to consequences over fairness and rights are called *consequentialists*. Let us look at a classic case to see how ethical theories involve their proponents in offering the solution to such dilemmas.

Some classic moral dilemmas

A classic moral dilemma is that of Jean Valjean in Victor Hugo's *Les Misérables*. Valjean has been an ex-prisoner living under an assumed name, in violation of parole for years and has been hunted relentlessly by a police officer named Javert. Javert, who is passionately committed to upholding the law, is obsessed with tracking Valjean down, and has reason to suspect that Valjean – who has changed his name, become mayor of a small French town, and the owner/ manager of the factory in the town – is the prisoner he seeks. To entrap Valjean, Javert lets it be known to Valjean that an innocent vagrant is about to be identified as Valjean and sent to prison.

Valjean realizes that if he does not reveal his true identity an innocent man will go to prison in his stead. What should Valjean do? It certainly won't benefit him to go to prison, nor will it benefit the town that depends on his managerial and governing skills. On the other hand it is not fair that an innocent vagrant should suffer in place of Valjean.

This is an example of a classic dilemma, the stuff that makes great drama. It presents a situation where whatever one does, one does something wrong and something right – where, so to speak, one is "damned if one does, and damned if one doesn't." In this case, doing what will benefit society will be unfair, or doing what is fair will harm society.

Another example of the same sort of dilemma (where the goodness of benefiting society is negated by the unfairness of the act) occurred when President Truman had to decide whether to drop an atomic bomb on Hiroshima and Nagasaki. People who defend the action say, among other things, that the taking of the 80,000 lives was justified by the saving of three million lives that would have been lost if Japan had been invaded. Those who condemn the action say that no matter what the consequences, the action was immoral and unjust because dropping the bomb involved the taking of innocent lives.

There are dilemmas of the same sort in accounting, though not as dramatic. Suppose you are a controller of a company, and you need a rather large influx of cash to develop and market a new product which will keep the company afloat. You are fairly sure you can get a loan from a bank, but not if you accurately report the expanding inventory you have on a now outmoded product at its true value. So, if you fudge the numbers and misrepresent the financial health of the company you can get the loan and keep the company going. Here again is a situation where the good consequences of benefiting a large number of people is negated or overridden by the necessity of being honest and preserving one's integrity.

Solving such dilemmas gives rise to ethical theory. We turn to a discussion of ethical theory in the next chapter.

▲ NOTES ▲

1. Miriam Hill, "Accountant Quit over Mistrust," *Philadelphia Inquirer*, November 19, 1999, section C, p. 1.
2. J. Edward Ketz and Paul B.W. Miller, "W.R. Grace's Disgraceful Abuse of Materiality," *Accounting Today*, May 24, 1999.
3. J. Edward Ketz and Paul B.W. Miller, ibid.
4. Gretchen Morgenson, "S.E.C. Seeks Increased Scrutiny and New Rules for Accountants," *New York Times*, May 11, 2000, section C, p. 1.
5. Adrian Michaels, "Big Five Must Unite to Avoid Return to Their Audit Days," *Financial Times* (London), Thursday, May 11, 2000, companies and finance section, p. 44.
6. Nanette Byrnes et al. "Accounting In Crisis," *Business Week*, January 28, 2002, pp. 44ff.

chapter three

Ethical Behavior in Accounting: Ethical Theory

Dilemmas help illuminate the nature of ethical theories. Competing contemporary ethical theories claim to provide an ultimate principle that can be used in solving a dilemma. If in the case of Victor Hugo's Jean Valjean we appeal to considerations of what is good for all the people affected, and allow those considerations to take priority over the fairness issue, we adopt the stance of those theorists who are called "utilitarians." For utilitarians, the ultimate justifying reason for an action is that the action brings about more good than harm for more people. If on the other hand in the Valjean case we appeal to considerations of fairness and let those take priority over the consequences of the action, we adopt the stance of those theorists who are called "deontologists," who think actions themselves are ethical in spite of their consequences. For deontologists the end doesn't justify the means. Finally, if we only allow considerations of what is good for oneself and that self-interested concern takes priority over considerations of what is good for others and what is fair, we adopt the stance of those theorists who are called "egoists." It is somewhat strange to talk of an "ethical" theory that gives priority to self-interest, but there are a few defenders of egoism, so we need to look at it briefly.

An *ethical theory*, then, *prescribes* a principle that provides the overriding justifying reason for pursuing any course of action.

Both egoism and utilitarianism use the good of consequences as the ultimate determinant of whether an action is ethically acceptable. Egoism gives priority to the reason, "It benefits me." When there is a conflict between something good for me and for society, or when there is a conflict between something good for me and its fairness, egoism recommends the self-serving action. Consequently, we can define egoism as the theory that maintains that, "One should always act in one's own best interest."

Utilitarianism gives priority to the concern for everybody's good, including one's own. But one's own interest is factored into the total overall good. If one's own interest conflicts with the overall good, it is set aside. Thus, utilitarianism maintains that, "Those actions should be done that bring about the greatest good for the greatest number of people."

Finally, there is the theory that gives precedence to the questions of fairness, rights and commitment, and that says the right thing should be done no matter what the consequences to myself and others. This is called deontological theory. It would maintain that, "The end does not justify the means."

Let us summarize. Many times in deciding what to do, no conflict arises between reasons. In many situations what is good for me is also good for society and is fair and just. At those times, we have every reason to perform the action and all three of the competing theories' principles would be fulfilled. But in the cases where there is conflict, the dramatic dilemmas, disagreement arises about which principle to follow. Which reason takes precedence? If we decide always for ourself, we are probably egoists. If we are moved by considerations of benefits to society, we have a utilitarian bent. If we are moved by questions of fairness or justice, we are following deontological lines. The plausibility of each of these theories rests on the fact that each of them appeals to a very important *reason* for choosing a course of action.

We all use all three reasons. Because at times these reasons conflict and we are unsure of what to do, some people conclude that we can't justify ethical beliefs, and are skeptical about the possibility of ethical knowledge. But, our contention is that it is only in the rare cases of dilemmas that we are not sure. In other cases a systematic investigation could lead to some resolution of the problem. We *can* determine what to do.

Let us turn, then, to a brief investigation of each of these positions; an investigation of contemporary ethical theory.

▲ EGOISM ▲

As mentioned above, egoists maintain a general principle of the following sort: "One ought always to act in one's own interest." Most people upon encountering such a principle think it is unethical. It is a principle that appears to promote selfishness, and in our society at least, if not in all societies, selfishness is considered wrong. How can a principle that promotes selfishness be an ethical theory? We would argue that it can't, and we will show why presently.

But why would some people pursue such a faulty theory? What insight are egoists tapping into? Usually egoists are objecting to those moralists who emphasize altruism over the pursuit of self-interest. The egoists want to claim what we have already noted, that pursuing one's self-interest is a good thing. However, we will see that the egoists go too far, because *always* pursuing one's interest necessarily leads, at times, to selfishness, and selfishness is immoral.

To see this more clearly it is necessary to define selfishness, and contrast it with *self-interest*, which is something quite different. Self-interested pursuits are not bad; they are good. It is healthy if everyone pursues their interests. Psychologists have pointed out the necessity of self-love and self-esteem, and the desirability of a robust pursuit of one's projects and dreams. After all, if I don't pursue my interests who will? That is why an action which benefits you is a good action, and a good *reason* for doing something is that it will be good for you.

The problem arises when the pursuit of your interests can only be done at the expense of others. If I can only make this sale by persuading a customer who can't afford the product to buy it, that is selfish behavior, and to justify it by saying it will aid me is to justify it egoistically. Thus a principle which says "*always* do that which is in your own interest" is a principle which *necessarily* promotes selfishness – that is, immoral behavior at times, those times when our interests can only be achieved at the expense of others. Since selfish behavior is probably the most common example of *unethical* behavior, and egoism mandates selfishness, it is rejected on those grounds as an ethical theory. Clearly it would not be acceptable in a profession such as accounting, where the code of ethics calls for the acceptance of the "obligation to act in a way that will serve the public interest."

There are other, more formal, objections to egoism that can be mentioned. First, egoism is incompatible with many accepted human activities, such as advice-giving and building true friendships, and, in the context of business, with being an agent for another. Simply ask yourself: how can one who is always acting in their own interest give advice? Suppose the advice would hurt the advisor. For accountants, there are times when they will not have the expertise necessary to render a client the best service. In such a situation, the accountant may have to recommend another professional and lose the business. You do not just do this because you are concerned about your long-term self-interest; you do this because it's your responsibility as a professional who has a duty to look out for the client's best interest.

The incompatibility of egoism with friendship is also easy to show. Who would consider a friend a "true" friend if they knew that "friend" was just around for what he could get out of the friendship? We expect friends to put themselves out for us, and we expect to put ourselves out for our friends. The consistent egoist, then, can be seen to be recommending against friendship.

A further difficulty with egoism is that it cannot resolve disputes. If everyone is to look out for themselves, what should two people do if both of them need the same thing? To say both should look out for their own interest does not solve the problem. Egoism can give no practical recommendation. For some, the task of ethics is to help settle disputes, so of what use is a theory that fails to adjudicate?

Further, there is a strange anomaly inherent in egoism – it cannot be promulgated (i.e. published, taught, or even spoken out loud). If I as an egoist seriously believed that I ought to act in my interest, and expect always to act in my interest, what is the effect of teaching that to others? It will put them on their guard in those situations where my interests conflict with theirs, and that is certainly not in my interest. If you are an egoist, your doctrine recommends that you do not teach your theory, for to teach your theory is not in your own interest. To teach the egoist theory is to act unethically according to that theory.

A standard objection of philosophers to egoism is that it cannot be formulated in any way that is not either illogical or absurd. For example, if I say, "Everyone ought to act in *their* own self-interest," it recommends an impossible situation in those cases where two people need the same thing. If we reformulate it to read, "Everyone ought to act in *my* own interest," to whom does the "my" refer? If it refers to whoever utters it, it is the same as the first formula, but if it refers to a specific person it becomes absurd. For example, if John utters it and says, "Everyone ought to act in my (i.e. John's) interest," isn't that absurd? Why should everyone in the world, billions of whom do not know John, act in John's interest? Why indeed should even those who know John act in John's interest? Perhaps it could be reformulated as "I ought always to act in my interest." But if the "I" means everyone uttering it, it is exactly the same as the first formula. If the "I" doesn't mean everyone, then it ceases to be a principle at all, for principles are supposed to be generally applicable.

There is a final objection to egoism. Egoism is based on a distorted egocentric view of the universe. Certainly, I am the most important person in my life. I am inside my own skin, so to speak. I am always with myself, and I see the world from my eyes and from my perspective. Thus, from my point of view, I am the center of the universe. But how limited that view is. The moral point of view demands that we expand beyond that view. An objective detached view recognizes that there are billions of other people in the world, more or less like me, all having a subjective viewpoint. Why then on objective grounds am I so important? The answer is, of course, that I am not. Not even the most influential person that ever lived is that important. He or she was just one among billions. Since egoism is thus limited we can see that it is inadequate. It is interesting to note that in the AICPA code of ethics this issue is addressed by the principle that states "a member should maintain objectivity."

If egoism is so inadequate, what is its appeal? The appeal seems to come because our self-interest is so strong. Economists like Adam Smith[1] thought that if a society set up a system that tapped into that strong self-interest, and legitimized it, the society would be more productive. It is even claimed by some philosophers, such as Thomas Hobbes,[2] that if you look deeply into human motivation all actions are directed by self-interest. "Everybody looks out for number one." Consider the following passage from *Catcher in the Rye*:

> Even if you did go around saving guys' lives and all, how would you know if you did it because you really wanted to save guys' lives, or whether you did it because what you really wanted to do was be a terrific lawyer, with everybody slapping you on the back and congratulating you in a court when the goddamn trial was over, the reporters and everybody? How would you know you weren't being a phony? The trouble is, you wouldn't.[3]

Salinger's Holden Caulfield says he doesn't know if we are acting in our own interest all the time, but there are philosophers who think that all human beings, when you look below the surface, already naturally act in their own interest. If everyone always does look out for their own interest, then recommendations of courses of action need to take that into account. My mother used to say, you'll catch more flies with honey than with vinegar. If something is naturally disposed one way, you'd better make recommendations that conform to that disposition rather than go against it.

Such a belief, that everyone always acts in their own interest, is called *psychological egoism*, because it is a theory about how people behave, and psychology is the study of human behavior. Psychological egoism is distinguished from ethical egoism, because psychological egoism is descriptive and tells how one *does* behave, whereas ethical egoism is prescriptive and tells us how one *ought* to behave. If psychological egoism is true, then any moral principle that prescribes that one act contrary to one's own interest would be sheer nonsense, since it would recommend that people do what is psychologically impossible.

Is psychological egoism true? It would seem not, for one can always find counter-examples like Mother Teresa, or one's own mother, or the soldier who throws himself on the grenade – examples of people who don't seem to be acting in their own interest all the time. Nevertheless, there is a strong contingent of thinkers who utilize psychological egoism as a model to explain human behavior and make predictions on the basis of that egoism. When economists do it, when they assume that all humans are selfish, it affects their view of what is acceptable and not acceptable in life, for it is foolhardy to tell people to go against their nature, just as it is foolhardy to expect stones to fly. Economists like Adam Smith say, "It is not from the benevolence of the butcher, the brewer, or the baker, that we expect our dinner, but from their regard to their own self-interest." But if that is so, then it makes sense to appeal to people's self-interest. Because of that belief, Smith continues, "We address ourselves, not to their humanity but to their self-love, and never talk to them of our own necessities but of their advantages."[4]

So economists and some philosophers and social scientists assume everyone is self-interested, and develop economic and business models based on that assumption. The self-interested rational maximizer is even given a name: *homo economicus*, economic man. The consequence, as Kenneth Lux points out, is that, "Economics is fundamentally different from every other discipline in the academic world, including the other social sciences. No other academic field, unless influenced by economics, teaches and promotes self-interest. All other fields essentially teach knowledge and truth."[5] In this way, economics, which looks value neutral since it assumes everyone always acts in their own interest, attempts to set up systems which will be most productive, systems which, if they are to work, must appeal to the way humans are. For the economist, that is selfish. No wonder, then, if selfishness is the opposite of ethical, and business is an activity in our economic system designed around facilitating selfishness, people often claim that business ethics is an oxymoron, a contradiction in terms. From that perspective it is difficult, if not impossible, to conceive of business as being ethical. To be ethical – if it means to sacrifice one's self-interest – would be bad business.

What can be said of this psychological egoism? Without getting too philosophically technical, we need only remind ourselves of the sacrifices that humans make for one another. Even if the psychological egoists call that "selfish" behavior, it's the kind of behavior we want. Even the most hardened economist, who recommends that we appeal to the self-interest of everyone, justifies that appeal by predicting that in the long run it will benefit society. Adam Smith's doctrine of the "invisible hand" does exactly that. It maintains that the invisible hand guides society, by assuring that self-interest will lead to societal benefits. The fact that it doesn't means that ethically we have to examine a system that justifies the unchecked pursuit of self-interest and at times check self-interest that occurs at the expense of others, the self-interest that we called selfishness. (Finally, it is interesting to note that Adam Smith does not believe self-interest is the only motivator.) Consider the following passage.

> Howsoever selfish he may be supposed, there are evidently some principles in his nature, which interest him in the fortune of others and render their happiness necessary to him, though he derives nothing from it except the pleasure of seeing it.[6]

But if egoism is inadequate as a theory, what of the other two theories – utilitarianism and deontological theory? We will examine them briefly.

▲ UTILITARIANISM ▲

The principal maxim of utilitarianism is best expressed by John Stuart Mill in his work by the same name. "Actions are right in proportion as they tend to promote happiness, wrong as they tend to produce the reverse of happiness." Mill continues, that "the happiness" he is talking about is "not the agent's own greatest happiness, but the greatest amount of happiness all together." The appeal to the happiness of all is Mill's answer to the egoists.[7]

Utilitarianism has recently been formulated in a slightly different way: "Do that action which will bring about the greatest good for the greatest number of people." Utilitarianism is significantly different from egoism because the consequences utilitarians use to judge the worth of an action are not simply the consequences for the agent but include the consequences for everyone concerned with or affected by the action, including the agent.

We can characterize the differences in the following chart. We have:

An Action   �️⎫ leads to ⎧ Consequences
Practice   ⎬   →   ⎨ (a) for self (egoism)
Institution ⎭   ⎩ (b) for all concerned, including self
                              (utilitarianism)

Good consequences make it a good action; bad make it a bad action.

Utilitarianism accords with our moral sensibilities much more than egoism, and reflects what we do quite often when we come up with reasons to justify an action or practice. Doing something to make myself happy is acceptable unless in doing so I made someone else miserable. If I do something that maximizes happiness for more than me while leaving precious few people miserable, that is a justifiable action.

Take an example. Suppose an accountant sets up a check-kiting scheme in which he takes the company's money for a few days and deposits it in his account before putting it in the company account, thereby gaining the interest on the money. It may be in his interest, but it is certainly not in the interests of the greatest number of people. It is an unethical action because clearly it will harm more people than it will help. According to the utilitarian principle, the action of kiting checks is wrong or unjustified because the action harms others. Utilitarians praise people and companies because the people or companies provide services or goods for society and do not do significant harm. Individuals and companies that cause more harm than benefit will come to be condemned by utilitarians.

A utilitarian uses the following procedure for justifying or condemning an action. Take any action. Compute the benefits and harms of the consequences for everyone affected. If the action brings more total happiness than unhappiness for more people, it is justified. If it brings about more total unhappiness for more people, it is wrong. Utilitarianism is the ethical theory that uses a cost–benefit approach.

However, there are some difficulties that arise in using the utilitarian approach. Suppose we recall the example of deceiving a bank about assets. It probably seems clear cut that deceiving a bank is wrong. It is just wrong for a company to misrepresent its worth to a bank that is considering giving you a loan. The bank has a right to know the company's true condition. But one often hears such behavior justified on the grounds that, "Well, in this case the bank is just too strict, so if I lie to the bank, I'll get the loan, save the business, and in the end everyone will be better off." But to justify lying by appealing to possible good consequences, even if you are sure those consequences would follow, shows one of the weaknesses of utilitarianism. This is typical of problems that arise if we use utilitarian principles. Let's examine some of them.

A major problem with utilitarian theory is *the distribution problem*. The phrase "the greatest good for the greatest number of people" is ambiguous. Are we obliged to bring about the maximum good, or are we obliged to affect the maximum number of people? Suppose I had five units of pleasure to *distribute* to five people. Let's make it five pickles. How, according to the formula, should I give them out? The easiest answer seems to be, give each one a pickle. Then supposedly each would get one unit of pleasure and we would have distributed to the greatest number of people, five. But suppose two people passionately love pickles and two people don't care one way or another about pickles. Then, wouldn't it make sense to give two apiece to the two people who passionately love pickles, and none to the two who don't care? This can be represented as follows.

(A)   A = 2 pickles = 2 units of happiness
           B = 2 pickles = 2 units of happiness
           C = 1 pickle   = 1 unit of happiness
           D = 0 pickle   = 0 unit of happiness
           E = 0 pickle   = 0 unit of happiness

   Totals   3 recipients   5 units of happiness

In the case where you distribute equally you get:

(B)   A = 1 pickle = 1 unit of happiness
           B = 1 pickle = 1 unit of happiness
           C = 1 pickle = 1 unit of happiness
           D = 1 pickle = 0 unit of happiness
           E = 1 pickle = 0 unit of happiness

   Totals   5 recipients   3 units of happiness

Thus, in case B you distribute to the greatest number of people but don't create the greatest amount of happiness, whereas in A you create the greatest amount of happiness, but don't distribute to the greatest number of people. This is the problem of distributive justice: a problem of fairness, a problem of how the goods and the burdens of the world are to be distributed. It is a problem that the utilitarian decision procedures do not deal with well, one that seems better handled by deontologists. One sees this problem arise in the utilitarian justification used in defense of capitalism. The claim is often made that the economic system of capitalism produces the highest standard of living in the history of mankind. That is probably true, but the rejoinder is that in maximizing all those goods, some people get much and others get little or nothing. Thus, the critics of capitalism say that while capitalism might create the greatest amount of material goods in history, it doesn't distribute those goods fairly to the greatest number of people. Utilitarianism leaves us with the question, "How are we to fairly distribute those goods?"

Another dilemma for utilitarianism is *the problem of deciding what counts as the good*. We adverted to this problem earlier, when we discussed the dimensions of human fulfillment, and contrasted the good, what we need, with what we desire. John Stuart Mill and his mentor Jeremy Bentham were *hedonists*. They equated the good with happiness, and happiness with pleasure. But there are numerous difficulties with hedonism. Philosophers usually view goods as objects of desire or objects we aim at, etc. Generally, they break them down into two types: intrinsic goods or extrinsic (instrumental) goods.

An intrinsic good is something desired or desirable for its own sake, whereas an extrinsic, or instrumental, good is good because it will lead to or is instrumental in obtaining another good. Money is an example of an extrinsic good. Happiness is clearly an intrinsic good. We show this by pointing out that when someone asks, "Why do you want money?" you can answer, "Because it will make me happy." But if they ask why you want to be happy, there is no further answer.

Mill recognizes happiness as the intrinsic good. Others recognize other things such as freedom or knowledge as intrinsic goods. Some claim there is a plurality of intrinsic goods. Thus, we have a disagreement among utilitarians about what counts as intrinsic goods – *pluralists* think there are a number of intrinsic goods; *eudaimonists* think happiness as well-being is the only intrinsic good; and, finally, *hedonists* think happiness is the same as pleasure. Mill, then, was a hedonistic utilitarian. Others, and especially economists, despair of identifying objective goods and appeal to individual preferences, or "satisficers" (i.e. what the people prefer or what they think will satisfy them).

However, such an identification is problematic because what I prefer is not always good for me, and/or what satisfies me is also not always good for me. Hence one can ask the utilitarian, "Are your promoting actions those which are *actually* good for people or only those which *seem* good for them?" If as in business and economics the notion of an objective good is dropped in favor of individual preferences, good can only be judged by demand. But that assumes that what people prefer (want) is what they need (good). We have seen that that assumption is unwarranted. For example, capitalism is often defended because it brought about the highest standard of living in the history of the world. But others criticize it because they think that a high standard of living is not necessarily a good thing. So we might agree about what an action will lead to, but disagree whether that goal is good or not. Anyone who does cost–benefit analysis will recognize that determining what will count as a cost and what will count as a benefit is a difficult matter. So the fact that there is disagreement about what counts as good should point out an area where we can expect disagreement in ethical matters.

Accountants, who deal in valuation, are especially sensitive to the problems of determining what counts as values. While a utilitarian approach would probably have a basic appeal to accountants because of their tendency to do cost–benefit analyses, it should make them wary because they, more than most, recognize the problem of judging the value of things where there is no clear standard. Utilitarians, then, along with other ethical theorists need to determine what things are good, a determination which often provokes ethical disputes, for, at times, one person's good is another person's poison.

A further quandary with utilitarianism is *the problem of predicting the future.* To decide whether an action is right by looking at the consequences means you have to look into the future and try to predict what will happen. Sitting looking out the window at a dismal day the weatherman predicted would be sunny reminds us how tenuous and risky predictions are. The inability to predict creates several problems. Should utilitarians do what they *think* will bring about good or should they do what they actually *know* will bring about good, and how are they to know? Very often what we think will be good turns out to be bad, or has unforeseen consequences. Economists speak of them as "externalities" – undesirable, unpredicted side effects of some activity.

Beyond these difficulties, there is one many critics of utilitarianism think is the most serious. We call it *the problem of illicit means*. Anyone who was raised with the maxim, "The ends don't justify the means," is familiar with the problem because from a utilitarian perspective, it is precisely the ends that do justify the means. So utilitarians are accused of letting the ends justify the means, even if the means are immoral. The example of misrepresenting assets to the bank is one such example. Even if we justify the misrepresentation by saying that no harm will be done, since the company will survive, and the bank will not get hurt, it is still lying. History is replete with examples of actions and practices we consider immoral being performed for the sake of bringing about some desirable end. Suppose I could save one hundred people by killing three innocent children. Should I do it? The happiness of the one hundred saved would seem to outweigh the pain of the loss of three dead children. But our ordinary moral sentiments are outraged at the suggestion, for they tell us that the taking of the life of these innocent children is immoral. Suppose I could achieve law and order by convicting a despicable character who happened to be innocent of the crime. Suppose I could benefit my company by misstating receivables. Suppose Lockheed could keep employees working by bribing Japanese government officials. Suppose I could keep my plant open and a hundred people employed by lying to a government inspector. Suppose I can keep a healthy economy in the southern US states by maintaining slavery. Suppose I can dampen inflation by keeping unemployment artificially high. These actions (means) are ordinarily viewed as immoral in spite of the good consequences (ends) they bring about. Utilitarians who justify an action by citing its good consequences are accused of missing an important part of ethics, the fact that some actions are wrong in principle, no matter what the consequences.

The philosopher W. D. Ross raises one more very important objection to utilitarianism which he calls its "essential defect."

> The essential defect of utilitarianism is that it ignores, or at least does not do full justice to, the highly personal character of duty. If the only duty is to produce the maximum of good, the question who is to have the good – whether it is myself, or my benefactor, or a person to whom I have made a promise to confer that good on him, or a mere

fellow man to whom I stand in no such special relation – should make no difference to my having a duty to produce that good. *But we are all in fact sure that it makes a vast difference.*[8]

Ross reminds us of how much we think ethical priority should be given to the duties one has because of special relationships. If you are uncomfortable with lying to the bank, it is because as an accountant you have a special duty to give accurate pictures of companies' financial positions. That is what accountants do.

Ross belongs to a group of ethical theorists who maintain that there are ethical concerns with the actions themselves that prohibit the actions in spite of the consequences. These theorists are called deontologists. The name deontologist comes from the Greek word "deontos," meaning "what must be done." It is sometimes translated as "obligation" or "duty." The foremost deontologist was the eighteenth-century philosopher Immanuel Kant.[9]

▲ KANT AND DEONTOLOGY ▲

Kant preceded Bentham and Mill, so he did not directly confront their utilitarianism. Still, if we apply his principles to utilitarianism he would say it is misguided as a theory because it fails to take into account one of the characteristics of a moral action, a moral motive. He calls the motive "duty." We can call it "a sense of moral obligation" and contrast it to "inclination" or "desire." For Kant, if you are acting merely from inclination or desire you are not acting morally at all. Rather, you are behaving pretty much the same as non-human animals. For Kant, it is the ability of humans to act on a *moral* level, to transcend animal instincts and inclinations, that makes human beings special, makes them moral and gives them a dignity and rights.

How does Kant establish this? Let's contrast and compare a human being's way of acting with a spider and a beaver. A spider spins webs. Why? Because of an "instinct" or "inclination." Nature makes spiders that way, and if they don't spin webs, they won't live. Beavers chew trees and build dams. Why? Because nature makes them that way. Notice it would be ridiculous to imagine a spider refusing to spin a web, or a beaver not chewing a tree. They have no *choice.* They are not *free.* They are inclined by nature to do those things and consequently will do them.

According to Kant, human beings, too, have inclinations. They are inclined to pursue things which they "want." They have psychological propensities for things and inclinations to pursue goals. But they have two capabilities other animals don't have. The first is to be able to choose between alternate means or ways of achieving the goals they are inclined to, and the second is the freedom to set aside those goals or inclinations and act out of a higher motive.

Being able to choose alternative means to a goal makes humans somewhat, but not significantly, different from other animals. A beaver has an inclination for food and shelter, yet is equipped by nature with only his instinct to chew bark and build dams to fulfill that inclination. Humans, even though they have the same inclination for food and shelter, can choose different means of achieving that; they can build lean-tos, dig caves, build houses, fish, plant crops, etc. They have choices about how to fulfill their inclinations. The second difference between humans and the rest of the animal kingdom, namely that humans can act against their inclinations for the sake of duty, is the one Kant thinks is particularly significant.

Deontological ethics

Human beings, because of their practical reason, ask the question, "What should one do?" But this question can take two forms. If we are interested in fulfilling our inclinations, the question is qualified: "What should I do, if I want to fulfill my inclinations?" However, at times the question is not what to do to fulfill our inclinations but what to do to fulfill our obligations or duty. Here the question is unqualified: "What should I do, no ifs, ands or buts?" The answers come out as rules. Kant calls these rules *imperatives*. For him all practical judgments – that is, judgments about what one ought to do – are imperatives. But, as we said, there are qualified oughts, oughts determined by some prior inclination, and unqualified oughts. The qualified oughts he calls *hypothetical* imperatives, and the unqualified oughts he calls *categorical* imperatives.

When we make decisions based on qualified oughts, what determines the goodness or badness is whether the decisions accomplish the goal. For example, if I'm in a third floor classroom, and I want to get to the cafeteria in the next building, what should I do? I could jump out the window, but then I'd probably break a leg, if not more, and not get to the cafeteria. Such a course of action would be *imprudent* for Kant. The *prudent* thing to do would be to take an elevator down or walk down the steps. Notice that in our opening remarks in this chapter, we talked about the advantages of being ethical in business. If we say we should be ethical because it accomplishes what we want, then we are saying it is prudent to be ethical.

Human beings, unlike animals, can be prudent or imprudent because they can choose effective or ineffective means to fulfill their inclinations. But by and large, aside from the fact that they have a brain to offer them options whereas other animals have only instincts, there is not much difference between humans and animals in striving to fulfill their inclinations. So, humans can be prudent, but that only gives them a hypothetical imperative, which for Kant is not an ethical imperative. Thus, for Kant, if we are being ethical because it's good business, we don't have the proper ethical concern. Note that Mill and utilitarians only deal with hypothetical imperatives (e.g. if you want the greatest good for the greatest number of people, do X). But Mill cannot answer two questions: first, "Why should anyone *want* the good of others over their own good?" and, second, "What difference does it make what motives anyone has for their action?" Where the latter is concerned, clearly it makes a difference. If someone gives to charity for a tax write-off, that isn't as fine a motive as giving because alms-giving is a duty. So, unless one is acting out of one's duty, one is not acting out of moral concern.

So, according to Kant, if you're doing something simply to fulfill a desire, you're not acting out of a moral motive. To act morally you do something simply because it is the moral thing to do, it's your duty. It follows, then, for Kant, that if you are doing the right things in business, simply because it will improve business, you may not be doing anything wrong, but you are certainly not acting from an ethical motive. These oughts of your duty are expressed in a *categorical* imperative. The categorical imperative simply says, "Do X." There are no ifs, ands or buts. If you ask, "Why do X?" the answer is because it's your duty. But notice that this is not a very informative answer, because a duty is what you're supposed to do. So we ask, "What is one's duty?" Kant gives several formulas to help decide what one's duty consists in.[10] We will look at two.

The first formula of the categorical imperative

The first formula for the categorical imperative is: *Act so that you can will the maxim of your action to become a universal law.* This needs explaining. A maxim is your reason for acting. Suppose you borrowed some money from a friend. When it came time to repay it, you didn't have the money. You then decided not to repay it, even though your friend needed it, because you didn't want to bother borrowing it from a bank, and you knew your friend would not press you on it. Your reason for not paying it is, then, that it's inconvenient to repay it. So, the maxim of your action becomes, "Don't repay debts (keep promises) if it's inconvenient to do so."

Now let's will that maxim to be a *universal law*; let's universalize our rule. What would happen if everybody broke promises because it was inconvenient? Well, the first thing is that such a universal practice would lead to chaos. Promises are made to guarantee that they will be kept, even when things are tough, when we are not inclined to keep them. So people would end up not trusting others and society would be chaotic. But notice that this is judging a universal practice by the consequences, and assuming chaos is not beneficial. Isn't that just a more complex utilitarianism, where we judge the universal practice rather than the particular action? Of course it is. Kant needs to go further, and does. He realizes that the consequence of not paying debts or keeping promises would be people not wanting to loan money or accept promises, but whether that consequence was unfavorable or not is not the determining factor.

The categorical imperative stresses that you must "will" the maxim to be a universal law. For Kant, the will is practical reason, and you cannot will promises not be kept, not because of unfavorable consequences, but because to will it is to involve yourself in a will-contradiction. A will-contradiction is when you want to eat your cake and still have it. In the case of promise-breaking, you are willing to break a promise. But if you universalize promise-breaking, no one would trust anyone, so no one could make a promise to another, since a precondition of promise-making is trust. So to will promise-breaking you must will promise-making. That's the contradiction and that's what goes wrong. The same sort of contradiction holds for stealing, lying, cheating, adultery, and any number of other activities we take to be immoral. The only way the action would work would be if others didn't all behave like you did. But that's a double standard.

The implications for business and accounting are obvious. There must be an atmosphere of trust to allow business to function. But to will to break promises is to will other people not to break them, for, if they did, promise-making would be impossible. But to will others not to follow your rule is to make an exception of yourself. When we universalize we get out of our egocentric view. We see that we are the same as others, and this is the basis for the rule of justice, which is: *Equals should be treated equally.*

The second formula of the categorical imperative

Kant does not stop with just the first formulation of the categorical imperative – he moves on to another. Unlike the other animals that are under the design of nature's inclinations, human beings can transcend these limitations. Humans can set projects by themselves; they are free or autonomous. Because of that, Kant calls humans *ends in themselves.* They are the ones who determine their moral life – they are autonomous, self-regulating. Consequently they are special, and all alike in that they make values and ends. Since they are so special, Kant thinks there is another formula that applies: *Act so as never to treat another rational being merely as a means.*

Based on this view, everyone is morally equal and ought to be treated with respect and dignity. Their rights ought to be respected and no one ought to be used *merely* as a means or instrument to bring about consequences that benefit the user. This is the deontological answer to the utilitarian's problem of illicit means. It is not justifiable to use someone or exploit someone to make society better. Hence Jean Valjean should not use the vagrant. Employers should not use employees. We call that "exploitation." Deceiving customers is a way to use them to make a sale and benefit ourselves. That's false advertising. Cooking the books to get a bank loan is using the bank. Breaking promises is using people. That's breaking contracts. This formula of the imperative shows what's wrong with slavery or sexism. It dehumanizes by turning a fellow human being into a thing or an instrument to be used by the person exploiting. Arguments for employees', customers', and other stakeholders' rights rest upon this kind of consideration. Businesses have no right to use stakeholders in the name of profit. They must respect the right and autonomy of customers, employees, and others they relate to. Thus, ethical reasons that rest on concerns for justice, fairness, dignity, and rights are quite often deontological in inspiration.

As you might expect, though, just as with every theory, there are some shortcomings of deontological thinking. The first is the criticism of the utilitarians. They want to know why one should do one's duty if it isn't going to lead to happiness. Why be moral just to be moral? The utilitarian might ask if the end doesn't justify the means, what does? They *suspect* that under Kant's deontological positions there is a belief that one ought to be moral because virtue will be rewarded. But if that is so, it reduces deontology to an egoistic or at least utilitarian reason.

Beyond that there is a problem of what to do when there is a conflict of duties. W. D. Ross, the contemporary deontologist we mentioned earlier, thought that we had certain duties that are prima facie – we should fulfill them unless they conflicted. They include duties to keep promises, to express gratitude, and to do good and to not do harm. Ross suggests that when prima facie duties conflict, we need to determine an actual duty. But what criterion of adjudication do we employ? Take an example. Suppose you promised your friend that the next time he was in town you would have a long-delayed heart-to-heart talk. Suppose also you promised your child you would take him to the ball game on Wednesday. Your friend calls Tuesday night and says he will be in town for a brief time tomorrow, and the time conflicts with the time of the ball game. Of course, you could probably get out of that particular conflict of obligations, but suppose there were really strong reasons for keeping both promises and you can't do both. How would you decide? Ironically, we decide by weighing the consequences and, if you keep the promise that causes the least harm, you are using a utilitarian reason to solve the conflict. Often the demands for justice for one person conflict with the demands of liberty for another. It is simply not enough to cite that we ought to provide liberty and justice for all. Utilitarians will insist that in such a conflict of rights, the only course of action is to consider the consequences of the action. So they insist that sooner or later deontologists have to give priority to considerations of consequences.

One last objection is sometimes raised against Kant's second formula. What exactly does it mean to say "merely" as a means? Very often we use people. Students use teachers; teachers use students. We use someone who is buying something from us, if only to help us make some money. Some relationships are defined in terms of use. But is someone being *merely* "used" if they give their permission to be used? Can an employee be exploited if he signs a contract specifying that he will perform certain services? The fault is that Kant's notion of "use" is quite unspecified. One person's use is another's exploitation.

▲ VIRTUE ETHICS ▲

Having examined utilitarian and deontological perspectives, we need to turn our attention to one more approach to ethics. It has recently been called the ethics of virtue or character. It addresses the question not of what one should do so much as the question of what one should be or become. What type of virtues should a person seek to develop? What makes a good businessman, or what makes a good person? Are these the same or compatible? Is honesty a virtue that businessmen ought to develop?

The word virtue comes from the Latin *virtus* meaning "power" or "capacity," and *virtus* was used to translate the Greek word *arete*, which means "excellent." For ancient Greek philosophers, especially Aristotle, the good life, the life of well-being, was a life where one did things in accord with one's excellent capacities: *activity in accord with virtue*.[11]

Which capacities were the excellent ones? Those that led, obviously, to well-being. Aristotle and his mentor Plato introduced a model for us to follow. A thing should fulfill its potential; be, so to speak, all that it could be. That potential was potential to a determinate end or goal or purpose. Just as a knife has a purpose to cut, and is a good knife if it cuts well, so humans have purposes, goals, ends, and are good if they accomplish or fulfill them.

Accountants have the goal to respond as truthfully as possible and will be excellent accountants if they accomplish that goal. But, since they are more than accountants, they have other goals that require some of the same and some different, and perhaps conflicting, virtues. Which of these virtues accountants are called upon to develop or utilize becomes an important question. For example, loyalty is often viewed as a virtue, but is it compatible with hard-nosed auditing practices? One problem will be to see if such conflicts can be reconciled.

What we have presented briefly are some ethical theoretical considerations that will be applicable to the issues we will be dealing with. These considerations give us a set of ethical approaches that the accountant should take seriously in evaluating his or her various practices. An accountant should benefit others and avoid harming them. An accountant should live up to his or her responsibilities because they have committed to them. An accountant should not exploit others. Finally, an accountant should develop virtues like integrity and honesty to assure a life practiced with virtue.

One can look at theory in several ways – as providing principles to be used in resolving ethical issues, or as describing to us what *underlying* principles inform people's ethical decision-making processes. Yet most people don't often reflect on those principles. They follow feelings, or intuitions or their guts. Or they follow the everyday rules they were trained into. The principles will allow us to analyze and evaluate these feelings and intuitions. But the everyday rules are important and we will take a brief look at them. Among these everyday rules, particularly in professions, is the code of ethics that provides ethical rules for any profession.

At this point, we turn to those issues. We will look at the accounting profession and then at the accountant's code of ethics.

▲ NOTES ▲

1. Adam Smith, *The Wealth of Nations*, 1776 (Ed. Edwin Canan. New York: Random House, 1937), IV, ii, 9.
2. Thomas Hobbes, *Leviathan*, chs 13 and 14.
3. J.D. Salinger, *Catcher in the Rye* (New York: Signet Books, 1960), p. 155.
4. Adam Smith, *The Wealth of Nations*, I, ii, 2.
5. Kenneth Lux, quoted in *Business Ethics*, May/June, 1991, p. 30.
6. Adam Smith, *The Theory of Moral Sentiments*, I.i.1.1.
7. John Stuart Mill, *Utilitarianism*, ch. 2.
8. W. D. Ross, *The Right and the Good* (Oxford University Press), p. 60.
9. The fundamental ethical theory of Immanuel Kant is found primarily in *The Groundwork of the Metaphysics of Morals*. See especially Chapter 1.
10. Kant, ibid., ch. 2.
11. Aristotle, *Nicomachean Ethics*, bk 1, ch. 10.

chapter four

Accounting as a Profession

In the mid-twentieth century in the United States, when the discipline of accounting was seeking the status of a profession, a Commission on Standards of Education and Experience for Certified Public Accountants issued a report that listed seven characteristics of a profession:

1. A specialized body of knowledge
2. A recognized formal education process for acquiring the requisite specialized knowledge
3. A standard of professional qualifications governing admission to the profession
4. A standard of conduct governing the relationship of the practitioner with clients, colleagues, and the public
5. Recognition of status
6. An acceptance of social responsibility inherent in an occupation endowed with the public interest
7. An organization devoted to the advancement of the social obligations of the group.[1]

That accounting meets the first two characteristics is plain. Accounting is a complicated discipline requiring formal study to become a competent expert. To become a Certified Public Accountant (CPA) usually requires a bachelor's degree in accounting as well as passing the rigorous CPA exam. Keeping one's status as a CPA requires staying abreast of the latest developments with continuing education.

In meeting the third standard, the accounting profession is like any number of groups who have banded together to give service to the general public from a position of expertise. Doctors, attorneys, teachers, engineers, and others each form a group and view themselves as professionals dedicated to serving their clients or patients.

Such professional groups generally determine who will be able to obtain membership in the group, and they do so by meeting the professional qualifications. But continued membership in the group also requires abiding by the standards of behavior of the group. Those standards generally include the requirement to look out for the client's best interest. Only those who meet the qualifications will be admitted into the profession, and individuals can be expelled from the profession if they do not live up to its standards.

Thus, standards four and six are quite interesting. Four indicates that a profession needs "a standard of conduct governing the relationship of the practitioner with clients, colleagues, and the public" and six indicates the need for "an acceptance of social responsibility inherent in an occupation endowed with the public interest." But what should be included in a standard of conduct which governs the relationship of practitioners with clients, colleagues, and the public? What should it prescribe? What does the professional owe to each of those constituencies?

One of the finest analyses of what the ethical standards of professionalism should be was developed by Solomon Huebner, the founder of the American College. Huebner founded the college to provide advanced education for insurance salesmen. He was concerned about turning insurance salesmen into professional agents. In 1915, seven years before he founded the college, Huebner delivered an address at the annual meetings of Baltimore Life and New York Life Underwriters, in which he laid out his vision of what he thought it meant to be a professional – arguably as fine a statement of what it takes to be a professional as exists.

Huebner cited four characteristics of the professional.[2]

1. The professional is involved in a vocation useful and noble enough to inspire love and enthusiasm on the part of the practitioner.
2. The professional's vocation in its practice requires an expert's knowledge.
3. In applying that knowledge the practitioner should abandon the strictly selfish commercial view and ever keep in mind the advantage of the client.
4. The practitioner should possess a spirit of loyalty to fellow practitioners, of helpfulness to the common cause they all profess, and should not allow any unprofessional acts to bring shame upon the entire profession.

If we apply Huebner's criteria to accounting it is evident that accountants are useful since modern organizations would be impossible to run without accounting skills. What about nobility? The code of ethics of the American Institute of Certified Public Accountants points out: "The accounting profession's public consists of clients, credit grantors, governments, employers, investors, the business and financial community, and others who rely on the objectivity and integrity of certified public accountants to maintain the orderly functioning of commerce."[3] Contributing to the orderly functioning of commerce certainly makes the profession useful and noble.

But the most interesting characteristic of the professional noted by Huebner is the third, for it offers a prescription to be followed in determining what standard of conduct should govern an accountant and what social responsibility is inherent in the occupation of accounting. Huebner's characteristic requires the professional to "abandon the strictly selfish commercial view and ever keep in mind the advantage of the client." Such a requirement is important because, as we have seen, the notion of professionalism has been utilized by many groups to bring ethical concerns to bear in the world of business. In appealing to one's profession, and the commitment one makes to that profession, one takes on ethical responsibilities. As the Commission on Standards of Education and Experience for CPAs points out, being a member of a profession involves one in *a standard of conduct* governing the relationship of the practitioner with clients, colleagues, and the public, as well as an *acceptance of social responsibility* inherent in an occupation endowed with the public interest. In short, to be a professional is to take on ethical responsibilities which require abandoning a strictly selfish commercial view.

But what is a strictly selfish commercial view? It is the view of those for whom the *only* concern of business is making money or increasing profit. It is a view voiced by extreme advocates of the free-market system, echoing the economist Milton Friedman and others who insist that "the primary and *only* responsibility of business is to increase profit."

Such a view distorts the position of Adam Smith, the father of the capitalistic free-market economy. As we mentioned earlier, Smith, the eighteenth-century economist-philosopher, in his book *The Wealth of Nations*, convinced economists that a great deal of good comes from a system that allows people to pursue their own interests. This became the theoretical foundation and justification of the capitalist free-market economic system. But Smith did not adopt a "strictly commercial point of view," for he insisted that the pursuit of self-interest be constrained by ethical considerations of justice and fairness. "Every man is left perfectly free to pursue his own interest, his own way, and to bring both his industry and capital into competition with those of any other man, or order of men, as long as he does not violate the laws of justice."[4] There are times when justice demands when it is ethically required to sacrifice one's own interests for the sake of others. Chief among those times is, of course, when one is meeting the obligations of a profession to look out for the best interest of a client.

The "strictly selfish commercial view" encourages the pursuit of self-interest with no limits – a pursuit that inevitably leads to selfishness. As we saw in our discussion of egoism in the last chapter, the English language uses two different words, self-interest and selfishness, to distinguish between behavior that is perfectly acceptable (self-interested behavior) and behavior that is ethically inappropriate (selfish behavior). The New Testament wisely prescribes that we love our neighbor as ourselves, thereby reminding us that if we don't have a healthy self-love and self-interest, we do both our neighbors and ourselves a disservice. Nevertheless, if we pursue our self-interest *at the expense of another*, we act unethically. In an ethical world, there are times people need to sacrifice their own interests for others or the common good – a need to abandon the "strictly selfish commercial view."

Further, one could argue that it is precisely because of the specialized knowledge that one should abandon this strictly selfish commercial view. Wherever there is specialized knowledge developed to provide services for other people, there exists a situation where there is asymmetry of knowledge and hence asymmetry of power, which gives rise to a dependency relationship (i.e. one person will need to depend on the word and advice of another, because they lack the knowledge). With such asymmetry of knowledge comes the potential to abuse one's position of power and take advantage of the other person. (For example, a doctor could recommend a procedure that a patient does not need, but that would bring the doctor extra compensation. The patient in such a case would depend on the recommendation of the doctor since the patient does not have the doctor's medical knowledge.) The ethics of our society insists that those in such a position of superior knowledge have an obligation not to abuse that knowledge or to use it on the unknowing to gain unfair advantage. Hence the professional has the obligation to abandon the strictly selfish commercial view and follow ethical precepts. But what are those obligations the professional needs to follow?

In the light of the above, one can argue that the accountant as professional has three obligations: (1) to be competent and know about the art and science of accounting; (2) to look out for the best interests of the client, avoiding the temptation to take advantage of the client; and (3) to serve the public interest.

We see these responsibilities clearly articulated in the AICPA code of ethics, which begins by asserting that the acquiring and maintaining of requisite knowledge is the CPA's individual responsibility.

> Competence is derived from a synthesis of education and experience. It begins with a mastery of the common body of knowledge required for designation as a certified public accountant. The maintenance of competence requires a commitment to learning and professional improvement that must continue throughout a member's professional life. *It is a member's individual responsibility.* In all engagements and in all responsibilities, each member should undertake to achieve a level of competence that will assure that the quality of the member's services meets the high level of professionalism required by these Principles.[5]

A second obligation, which accountants have and which accrues to all professionals, is the obligation to look out for the best interest of the client. The accountant is hired to perform a service for the client. Given that, it goes without saying that when an accountant accepts a position with a client, there is at the very least an implied understanding that the accountant will look out for the interests of the client. As the code states, "A distinguishing mark of a profession is acceptance of its responsibility to the public . . . which consists of clients."[6]

But that same passage of the code also takes note of a further quite interesting but often overlooked obligation specific to the accountant, the obligation to the public.

> A distinguishing mark of a profession is acceptance of its responsibility to the public. The accounting profession's public consists of clients, credit grantors, governments, employers, investors, the business and financial community, and others who rely on the objectivity and integrity of certified public accountants to maintain the orderly functioning of commerce. This reliance imposes a public interest responsibility on certified public accountants. The public interest is defined as

the collective well-being of the community of people and institutions the profession serves.[7]

Thus, the accountant has to accept the "social responsibility inherent in an occupation endowed with the public interest." Accountants as professionals therefore have this social responsibility inherent in their occupation. It is important to note that this responsibility arises because of the purpose of accountants, cited above, which is "to maintain the orderly functioning of commerce." It is also interesting to note that the public interest, defined as "the collective well-being of the community of people and institutions the profession serves," sounds remarkably like "stakeholder" interests, a concept current in much business ethics literature. In the light of Arthur Andersen's role in the Enron debacle, it is important to note that, no matter what the facts, Arthur Andersen had an obligation to look out for the public interest, to protect the integrity of the free-market system.

This brings us to the last characteristic of a profession, "an organization devoted to the advancement of the social obligations of the group." The AICPA in the United States and professional organizations in other countries do that. This would lay an important obligation on the AICPA to devote itself to the advancement of the social obligations of the group. The AICPA would be mandated by this proviso to promote the obligation of accounting firms to the general public. If performing auditing and consulting services for the same company stands in the way of an accountant being objective, then the AICPA has a responsibility to promote ways that will allow the accountant to meet his or her obligations.

It follows that if accountants are responsible to various groups – clients, colleagues, and the public – they will inevitably face conflicting pressures from each of the groups. How is one to handle these pressures? The code of ethics suggests that, "In resolving those conflicts, members should act with integrity, guided by the precept that when members fulfill their responsibility to the public, clients' and employers' interests are best served."[8]

This passage reveals an interestingly optimistic motivation for being ethical. It claims that there cannot be a substantial conflict between the public, clients', and employers' interests. In doing what is right for the public, the clients' and employers' interests are best served. Hence, if an employer pressures a management accountant to "cook the books" the accountant should not acquiesce, not only because it would not be in the public's best interest, but also because it would not be in the employer's interest. Would Enron have been better off if its accountants had vigorously called to attention some of its more opaque transactions? In short, there are assumptions made in the code that honesty is always the best policy, and that ethical business is always good business. In effect this means one has to read interests in such a way that even though something appears to be in a client's or employer's interests, if it is not in the public's interest, that appearance is false and misleading.

Given the accountant's purpose to maintain the orderly functioning of commerce, without succumbing to the strictly commercial point of view, it is not a far reach to suggest that the public has a right to expect public accountants to act with ethical probity. As the code says,

> Those who rely on certified public accountants expect them to discharge their responsibilities with integrity, objectivity, due professional care, and a genuine interest in serving the public. They are expected to provide quality services, enter into fee arrangements, and offer a range of services – all in a manner that demonstrates a level of professionalism consistent with these Principles of the Code of Professional Conduct.[9]

Joining a professional group such as the AICPA is tantamount to making a promise to abide by the ethical standard set up by that group. As such, that promise must be kept. As we have seen in our examination of Immanuel Kant, not keeping promises is unacceptable, because breaking promises is usually done to pursue one's own inclinations without giving due attention to the necessities of others in the light of which the promise was made. The code specifically points out that joining the AICPA puts an ethical burden upon the member.

> All who accept membership in the American Institute of Certified Public Accountants commit themselves to honor the public trust. In return for the faith that the public reposes in them, members should seek continually to demonstrate their dedication to professional excellence.[10]

But what are the principles enumerated by the Code of Professional Conduct? We will turn to an examination of those principles and the rules derived from them in the next chapters. However, an interesting question remains. If being a professional requires membership in an organization, and we know all accountants are not CPAs and do not all belong to the AICPA, are they professionals? Are all accountants professionals? If not, are they bound by the same ethical obligations?

It seems clear that all CPAs meet the criteria of being professionals. They are admitted into the CPA fraternity by meeting the standards of professional qualification. They have to pass the rigorous CPA exams to show they have the requisite expertise. The exams act as monitoring devices to see who has the competence to be accepted into and remain in the CPA profession.

But what about the accountants who have not acquired their CPA designations? They certainly may have the expert knowledge required. It's just that they failed to pass through the rigorous testing procedures required for acceptance in an organization like the AICPA. One can easily argue that even if they failed to be admitted to the organization or chose not to join it, since they have the expert knowledge, and they will be in a position of dealing with clients who are vulnerable to their exploitation because of lack of knowledge, they have pretty much the same obligations as those accountants who have attained the CPA designation.

We would argue that they certainly should be subject to some of the other standards. Just because an individual is not a CPA nor a member of the AICPA or any other professional group of accountants, it does not follow that that individual is not obligated to live by the provisions of the code of ethics. The codes of ethics of the various accounting constituencies, upon examination, render mostly commonsensical readings of what would be ethical responsibilities of any person in the situation of advisor to advisee or provider to dependent or professional toward a vulnerable client, and to the general public. The standards of behavior do not rest on the code. Rather the code specifies more or less universally valid standards that should be followed. However, since the standards can be found in the codes it will be helpful to examine the codes of ethics to see the principles and standards on which they are based. We now turn to examining those codes.

▲ NOTES ▲

1. From "Background Paper on CFP Board's Initiatives." Announced June 14, 1999. On Internet site http://natasha.cfp-board.org/internet/ WP_text.html.
2. Solomon S. Huebner, "How the Life Insurance Salesman Should View the Profession." Address to Annual Meeting of the Baltimore Life Underwriters Association, February 20, 1915.
3. AICPA Code, 53.II.01.
4. Adam Smith, *The Wealth of Nations*, IV, ix 5s.
5. AICPA Code, 56.V.02.
6. AICPA Code, 53.II.01.
7. AICPA Code, 53.II.01.
8. AICPA Code, 53.II.02.
9. AICPA Code, 53.II.03.
10. AICPA Code, 53.II.04.

chapter five

Accounting Codes of Ethics: The Principles

Accountants have a responsibility to present or aid in presenting the most truthful and accurate financial pictures possible of the organization they are portraying, or, as auditors, a responsibility to evaluate other accountants' pictures and attest to their truthfulness and accuracy. In such ways accountants carry out the purposes of their profession – to meet the needs of the clients or companies they work for, or to serve the best interests of those stockholders and stakeholders who are entitled to accurate financial pictures of organizations with which they are involved.

Since one of the clearest ethical obligations is, all things being equal, to do one's job (since the act of accepting a job entails a promise to do that job, and promises should be kept), providing or attesting to accurate financial pictures for organizations is a basic accounting responsibility. The responsibilities of a job can be ascertained by looking in any number of places. Usually they are spelled out in some form or other, either in the job description, the employees' handbook, the managerial guide book, the company's code of conduct, and/or finally in a profession's code of conduct or ethics.

The accounting profession has developed multiple codes of ethics that set the standards for the way accountants ought to behave and, most importantly, in the light of incidents like the Enron debacle, which require more than simply adhering to the letter of the law. *We suggest that these sophisticated codes are the equivalent of a binding organizational moral law,* and consequently will prove quite useful for spelling out what is ethically required of accountants in a number of ways.

There are six ways codes of conduct are useful.[1]

1. A code can motivate through using peer pressure, by holding up a generally recognized set of behavioral expectations that must be considered in decision making.

2. A code can provide more stable permanent guides to right or wrong than do human personalities or continual ad hoc decisions.
3. Codes can provide guidance, especially in ambiguous situations.
4. Codes not only can guide the behavior of employees, they can also control the autocratic power of employers.
5. Codes can help specify the social responsibilities of business itself.
6. Codes are clearly in the interest of business itself, for if businesses do not police themselves ethically, others will do it for them.

Given the usefulness of codes, we propose to look at specific codes of accounting ethics to examine what they say is appropriate behavior for accountants.

There are two major codes for the accounting profession in the United States – *The Code of Professional Conduct of the American Institute of Certified Public Accountants*, adopted in its current form in 1973 and significantly revised in 1988, and *Standards of Ethical Conduct for Practitioners of Management Accounting and Financial Management*, adopted in April of 1997. These are also codes for accountants in other countries, such as England, Canada, Germany, and Australia, to name but a few, which are quite similar. Because we do not have the time or space to examine them all, we will concentrate on the Code of the American Institute of Certified Public Accountants (AICPA) and then briefly at the Management Accounting Code.

▲ THE AICPA CODE ▲

The AICPA Code is composed of two sections – one treating the principles and the second treating the rules. The principles are general norms of behavior and provide the framework for the more specific rules. The Council of the AICPA designates bodies to interpret the rules and provide technical standards for them. These interpretations result in *ethical rulings*, which govern specific activities but can be applied to other similar activities.

The AICPA Code begins by detailing the purpose and scope of the Code. It "was adopted by the membership to provide guidance and rules to all members – those in public practice, in industry, in government, and in education – in the performance of their professional responsibilities."[2] Its purpose, then, is to guide, and its scope includes all certified public accountants who belong to the AICPA. It is binding on them and them only. However, since the purpose of the Code, as stated in the preamble, is "to give the basic tenets of ethical and professional conduct for accountants," it can serve as a basic handbook on ethics for all accountants.

The Code specifies three constituencies to whom accountants have ethical responsibilities – the public, clients, and colleagues. Different from a number of professions, such as law and medicine, in which the professional has a primary responsibility to the client or patient, for the accounting profession, particularly in the case of the "public" accountant, the responsibility to the public is paramount. This responsibility to the public for accountants is so important that at times it overrides accountants' obligations to clients or to those who hire them. As we have seen in numerous cases in the past several years, in the case of an external audit, even though the firm being audited hires the accountant and pays the accountant, the accountant's first responsibility is to those in the public who are entitled to view the financial statements of the company rather than to the company that hired them. This creates an anomalous situation where the accountant is technically not working for the person or company paying him or her.

Still, even though the public accountant who is auditing has a primary responsibility to the public, the accountant has responsibilities to other constituents. Hence there is a need to examine all the various relationships an accountant has and the obligations consequent upon those relationships. The provisions of the AICPA Code help to specify those various relationships, so it will be useful to examine them. We will begin by examining the principles of the Code. That will be the main focus of this chapter. In the next chapter we will engage in a detailed examination of the rules of the Code.

▲ THE PRINCIPLES ▲

"The Principles of the Code . . . express the profession's recognition of its responsibilities to the public, to clients, and to colleagues. They guide members in the performance of their professional responsibili-

ties and express the basic tenets of ethical and professional conduct. The Principles call for an unswerving commitment to honorable behavior, even at the sacrifice of personal advantage."[3]
There are six principles.

1. In carrying out their responsibilities as professionals, members should exercise sensitive professional and moral judgments in all their activities.
2. Members should accept the obligation to act in a way that will serve the public interest, honor the public trust, and demonstrate commitment to professionalism.
3. To maintain and broaden public confidence, members should perform all professional responsibilities with the highest sense of integrity.
4. A member should maintain objectivity and be free of conflicts of interest in discharging professional responsibilities. A member in public practice should be independent in fact and appearance when providing auditing and other attestation services.
5. A member should observe the profession's technical and ethical standards, strive continually to improve competence and the quality of services, and discharge professional responsibility to the best of the member's ability.
6. A member in public practice should observe the Principles of the Code of Professional Conduct in determining the scope and nature of services to be provided.

Looking at these principles, one sees considerations similar to those that appear in most professional codes – service to others, competency, integrity, objectivity and independence, professionalism, including continuing education, and accountability to the profession. Each of these principles is explained in greater detail in the code, and we will take some time to comment on those explanations.

Principle I. Responsibilities: *In carrying out their responsibilities as professionals, members should exercise sensitive professional and moral judgments in all their activities.*
This principle simply and clearly states that professional responsibilities require moral judgment in all activities, thereby equating professional behavior with moral behavior. The explanation of the principle reads as follows.

As professionals, certified public accountants perform an essential role in society. Consistent with that role, members of the American Institute of Certified Public Accountants have responsibilities to all those *who use* their professional services. Members also have a continuing responsibility to cooperate with each other to improve the art of accounting, maintain the public's confidence, and carry out the profession's special responsibilities for self-governance. The collective efforts of all members are required to maintain and enhance the traditions of the profession.[4]

This paragraph is full of meaning. It begins by calling attention to the essential role that certified public accountants play in society. We have seen in chapter 2 how crucial accounting is to the health of the free-market system. Accountants have a responsibility to "all those who use their professional services." Here again is the anomaly we have noted. Most professionals, as professionals, have an overriding responsibility to their client. But accountants, whose role in the financial markets is so crucial, since they give the financial picture of organizations, data that is essential to doing business, have numerous constituencies depending on that information. Because the scope of their responsibility extends to all those who use the information, they have prima facie responsibilities beyond those to their clients, or to those who pay their fees. In a real sense, for example, even though Arthur Andersen was paid by Enron, as an external auditor, they did not work for Enron. Their primary responsibility was to the general public.

The explanation of the first principle also points out the responsibility to cooperate with fellow professionals to keep the integrity of the accounting profession. We have already seen in the section on professionalism that one of the obligations of a professional is to the profession itself. Specifically, the Code mentions three areas: (1) to improve the art of accounting, (2) to maintain the public's confidence, and (3) to carry out the professional responsibility for self-governance. While little is said about the obligation to improve the art of accounting, the Code goes on and devotes specific attention to the obligation to maintain the public's confidence in the profession and the obligation to self-governance. We will mention those specifics when we address the rules. For now we need only mention that for a number of years critics of the accounting profession, most of whom are accountants themselves, have maintained that the accounting standards are not sufficient for the complex financial transactions of today. Their inadequacies have become only too clear in recent years. Further, recent events such as the collapse of companies such as Enron have eroded the public's confidence in the profession. Thus, it is ethically imperative that the profession "carry out its responsibility for self-governance." Once can ask whether the current practice of peer review is sufficient to carry out that responsibility.

To fulfill the above mentioned moral obligations, the code indicates that the accountant needs to practice sensitive moral judgment. For sensitive moral judgment, the accountant will need to evaluate his or her activities in the light of the reasons we discussed in the second chapter. The accountant will need to consider whether their activities benefit or harm; whether they are respectful of others and their rights; whether they are fair; and whether they are in accord with the commitments the accountant has made. As we have seen, sensitive moral judgment has no place for *selfish* behavior. Consequently the accountant like so many of his or her colleagues in other professions will be bound by some version or other of the golden rule: "do unto others as you would have them do unto you."

Principle II. Serve the Public Interest: *Members should accept the obligation to act in a way that will serve the public interest, honor the public trust, and demonstrate commitment to professionalism.*
In the explanation of this principle, the Code states that responsibility to the public is a distinguishing mark of a profession. That is a somewhat idiosyncratic view of a profession. As we mentioned above, professions such as law and medicine and even to an extent teaching are clearly client oriented. Doctors and lawyers would state that their first, and possibly only, obligation is to their patient or client, subject only to the constraints of some higher moral principle, were that violated, in the pursuit of their serving their client. For example, a lawyer cannot suborn perjury. A distinguishing mark, if not the distinguishing mark, of a "public" accountant is that their primary obligation is to the public, and in a broader sense to the truth – the accuracy or veracity of the financial statements they deal with.

This, of course, leaves a question: if all accountants are not public accountants, do they have this responsibility to the public? If we construe the function of accounting narrowly as public accounting involved in external auditing, then of course the responsibility to the public is clear. But is that the case with tax accounting and management accounting, or even internal auditing? We will need to examine this question more at length later.

Be that as it may, the explanation of service to the public continues and spells out who is included in the public, naming "clients, credit grantors, governments, employers, investors, the business and financial community, and others who rely on the objectivity and integrity of certified public accountants to maintain the orderly functioning of commerce."[5] This principle shows us that the public nature of accounting is grounded in the social purpose of the orderly functioning of commerce. To achieve that goal, ethical behavior is necessary. "The public interest is defined as the collective well-being of the community of people and institutions the profession serves."

At this point in the explanation, a remarkable passage appears: "In discharging their professional responsibilities, members may encounter conflicting pressures from among each of those groups. In resolving those conflicts, members should act *with integrity*, guided by the precept that when members fulfill their responsibility to the public, clients' and employers' interests are best served."[6] Conflicts of interest between clients and the public or between employers and public are bound to occur. What is remarkable about this passage is that the Code states unequivocally that the accountant in such a case needs to act with integrity (we will discuss that shortly, since the Code takes up the principle of integrity as the next point) and insists that when the accountant fulfills his or her responsibility to the public, clients' or employers' interests are best served.

Is it true that a client's interest is always best served when an accountant fulfills his or her responsibility to the public? A situation where a client's business might go bankrupt if no loan is attained from a bank, and where no loan will be attained unless the financial status of the company is misrepresented or hidden, seems to belie that claim. At worst, though, the precept would maintain that in most cases good ethics is good business, and when the accountant tells the truth everyone will be better off, even if at first glance it does not look that way. Whether it is always workable, the precept is a powerful normative principle in the heart of the Code, one worth looking at, arguing for, and developing.[7] The explanation continues by noting that those who rely on certified public accountants expect them to discharge their responsibilities with integrity, objectivity, due professional care and a genuine interest in serving the public, and offer services at a level of professionalism. It identifies the principles of the Code as being the characteristics the public expects of the accountant.

The explanation of public trust ends by stating that all who voluntarily accept membership in the AICPA "commit" themselves to honor this public trust. In short, if one is a member of the AICPA, one has promised or contracted to act on behalf of the public interest, defined as "the collective well-being of the community of people and institutions" one serves as a professional. If, as we saw in chapter 2, promises need to be kept, this becomes a primary responsibility for any AICPA member. Whether it is so for accountants who do not belong to the AICPA remains a question. We would need other grounds to establish their responsibility to the public.

Principle III. Integrity: *To maintain and broaden public confidence, members should perform all professional responsibilities with the highest sense of integrity.*

In the explanation of principle II, the Code called for resolving conflicting pressure from among groups with *integrity*. Principle III is the principle that specifies the requirements of that integrity.

The Code defines integrity in the following way: "Integrity is an element of character fundamental to professional recognition. It is the quality from which the public trust derives and the benchmark against which a member must ultimately test all decisions . . . [It] requires a member to be, among other things, honest and candid within the constraints of client confidentiality. Service and the public trust should not be subordinated to personal gain and advantage . . . [It] is measured in terms of what is right and just."

Such an explanation is, of course, quite general. It identifies integrity as an element of character that is fundamental to professional recognition, indicating that from the recognition of integrity, public trust would be derived. It further identifies it as a benchmark against which a member must ultimately test all decisions. But none of this tells us what integrity is.

Clearly one can say that a decision to misrepresent the financial picture of a company or to overlook some suspicious red flags in a company's financial statement would violate an accountant's integrity, but what is that integrity which is being violated? Of course the obvious answer is that such behavior would involve the accountant in being dishonest. And indeed, integrity, as is evident from the statements, is often taken to be synonymous with honesty. But to stop with that meaning is not enough. Nor does it help much to indicate that integrity involves subordinating personal gain and advantage to the public trust or doing what is right and just. Exactly what do all those things mean?

We need further analysis. Integrity being described as an element of character brings up a consideration of what is called virtue or character ethics. One can ask, what sort of character does a person of integrity have? To get to the most basic meaning of the word integrity, we need to recall that the word was originally used in mathematics. *Integrity* is related to the word *integer*, which refers to *whole* numbers. Thus, the primary dictionary definition of integrity is "the quality or state of being complete or undivided." Integrity means wholeness, the kind of wholeness referred to when people are praised for "having themselves together." But what does it take to *have it all together*? A secondary dictionary definition of integrity is useful: "firm adherence to a code of especially moral or aesthetic values." That means having a good conscience and adhering to it by doing the right things. Still, that is pretty vague.

Recently when I had the pleasure of reading the Walt Disney version of Pinocchio[8] to my young daughter, it occurred to me that this story goes a long way toward illuminating the notion of integrity. Limiting the notion of integrity to simply being honest is analogous to simply concentrating on the fact in the story of Pinocchio that his nose grew when he lied. Certainly the story tells us not to lie, just as integrity tells us to be honest. But honesty is not a synonym for integrity. Lying and dishonesty are merely symptoms of the lack of integrity, and the identification of integrity with lying doesn't quite get to the core meaning, any more than Pinocchio's growing nose is the whole story of Pinocchio.

What does the story tell us? Think back to the story. Gepetto makes a puppet, a special puppet. It walks and talks by itself. But it's a puppet, not a real boy. Being a "real boy" is the goal and ideal that Gepetto and Pinocchio seek – their highest value. However, for Pinocchio to become a real boy he must become morally complete. What does it take for Pinocchio to become whole and complete, to achieve integrity – to become a real boy?

The first thing necessary is to develop a conscience. Since puppets don't come equipped with consciences, he is given Jiminy Cricket. But Jiminy is external to Pinocchio. With Jiminy, Pinocchio hears from the outside what is right and wrong. The code of conduct, which Jiminy represents, is not yet part of Pinocchio. He needs to internalize that code and make it a part of himself. Similarly, learning the rules of a profession are not enough. We must internalize and live by the rules.

In this incomplete state, Gepetto sends Pinocchio off to school, and on the way he meets Gideon and Honest John, who is anything but honest. When Jiminy gets left behind, Gideon and Honest John entice Pinocchio to join a puppet show. They promise him fame, convincing him that a puppet who can walk without strings and talk by himself will become an instant celebrity. But Pinocchio soon learns that celebrity and fame are not values that will make him complete. As a matter of fact, celebrity and fame entrap Pinocchio, since Stromboli, the puppet-master, puts Pinocchio in a cage because he is too valuable to be set free.

Jiminy helps Pinocchio escape, only to see him get enticed into going to Pleasure Island, where one can engage in the self-centered pursuit of pleasure with no restraint. However, unrestrained pleasure seeking does not help one achieve completeness. Rather it turns the inhabitants of Pleasure Island into jackasses. After he grows ears and a tail, the light of wisdom dawns on Pinocchio and, with Jiminy's help, he escapes. At this point Pinocchio, besides being wiser, is beginning to develop self-control. After escaping, Pinocchio and Jiminy search for Gepetto, only to discover that the whale, Monstro, has swallowed him. With courage and selflessness, Pinocchio and Jiminy succeed in going into Monstro's belly, from which they help Gepetto escape. Having performed such a brave and selfless act, Pinocchio finally becomes a real boy. He is complete. He has integrity.

The story of Pinocchio shows us that lying is only a symptom of the lack of integrity. People lie because they are self-absorbed. They do it to avoid unpleasantness, to look better, avoid a harm or gain an advantage. People with integrity do not need to lie, because their values are sound and they have the *wisdom* to see that there is nothing for which it is worth compromising those values. They will be *in control* and *courageous* enough to live with the consequences of the truth, and will be self-assured enough to give others their due (*justice*) without unduly fearing for themselves.

Beginning with Plato and Aristotle, traditional ethical theories put high emphasis on integrity or wholeness. In their theories one was not whole unless one possessed what came to be called the four cardinal virtues – wisdom, justice, temperance, and courage. One only had integrity if one possessed all of them together. Each virtue required the others. The story of Pinocchio is the story of how he

acquired all of them. He became wise enough to know *what* to value
– to know that celebrity and pleasure by themselves do not constitute
a good life. He developed temperance, or self-control, by fleeing
Pleasure Island, and coupled that with courage and justice when
sacrificing himself for Gepetto – since the willingness to sacrifice
oneself when required marks the beginning of justice. So, Pinocchio
became a "real" boy when he acquired all the cardinal virtues, thus
achieving integrity.

The lessons of Pinocchio and traditional ethics are obvious when
we apply them to the accountant. Fame or the pursuit of pleasure
should not cloud one's judgment. Misrepresenting a financial statement to keep a client sounds suspiciously like doing what Pinocchio
did before he became a real boy – before he got integrity. Those
tempted to do those sorts of things need to undergo a transformation
similar to Pinocchio's – to become "real" professionals. They need
the wisdom, courage, and self-control to set their goals correctly,
internalize them and remember that being a professional requires a
commitment to fairness and justice. And indeed, the Code insists
that integrity be "measured in terms of what is right and just." Thus,
the Code states:

> Integrity is measured in terms of what is right and just. In the absence
> of specific rules, standards, or guidance, or in the face of conflicting
> opinions, a member should test decisions and deeds by asking: "Am I
> doing what a person of integrity would do? Have I retained my
> integrity?" Integrity requires a member to observe both the form and
> the spirit of technical and ethical standards; circumvention of those
> standards constitutes subordination of judgment.[9]

This principle leaves a great deal up to the judgment of the
individual, for it says "in the absence of specific rules, standards, or
guidance, or in the face of conflicting opinions, a member should
test decisions and deeds by asking: 'Am I doing what a person of
integrity would do?'" And that seems to be to do what is right and
just. Since, as we have seen, determining what is right and just might
be difficult, we seem to be caught in a vicious circle. But there may
be a way out. One can always employ something like the golden rule
to determine the justice and rightness of an action. Propose a course
of action and ask whether one would approve of that action if it were
done to oneself. Generally, but not always, that is a reasonable test.
At least it assures that one's interests won't be followed exclusively

and that there is concern for the needs and dignity of the other. Add to the golden rule the test of whether you will be able to live with yourself after making a decision. If you can't you are being torn apart and your integrity is being sundered.

There is another important aspect of the principle, near the end of the explanation, which says explicitly that integrity requires a member to observe both the form and *the spirit* of technical and ethical standards. "To circumvent those standards means subordination of judgment." Consequently, in the light of this, the utilization of technical standards, say in tax accounting, to bypass the intent of the tax legislation would be looked upon as unethical according to the Code. The invention of "black box" accounting, to circumvent the responsibility to present accurate pictures of the financial status of a company, the deliberate listing of assets or liabilities off the books to make the company look more profitable than it is, clearly violates the *spirit* of accounting standards, which were set up precisely to guarantee the public and other users as accurate pictures as possible. It is difficult to imagine how an accountant can defend such behavior by saying they have broken no law, when they have clearly violated the spirit of the law.

The final point in the Code's explanation of integrity bring up the notions of objectivity, independence, and due care, for it says "integrity requires a member to observe the principles of objectivity and independence and of due care." Objectivity and independence are perhaps the most important of the principles in the AICPA Code.

Principle IV. Objectivity and Independence: *A member should maintain objectivity and be free of conflicts of interest in discharging professional responsibilities. A member in public practice should be independent in fact and appearance when providing auditing and other attestation services.*

The explanation of the principle tells us that objectivity is a state of mind, a quality. Hence it is a virtue, some habit to be developed. The principle requires that the objective person be impartial, intellectually honest, and free of conflicts of interest. It "precludes relationships that may appear to impair a member's objectivity in rendering attestation services." In the light of this it is difficult to imagine anyone thinking that Arthur Andersen could "appear" to be objective with respect to Enron, when it "depended on Enron for $52million in fees, more than half of which, $27 million, was 'derived not from auditing its books, but from providing other services'."[10]

Objectivity and the demand for it reminds one of the difference between "he believed because it was a fact" or "because he believed it was a fact." Human beings are notorious for seeing things as they think they are or as they want them to be, rather than seeing them the way they actually are. This will apply to accountants as well. If you believe the company you are auditing is filled with honest people, you give the benefit of the doubt to them and don't see things that more skeptical auditors would see. It is interesting that in the interpretations of the Code, auditors are called upon to adopt a skeptical attitude. Achieving objectivity is not easy and one must bend over backwards at times to accomplish the objective point of view. Specifically, the principle lays three obligations on the accountant:

1. The member should be impartial. This means the member must try to remove his personal feelings and interests from any judgments or recommendations being made or from any actions being taken. The member must detach himself from the situation and look on it as a third party with a disinterested attitude.
2. The member should be intellectually honest.
3. The member should be free of conflicts of interest. If one is auditing a company in which one has stock, and if an unfavorable audit would hurt the worth of the stock, the person involved has a conflict of interest. Similarly, if the accountant is consulting with one client and the advice would hurt another client, there is a conflict of interest. Members should either avoid such conflicts or free themselves from them.

Along with the three obligations, there is a fairly strong statement that, "Independence precludes relationships that may *appear* to impair a member's objectivity in rendering attestation services."[11] It is not only real conflicts of interest that are prohibited. If one gives attestation services, there needs to be an avoidance of even the appearance of a conflict of interest. The member *in public service* (this does not apply to those in private service) should be independent in fact and appearance.

> For a member in public practice, the maintenance of objectivity and independence requires a continuing assessment of client relationships and public responsibility. Such a member who provides auditing and other attestation services should be independent in fact and appear-

ance. In providing all other services, a member should maintain objectivity and avoid conflicts of interest.[12]

This is important because of the insistence here of the appearance of independence.

One might object, that while one providing attestation services needs to be objective and independent, that is hardly possible for internal auditors or management accountants. Yet the Code does not make that allowance. As a matter of fact, it recognizes those different interests, "Members often serve multiple interests in many different capacities," but concludes that they "must demonstrate their objectivity in varying circumstances."[13] It describes the various functions AICPA members perform. "Members in public practice render attest, tax, and management advisory services. Other members prepare financial statements in the employment of others, perform internal auditing services, and serve in financial and management capacities in industry, education, and government. They also educate and train those who aspire to admission into the profession."[14] But note that in spite of those different roles that they play for different constituencies, the Code calls for them to maintain their objectivity. "Regardless of service or capacity, members should protect the integrity of their work, maintain objectivity, and avoid any subordination of their judgment."[15]

Just as the ideal researchers are motivated by the search for true knowledge, the ideal accountants are responsible for presenting as true a picture as possible. That cannot be done if they subordinate their judgment to others, or if out of fear (note the need for courage) or greed (note the need for temperance) they tell the boss what he or she wants to hear. They must be true to themselves and their calling as accountants first and foremost to keep their integrity. Thus, the explanation of the principle of objectivity concludes with the following very strong remarks about the responsibilities of members not in public practice, who by nature of their job are not independent.

> Although members not in public practice cannot maintain the appearance of independence, they nevertheless have the *responsibility* to maintain objectivity in rendering professional services. Members employed by others to prepare financial statements or to perform auditing, tax, or consulting services are charged with the same responsibility for objectivity as members in public practice and must be *scrupulous* in their application of generally accepted accounting

principles and candid in all their dealings with members in public practice.[16]

We will be looking at a number of cases in management accounting where supervisors pressured accountants to stray from an appropriate application of accounting principles or to hide elements of a financial statement from auditors. Clearly such activity, even if it is generally practiced, is unethical according to the Code, and even if it is legal but violates the spirit of the principles it is still unethical.

The last few conditions are especially intriguing. Members working in private practice are "charged with the same responsibility for objectivity as members in public practice." We have seen why in the preceding paragraph. They must be "scrupulous in their application of generally accepted accounting principles" (GAAP), and "candid in all their dealings with members in public practice."[17] There must be honesty and forthrightness in their accounting work and communications. Hence, one could conclude that all accountants have one primary responsibility, *to make their work as honest and true as possible.* Anything short of that, for whatever reason, damages their integrity and their dedication to the goals of their profession. These are the very stringent requirements of integrity, objectivity, and independence. We will return to a discussion of objectivity and independence in the chapter on auditing.

Principle V. Due Care: *A member should observe the profession's technical and ethical standards, strive continually to improve competence and the quality of services, and discharge professional responsibility to the best of the member's ability.*

The principle of due care sets a very high bar for the accountant. The explanation of the principle indicates that it involves the "quest for excellence" that is identified as the *essence* of due care. That excellence requires both competence and diligence. The accountant must perform to the best of his or her ability with a "concern for the best interest of those for whom the services are performed and consistent with the profession's responsibility to the public."[18]

The competence the accountant is required to achieve will come from education and experience. The common body of accounting knowledge must be learned and then supplemented by a continuous commitment to learning and professional improvement. The level that must be achieved is one of facility and acumen, and due care requires that when an accountant recognizes the limitations of his competence, he consult with others or at least refer the client to another who has the requisite competence. As the Code says, "Each member is responsible for assessing his or her own competence – of evaluating whether education, experience, and judgment are adequate for the responsibility to be assumed."[19]

Diligence is another aspect of due care, which "imposes the responsibility to render services *promptly and carefully*, to be thorough, and to observe applicable technical and ethical standards."[20] Of course, to be prompt, careful, and thorough requires that an accountant "plan and supervise adequately any professional activity for which he or she is responsible."[21] Hence, it could be argued that sloppy planning which leads to less than competent service to clients is unethical behavior. Many accountants would disagree that sloppiness is an ethical dimension, but the argument could be made that the principle of due care sets the ethical bar rather high.

Principle VI. Scope and Nature of Services: The final principle of the Code states: *A member in public practice should observe the Principles of the Code of Professional Conduct in determining the scope and nature of services to be provided.*

This is the summary principle that ties all the principles together. Note that the opening explanation mentions professionalism. The public interest aspect of certified public accountants' services requires that such services be consistent with acceptable professional behavior for certified public accountants. It calls for integrity that "requires that service and the public trust not be subordinated to personal gain and advantage." It reiterates objectivity and independence that requires members to be free from conflicts of interest in discharging professional responsibilities. Finally, it recalls due care that requires that services be provided with competence and diligence.

A member has to decide whether or not to provide specific services in individual circumstances by considering each of these principles. The explanation of what constitutes the proper scope and nature of services insures that in some cases the principle may represent "an overall constraint on the non-audit services that might be offered to a specific client. No hard-and-fast rules can be developed to help members reach these judgments, but they must be satisfied that they are meeting *the spirit of* the Principles in this regard."[22] In other words, the application of the principles is an act that is best done in the spirit of justice by a prudent practitioner.

As the Code states: "In order to accomplish this, members should

- Practice in firms that have in place internal quality-control procedures to ensure that services are competently delivered and adequately supervised
- Determine, in their individual judgments, whether the scope and nature of other services provided to an audit client would create a conflict of interest in the performance of the audit function for that client
- Assess, in their individual judgments, whether an activity is consistent with their role as professionals (for example, Is such activity a reasonable extension or variation of existing services offered by the member or others in the profession?)"[23]

The practical implications of this are monumental. It means, according to the Code, members should *not* practice in firms that don't have internal quality control procedures for competent services adequately supervised. They must be aware of and determine whether other services for a client would create a conflict of interest for an audit client. Finally, they must assess the propriety of their activities against what the true professional would do.

In summary, then, we can say that the codes of ethics lay out, at least in their principles, an outline or framework of the ethical approach accountants should take to their work.

It has been argued that such codes suffer from at least two insufficiencies: they are too broad and amorphous, and they lack sanctions.

Concerning codes being too broad or amorphous one could cite the first principle of the AICPA Code. It states that, "In carrying out their responsibilities as professionals, members [of the AICPA] should exercise sensitive professional and moral judgments in all their activities." That is too broad because professionals do not act as certified public accountants in "all their activities," and it is too amorphous because it does not specifically define "sensitive" professional judgments. However, one can rejoin that language is always general and in need of interpretation. Further rules and interpretation of code principles attempt to address the lack of specificity problem. Principles are meant to be inspirational and rules more concrete.

The second drawback to codes is that they are seldom enforced. They need to be enforced, for a code without enforcement can be worse than no code at all. In the case of accounting codes, that is an issue that is currently being studied in the light of the Enron case. Before Enron, the Securities and Exchange Commission was studying the feasibility of accounting's self-regulation and the worth and effectiveness of the Financial Accounting Standards Board. There was also an Independence Standards Board (ISB) until its recent dissolution. We will examine these attempts at enforcement later.

Despite these drawbacks, we would argue that codes can be immensely helpful in pointing out standards to be followed in following one's profession. As to vagueness, some of the vagueness can be cleared up with more specific rules. The AICPA Code achieves some specificity with its section on the rules that derive from the principles. We now turn our attention to that part of the Code.

▲ NOTES ▲

1. Norman Bowie and Ronald Duska, *Business Ethics* (Prentice Hall, 1985).
2. AICPA Code, Preamble.
3. AICPA Code, Preamble, Section 50.02.
4. AICPA Code, 52.I.01.
5. AICPA Code, 53.II.01.
6. AICPA Code, 53.II.02.
7. Cf. Ronald Duska, "Business Ethics, an Oxymoron or Good Business?" *Business Ethics Quarterly*, vol. 10, no. 1.
8. The original version was written in Italian by Carlo Collodi in 1881 and 1882 in serial form, and differs somewhat from the Disney version. But the lessons still hold.
9. AICPA Code, 54.III.03.
10. "The Twister Hits," *The Economist*, January 19, 2002, p. 59.
11. AICPA Code, 55.IV.01.
12. AICPA Code, 55.IV.03.
13. AICPA Code, 55.IV.02.
14. AICPA Code, 55.IV.02.
15. AICPA Code, 55.IV.02.
16. AICPA Code, 55.IV.04.
17. AICPA Code, 55.IV.04.
18. AICPA Code, 56.V.01.
19. AICPA Code, 55.V.03.

20. AICPA Code, 55.V.04.
21. AICPA Code, 55.V.04.
22. AICPA Code, 55.VI.02.
23. AICPA Code, 55.VI.03.

chapter six

Accounting Codes of Ethics: The Rules

Following the enunciation of the principles of the code of ethics, the AICPA Code develops a section on the rules: "The bylaws of the American Institute of Certified Public Accountants require that members adhere to the Rules of the Code of Professional Conduct. Members must be prepared to justify departures from these Rules." Now, these rules are formally only applicable to members of the AICPA and people under members' control; if members violate the rules they are subject to disciplining by the AICPA. Nevertheless, it is useful to examine the rules to appreciate what sorts of expectations the professional association has with respect to specific kinds of behavior by accountants.

The rules section of the Code breaks down into five sections: (1) independence, integrity, and objectivity, (2) general standards, accounting principles, (3) responsibilities to clients, (4) responsibilities to colleagues, and (5) other responsibilities and practices.

In most cases, the rule is followed by interpretations of that rule which address the acceptability of specific types of activities. Finally, under each of the rules, still more specific ethic rulings are given – 111 rulings on independence, integrity, and objectivity, 11 rulings on general standards (six that have been deleted and one transferred), 25 rulings on responsibilities to clients, and 192 rulings on other responsibilities and practices (153 of which have been deleted, and six of which have been superseded).

In this chapter we will enumerate the rules of the Code (anyone who wishes to examine the entire Code can obtain it by contacting the AICPA at www.aicpa.org).

▲ SECTION 100 ▲

The independence rule (Rule 101): The rule governing independence reads: *A member in public practice shall be independent in the performance of professional services as required by standards promulgated by bodies designated by Council.*
Under the interpretation of Rule 101, the Code specifies what bodies a member should consult. Among these bodies the interpretation lists the following: the accountant's "state board of accountancy, CPA society, the Independence Standards Board if the member's report will be filed with the US Securities and Exchange Commission (SEC), the US Department of Labor (DOL) if the member's report will be filed with the DOL, the AICPA SEC Practice Section (SECPS) if the member's firm is a member of the SECPS, and any organization that issues or enforces standards of independence that would apply to the member's engagements." Those bodies might have independence requirements or rulings that are different from, including more restrictive than, the requirements or rulings of the AICPA.
But, in general, what does independence require? The interpretation in the Code does not give a positive account of independence, which would simply be freedom from interests which conflict with the accountant's basic responsibilities. Rather, the interpretation gives a negative account by citing when independence will be impaired. Independence shall be considered to be impaired if, for example, a member had any of the following transactions, interests, or relationships:

A.　During the period of a professional engagement or at the time of expressing an opinion, a member or a member's firm
1.　Had or was committed to acquire any direct or material indirect financial interest in the (client's) enterprise.
2.　Was a trustee of any trust or executor or administrator of any estate if such trust or estate had or was committed to acquire any direct or material indirect financial interest in the enterprise.
3.　Had any joint, closely held business investment with the enterprise or with any officer, director, or principal stockholders thereof that was material in relation to the member's net worth or to the net worth of the member's firm.
4.　Had any loan to or from the client enterprise or any officer,

director, or principal stockholder of the enterprise except as specifically permitted in interpretation 101–5.

B. During the period covered by the financial statements, during the period of the professional engagement, or at the time of expressing an opinion, a member or a member's firm

1. Was connected with the enterprise as a promoter, underwriter or voting trustee, as a director, officer, or employee, or in any capacity equivalent to that of a member of management.

2. Was a trustee for any pension or profit-sharing trust of the enterprise.[1]

In summary, independence is threatened if an accountant, while professionally engaged with an enterprise: had a financial interest in this enterprise; was a trustee of an estate with such an interest; had closely held business investments with any principal of the enterprise; or was invested in the enterprise or had a loan from the enterprise. Further, if the CPA held any position equivalent to a management position in the enterprise, or was trustee for pension or profit sharing trusts of the enterprise, his or her independence would be deemed to be impaired.

Such entanglements would compromise the independence of the accountant and possibly jeopardize the accountant's integrity and objectivity because they would or could create a real or perceived conflict of interest, a topic which is specifically covered in Rule 102.

Integrity and objectivity (Rule 102): *In the performance of any professional service, a member shall maintain objectivity and integrity, shall be free of conflicts of interest, and shall not knowingly misrepresent facts or subordinate his or her judgment to others.*

Rule 102, then, calls for four things in performing professional service: (1) maintaining integrity and objectivity, (2) being free from conflicts of interest, (3) not knowingly misrepresenting facts, and (4) not subordinating one's judgment to others.

We have already looked at integrity under the principles. But what of objectivity? As we saw in the principles, it imposes the obligation to be impartial, intellectually honest, and free of conflicts of interest. The notion of objectivity comes from the notion of a scientific approach wherein one stands back as a third party observer. One's own interests are set aside and the situation is appraised on its own merits. Intellectual honesty requires looking at a situation from all possible perspectives.

Ethical theory gives us a number of ways to achieve this point of view, such as Kant's universalizability principles which ask, what if everyone did this? But the most common way in ethics to attempt to reach objectivity is to invoke the *golden rule* – "Do unto others as you would have them do unto you." Ask the question, what would you have done to you and you leave the perspective of the doer of the action and take on the perspective of the receiver. In this way you cognitively get outside yourself to consider the issue. You adopt the perspective of the detached, disinterested, outside observer (i.e. you become impartial and objective). If one can do this effectively – become impartial and detached – it helps one to avoid conflicts of interest (the second element in Rule 102).

Conflicts of interest are described in the Code as situations where certain relationships impair the member's objectivity. We don't recommend doctors diagnose their loved ones. We don't recommend colleagues get romantically involved with subordinates whose work they need to evaluate. Judges recuse themselves in cases where they have an interest in a case. Similar recommendations hold for accountants.

> A conflict of interest may occur if a member performs a professional service for a client or employer and the member or his or her firm has a relationship with another person, entity, product, or service that could, in the member's professional judgment, be viewed by the client, employer, or other appropriate parties as impairing the member's objectivity.

An important element of this interpretation is that it goes beyond the mere existence of a conflict of interest. It even includes the *appearance* of a conflict of interest, a point that has become highly contentious. Some think the mere appearance of a conflict is not enough to disqualify an accountant from doing an audit. Others insist that even the appearance of a conflict of interest undermines the trust that the general public must have in the integrity of the accountant's work. The interpretation of a conflict of interest notes that a member is to avoid a situation which can be *viewed* by the client, or other appropriate parties, as one which *could* impair the member's objectivity.

As far back as 1974, the AICPA's Commission on Auditors' Responsibilities, usually known as The Cohen Report after its chairman, stated that, "It is obvious the auditing firms' aspirations to maximize the number of well paying clients provides them considerable interest in their client's financial success."[2] Because of this obvious fact, Arthur Levitt of the SEC, over a quarter of a century later, cautions: "It is not enough that the accountant in an engagement act independently. . . . For investors to have confidence in the quality of the audit, the public must perceive the accountant as independent."

The interpretation seems to be in agreement with Levitt's point. However, it seems not to initially, for it goes on to make allowances for apparent but not real conflicts of interest, but only under circumscribed conditions. "If the member believes that the professional service can be performed with objectivity, and the relationship is disclosed to and consent is obtained from such client, employer, or other appropriate parties, the rule shall not operate to prohibit the performance of the professional service."

However, the interpretation cautions that in the case of attest services, disclosure and consent cannot eliminate independence impairments. "Certain professional engagements, such as audits, reviews, and other attest services, require independence. Independence impairments according to rule 101, its interpretations, and rulings cannot be eliminated by such disclosure and consent."[3]

The apparent versus real conflict debate notwithstanding, the Code goes on to offer several examples of situations that should cause a member to consider whether or not the client, employer, or other appropriate parties could *view* the relationship as impairing the member's objectivity:

- A member has been asked to perform litigation services for the plaintiff in connection with a lawsuit filed against a client of the member's firm.
- A member has provided tax or personal financial planning (PFP) services for a married couple who are undergoing a divorce, and the member has been asked to provide the services for both parties during the divorce proceedings.
- In connection with a PFP engagement, a member plans to suggest that the client invest in a business in which the member has a financial interest.
- A member provides tax or PFP services for several members of a family who may have opposing interests.
- A member has a significant financial interest, is a member of management, or is in a position of influence in a company that is

a major competitor of a client for which the member performs consulting services.

- A member serves on a city's board of tax appeals, which considers matters involving several of the member's tax clients.
- A member has been approached to provide services in connection with the purchase of real estate from a client of the member's firm.
- A member refers a PFP or tax client to an insurance broker or other service provider, which refers clients to the member under an exclusive arrangement to do so.
- A member recommends or refers a client to a service bureau in which the member or partner(s) in the member's firm hold material financial interest(s).

Misrepresentation: The third aspect of Rule 102 is to proscribe deliberate, knowing misrepresentation of facts. This is simply an appeal to honesty on the part of an accountant. Misrepresentation is lying, and lying, as we saw, is a process of using someone to get our own way. While the Code only applies to AICPA members, the spirit of this rule will apply to all accountants, prohibiting auditors from misrepresenting whether a financial statement is truthful and in accordance with GAAP, tax accountants from misrepresenting income or assets, or management accountants from misrepresenting inventories. The accounting professional must be truthful, since to misrepresent is to use the person to whom the misrepresentation is given merely as a means to the misrepresenter's end.

Subordination of judgment: The final aspect of Rule 102 is the proscription against subordinating one's judgment to others. It may take courage and self-control to fend off the threats and subtle bribes of one's client, but it is unethical to portray a financial picture as a client wishes if the accountant's best judgment indicates they should be pictured otherwise.

Rule 102, in prohibiting a member from knowingly misrepresenting facts or subordinating his or her judgment when performing professional services, specifies rather clearly a set of steps that must be followed to ensure that there is no subordination of judgment. "Under this rule, if a member and his or her supervisor have a disagreement or dispute relating to the preparation of financial statements or the recording of transactions, the member should take the following steps to ensure that the situation does not constitute a subordination of judgment [effective November 30, 1993].

1. The member should consider whether (a) the entry or the failure to record a transaction in the records, or (b) the financial statement presentation or the nature or omission of disclosure in the financial statements, as proposed by the supervisor, represents the use of an acceptable alternative and does not materially misrepresent the facts. If, after appropriate research or consultation, the member concludes that the matter has authoritative support and/ or does not result in a material misrepresentation, the member need do nothing further.

2. If the member concludes that the financial statements or records could be materially misstated, the member should make his or her concerns known to the appropriate higher level(s) of management within the organization (for example, the supervisor's immediate superior, senior management, the audit committee or equivalent, the board of directors, the company's owners). The member should consider documenting his or her understanding of the facts, the accounting principles involved, the application of those principles to the facts, and the parties with whom these matters were discussed.

3. If, after discussing his or her concerns with the appropriate person(s) in the organization, the member concludes that appropriate action was not taken, he or she should consider his or her continuing relationship with the employer. The member also should consider any responsibility that may exist to communicate to third parties, such as regulatory authorities, or the employer's (former employer's) external accountant. In this connection, the member may wish to consult with his or her legal counsel.

4. The member should at all times be cognizant of his or her obligations under interpretation 102–3."

This rule prohibiting the subordination of judgment lays a heavy responsibility on an accountant who disagrees with his or her supervisor's auditing or reporting actions, up to and including resigning from one's position if the disagreement cannot be worked out. Section 102–3 covers the obligations of a member to his or her employer's external accountant. It requires that a member be candid and not misrepresent facts or fail to disclose material facts; if there are irregularities it would seem that they should be made known to an external accountant. Hence, Rule 102 is a very powerful governing rule in accounting ethics.

▲ SECTION 200 ▲

Rule 201: At this point, we move to Section 200 of the code and examine the rule governing general standards – Rule 201. The rule reads: *A member shall comply with the following standards and with any interpretations thereof by bodies designated by Council.* The rule lists four standards: professional competence, due professional care, planning and supervision, and sufficient relevant data. We quote from the rule.

    A. *Professional Competence.* Undertake only those professional services that the member or the member's firm can reasonably expect to be completed with professional competence.

    B. *Due Professional Care.* Exercise due professional care in the performance of professional services.

    C. *Planning and Supervision.* Adequately plan and supervise the performance of professional services.

    D. *Sufficient Relevant Data.* Obtain sufficient relevant data to afford a reasonable basis for conclusions or recommendations in relation to any professional services performed.

This rule reiterates the prescriptions we saw under the principle of due care. This brings us to Rule 202.

Rule 202 – Compliance with standards: *A member who performs auditing, review, compilation, management consulting, tax, or other professional services shall comply with standards promulgated by bodies designated by Council.*
Those bodies that set up the generally accepted accounting principles are the Financial Accounting Standards Board (FASB) and the Governmental Accounting Standards Board (GASB) for audited statements, and the AICPA Auditing and Review Services Committee with respect to standards for unaudited financial statements and other unaudited financial information. Finally, the Auditing Standards Board establishes standards for disclosure of financial information outside financial statements. Standards with respect to offering consulting services will be handled by the AICPA Consulting Services Executive Committee.

Council has designated the Financial Accounting Standards Board (FASB) as a body to establish accounting principles and has resolved that FASB Statements of Financial Accounting Standards, together with those Accounting Research Bulletins and APB Opinions which are not superseded by action of the FASB, constitute accounting principles as contemplated in rule 203. Council has also designated the Governmental Accounting Standards Board (GASB), as the body to establish financial accounting principles for state and local governmental entities pursuant to rule 203. Council has also designated the Federal Accounting Standards Advisory Board (FASAB), with respect to Statements of Federal Accounting Standards adopted and issued in March 1993 and subsequently, as the body to establish accounting principles for federal government entities pursuant to rule 203.

In determining the existence of a departure from an accounting principle established by a Statement of Federal Accounting Standards, Accounting Research Bulletin or APB Opinion encompassed by rule 203, or the existence of a departure from an accounting principle established by a Statement of Governmental Accounting Standards or a Statement of Federal Accounting Standards encompassed by rule 203, the division of professional ethics will construe such Statements, Bulletin or Opinion in the light of any interpretations thereof issued by the FASB or the GASB.

Rule 203 – Accounting Principles: The final rule dealing with Standard Accounting Principles is Rule 203, which governs the attestation of the use of generally accepted accounting principles. The first part of the rule reads as follows:

A member shall not (1) express an opinion or state affirmatively that the financial statements or other financial data of any entity are presented in conformity with generally accepted accounting principles (GAAP) or (2) state that he or she is not aware of any material modifications that should be made to such statements or data in order for them to be in conformity with generally accepted accounting principles, if such statements or data contain any departure from an accounting principle promulgated by bodies designated by Council to establish such principles that *has a material effect* on the statements or data *taken as a whole.*

Thus, the rule prescribes that a member not certify that financial statements or data are in accord with GAAP if there is a departure from those principles that has a material effect on the statements or data. We will have to return to the notion of a material misstatement. But there is a provision to the rules: "If, however, the statements or data contain such a departure and the member can demonstrate that due to unusual circumstances the financial statements or data would otherwise have been misleading, the member can comply with the rule by describing the departure, its approximate effects, if practicable, and the reasons why compliance with the principle would result in a misleading statement." [As adopted January 12, 1988.]

So, one should follow GAAP unless there is a reason to depart from them, and the accountant can show reasons justifying said departure. Of course this brings up the now heated debate about whether GAAP provide sufficient tools for determining the worth of large corporations in contemporary times, or whether techniques such as "pro forma" accounting, and other valuational techniques are sufficient for providing users with adequate information about the financial status of companies. There is a loud call to the FASB for needed reform of those principles. But the strengths and weaknesses of those standards are a technical question beyond the scope of this book.

▲ SECTION 300 ▲

This brings us to the section of the rules that deals with accountants' relational responsibilities. Section 300 deals with responsibilities to clients and colleagues. While the Code has already dealt in Rule 201 with the responsibility to offer competent service with due care, Section 300 deals with the specific areas of confidentiality and contingent fees.

Rule 301 – Confidential client information: This is rather straightforward: *A member in public practice shall not disclose any confidential client information without the specific consent of the client.* However, the rule nowhere specifies what counts as confidential information. Supposedly such information would include income figures, debts, and such that were not part of the public record, and which a third party had no legitimate claim to know.

Rule 302 – Contingent fees: Rule 302 deals with contingent fees, which is a rather complex issue. It prohibits members from accepting fees contingent upon audits or reviews of financial statements, or compilations of statements to be used by a third party, which don't disclose a lack of independence. Thus, accountants who engage in opinion shopping, or offer auditing guaranteed to make the company look good, no matter how subtly these are marketed, are in violation of Rule 302. As would follow, the rule also prohibits preparing original or amended tax returns for a contingent fee.

This becomes clear when we explain what constitutes a contingent fee. According to the Code, "a contingent fee is a fee established for the performance of any service pursuant to an arrangement in which no fee will be charged unless a specified finding or result is attained, or in which the amount of the fee is otherwise dependent upon the finding or result of such service." Fees fixed by public authorities are not considered contingent in this area.

▲ SECTION 400 ▲

The next section of the code, which includes rules in the 400 series, is dedicated to an accountant's responsibilities to colleagues. Whereas other professional codes deal extensively with the importance of fellow professionals encouraging, aiding, and mentoring each other, and with responsibilities toward self-policing, the AICPA Code currently contains nothing in this area. According to William Keenan, Technical Manager of Professional Ethics, ". . . the section was reserved for addressing possible future rules and interpretations dealing with responsibilities to colleagues." Keenan indicates that "there is nothing in the offing at present and nothing to my knowledge that has been issued in the past in exposure draft form to the membership."[4]

There are certainly issues that face accountants about what to do with respect to other accountants who commit illegal or unethical actions in pursuing their work. There are issues that come up with respect to cooperation with other professionals in such things as multi-disciplinary financial planning groups. However, we will deal specific ethical issues such as these as they come up in the course of the book.

▲ SECTION 500 ▲

The final section of the Code is the section dealing with **Other responsibilities and practices.**

Rule 501 is a comprehensive rule prohibiting a member from committing acts that would be discreditable to the profession.

Rule 502 prohibits a member in public practice from false advertising or other forms of solicitation that is misleading or deceptive. It also prohibits solicitation by the use of coercion, overreaching, or harassing conduct.

Rule 503 deals with the prohibition of commissions and referral fees.

> An accountant while auditing, reviewing, compiling statements for third party use or examining prospective financial information, shall not recommend or refer any product or service, or recommend or refer any product or service to be supplied by a client, for a commission.

This section has created problems for those accountants who take on the function of a financial or estate planner for their client. It is argued that because an accountant knows the financial affairs of clients better than most, it is prudent for the accountant to take on financial planning services where the accountant is trained and has the competence to offer such services. Since those services often involve brokering products for a commission, it seems only fair that the accountant be entitled to the commission on selling those products. The Code, though, wisely sees the potential conflict of interest that commission-based sales can generate.

The section that deals with the prohibition against receiving certain commissions is followed by standards of disclosure for permitted commissions.

> A member in public practice who is not prohibited by this rule from performing services for or receiving a commission and who is paid or expects to be paid a commission shall disclose that fact to any person or entity to whom the member recommends or refers a product or service to which the commission relates.

Rule 503 also goes on to cover referral fees. It states, "any member who accepts a referral fee for recommending or referring any service of a CPA to any person or entity or who pays a referral fee to obtain a client shall disclose such acceptance or payment to the client." In short, if an accountant is receiving commissions or referral fees, he or she is obliged to disclose that fact to the client.

The final rule of the Code, Rule 505, deals with the form of organization and name. Simply, a member shall not practice public accounting under a firm name that is misleading, and a firm may not designate itself as "Members of the American Institute of Certified Public Accountants" unless all of its CPA owners are members of the Institute.

To summarize, the rules of the Code break down into five sections: (1) independence, integrity, and objectivity, (2) general standards, accounting principles, (3) responsibilities to clients, (4) responsibilities to colleagues, and (5) other responsibilities and practices. They are informed by the general principles of honesty, integrity, and independence. The accountant has a function to fulfill, that is to present as accurate a picture as possible of the financial condition of a company or client, a picture which affords the proper information to those who have a legitimate claim to the use of such information. We turn now to an examination of how these responsibilities work out in the various fields of accounting – auditing, financial or management accounting, and tax accounting.

▲ NOTES ▲

1. AICPA Code, 101.07.
2. The Commission on Auditors' Responsibilities, "Report, Conclusion and Recommendations" (New York: Commission on Auditors' Responsibilities, 1978), p. 2.
3. AICPA Code, 101.01.
4. William L. Keenan, Technical Manager, Professional Ethics. "There is nothing in existence at present to be included in Section 400. I believe the section was reserved for addressing possible future rules and interpretations dealing with responsibilities to colleagues but there is nothing in the offing at present and nothing to my knowledge that has been issued in the past in exposure draft form to the membership." Email, March 25, 2001.

chapter seven

Ethics in Auditing: The Auditing Function

In an article entitled "Arthur Andersen's 'Double Duty' Work Raises Questions About Its Independence" in the *Wall Street Journal*, Jonathan Weil reported:

> In addition to acting as Enron Corp.'s outside auditor, Arthur Andersen LLP also performed internal auditing services for Enron, raising further questions about the Big Five accounting firm's independence and the degree to which it may have been auditing its own work.
>
> That Andersen performed "double duty" work for the Houston-based energy concern likely will trigger greater regulatory scrutiny of Andersen's role as Enron's independent auditor than would ordinarily be the case after an audit failure, accounting and securities-law specialists say . . .
>
> Such arrangements have become more common over the past decade. In response, the Securities and Exchange Commission last year passed new rules [effective August 2002], restricting the amount of internal audit work that outside auditors can perform for their clients, though not banning it outright . . .
>
> Andersen officials say their firm's independence wasn't impaired by the size or nature of the fees paid by Enron – $52 million last year. ($25 million for audit fees, $27 million for other services, including tax and consulting work.) An Enron spokesman said, "The company believed and continues to believe that Arthur Andersen's role as Enron's internal auditor would not compromise Andersen's role as independent auditor for Enron." . . .
>
> Accounting firms say the double-duty arrangements let them become more familiar with clients' control procedures and that such arrangements are ethically permissible, as long as outside auditors don't make management decisions in handling the internal audits. Under the new SEC rules taking effect next year, an outside auditor impairs its independence if it performs more than 40% of a client's internal-audit work. The SEC said the restriction wouldn't apply to

clients with assets of $200 million or less. Previously, the SEC had imposed no such percentage limitation.[1]

This Enron/Arthur Andersen case raises many ethical questions about what is appropriate behavior for auditors. We propose to examine them by taking a look at what the proper function of the auditor is and what sorts of things stand in the way of an auditor performing that function. To begin, consider the following scenario.

Nancy is an audit partner with a large regional CPA firm, Accountants & Co. She is auditing Golf Manufacturers, a company that produces golf clubs. A senior accountant on the job has brought to Nancy's attention that a review of the cost accounting system has revealed an extremely large unfavorable material quantity variance. From Nancy's perspective, the variance is so large that it is material, and should be placed on the income statement as a non-recurring item.

Two years ago, the management advisory services (MAS) department of Accountants & Co. had contracted with Golf Manufacturers to examine their cost accounting and control system. Because of the MAS department's recommendation Golf Manufacturers implemented a major overhaul of its cost accounting and control system throughout the company. Nancy thinks this new system contains a major flaw that is directly responsible for the large unfavorable material quantity variance. Nancy decides to talk this over with her managing partner, Peter, before taking her findings to the management of Golf Manufacturers.

Peter reviews the working papers sent by Nancy and concludes the unfavorable materials quantity variance has been properly calculated. Peter also consulted with the MAS department and reached the same conclusion as Nancy, that the variance can be traced to the new system that the MAS department recommended.

In a conversation with Nancy, Peter admits that the MAS staff has made a huge blunder. But he says the theory experts at the head office say this can be handled in two ways. Under standard cost theory Nancy's approach is correct. But under actual cost theory the variance can be prorated among several inventory accounts and cost of goods sold. That way we can wash it out of the system.

Peter suggests that given the competition for clients it would not be wise to go with Nancy's plans. Besides, actual cost theory has as much, if not more support than standard cost theory.[2]

This case is an example of the sort of serious ethical pressures that beset the accounting profession today – the risks and dangers to the integrity of the accounting practice created by conflicts of interest and the necessity of surviving in a competitive market. To increase profit, accounting firms add consulting services, quite often for the same companies that they are simultaneously auditing, thus creating at least apparent if not real conflicts of interest. This kind of practice has been going on for years, but until recently has remained under the radar. With the eruption of the Enron case, accounting firms have come under new scrutiny. The conflict of interest was writ large in stories like the following:

> Arthur Andersen LLP's role in Enron Corp.'s accounting problems is more proof of a need for tighter controls of the accounting industry, says former Securities and Exchange Commission Chairman Arthur Levitt . . . Arthur Andersen's Enron audit work is being scrutinized by the SEC, the Justice Department and six congressional committees.
>
> Mr. Levitt, despite his efforts, failed in late 2000 to enact rules banning auditors from acting as consultants for companies they audit. He argued that potential profits from consulting could create a conflict of interest that undermines auditors' independence. He also proposed that outside auditors be barred from working with company accountants on company financial reports. Otherwise, Big Five firms could be auditing their own work.
>
> Faced with opposition from three of the Big Five, including Andersen, the SEC eventually adopted new rules requiring corporate-board audit committees to monitor potential conflicts and banning auditors from providing some specific consulting activities, such as tax work. But the rules stop short of a total ban on auditors doing any consulting work for audit clients.
>
> Arthur Andersen collected $52 million in fees in 2000 from Enron: $25 million in audit fees and $27 million for other services, including consulting work.[3]

Human nature being what it is, it seems less likely that one will be able to keep a client on the consulting side if the client is given an unfavorable audit. The client might go shopping for an audit firm that would give a more lenient reading of the books. On the other hand, if the audit is inadequate and people suffer from misinformation that the accountants should have uncovered, the accounting firm might get sued, because auditors are expected to look out for the interests of the public before looking out for the best interest of the client. The fact that, as Steven Silber said, lawsuits happen to auditors with great frequency, only reinforces the point that the role of the auditor in financial services is so critically important.[4]

Independence of management advisory services for auditors is required. Suppose an auditor questions a technique the consulting branch of his company employed. He might be asked to overlook it for any number of reasons. At any rate, to begin to worry about the interests of the firm being audited – which is paying the accountant – more than the truth is to violate the duty of accountants to immediate third party users.[5]

Given the way financial markets and the economic system have developed, society has carved out a role for the independent auditor, which is absolutely essential for the effective functioning of the economic system. If accounting is the language of business, it is the auditor's job to see the language is used properly so that the relevant message is communicated properly. This means that, in the system, the role of the independent auditor is "to see whether the company's estimates are based on formulas that seem reasonable in the light of whatever evidence is available and that choice formulas are applied consistently from year to year."[6]

Most times, when people talk about the ethics of public accounting, they are talking about the responsibilities of the independent auditor. Auditing the financial statements of publicly owned companies is certainly not the only role of an accountant, but an argument can be made that it is one of the, if not *the*, most important roles in the current economic system. John C. Bogle, founder of The Vanguard Group, puts it succinctly:

The integrity of financial markets – markets that are active, liquid, and honest, with participants who are fully and fairly informed – is *absolutely central* to the sound functioning of any system of democratic capitalism worth its salt. It is only through such markets that literally trillions upon trillions of dollars – the well-spring of today's powerful American economy – could have been raised in the past decade to become capital for the plant and equipment of our Old Economy and the capital for the technology and innovation of our New Economy. Only the complete confidence of investors in the integrity of the financial information they received allowed these investment needs to be met at the lowest possible cost of capital.

Sound securities markets require sound financial information. It is as simple as that. Investors require – and have a right to require – complete information about each and every security, information that fairly and honestly represents every significant fact and figure that might be needed to evaluate the worth of a corporation. Not only is accuracy required but also, more than that, a broad sweep of information that provides every appropriate figure that a prudent, probing, sophisticated professional investor might require in the effort to decide whether a security should be purchased, held, or sold. Those are the watchwords of the financial system that has contributed so much to our nation's growth, progress, and prosperity.

It is unarguable, I think, that the independent oversight of financial figures is central to that disclosure system. Indeed independence is at integrity's very core. And, for more than a century, the responsibility for the independent oversight of corporate financial statements has fallen to America's public accounting profession. It is the auditor's stamp on a financial statement that gives it its validity, its respect, and its acceptability by investors. And only if the auditor's work is comprehensive, skeptical, inquisitive, and rigorous, can we have confidence that financial statements speak the truth.[7]

For years, independent auditing was the primary occupation of the large accounting firms. But that has changed. As we have been made aware of in the case of Arthur Andersen, which is by no means alone in this practice, large accounting firms in order to generate more income for the firm have taken on other tasks, particularly consulting. As one report says:

> In 1993, 31% of the industry's fees came from consulting. By 1999, that had jumped to 51%. In 2002, for example Pricewaterhouse-Coopers earned only 40% of its worldwide fees from auditing, 29% coming from management consulting and most of the rest from tax and corporate finance work . . . More telling, in a study of the first 563 companies to file financials after Feb. 5, 2001, . . . for every dollar of audit fees, clients paid their independent accountants $2.69 for non-audit consulting. . . . Marriott International Inc. . . . paid Andersen just over $1 million for its audit, but more than $30 million for information technology and other services. . . . It simply looks bad to have Andersen earning more on consulting to Enron than on auditing.[8]

However, even though the structure of the large accounting firms has changed, the need for the independent external auditor has grown while society's need to be able to trust the fidelity of the external corporate audit remains as strong as ever.

As Bogle notes, a free-market economy needs to base transactions and decisions on truthful and accurate information. In market transactions the financial status of a company is vital information on which a choice to purchase is to be based. The role of the auditor is to attest to the fact that the financial picture of a company, presented to any user who needs to make a decision on the basis of that picture, is as accurate as possible.

This function and responsibility is not new; it has only come under the harsh glare of public scrutiny with the eruption of the Enron/ Arthur Andersen debacle. The classic statement of this function and responsibility of the auditor is the opinion given by Justice Burger in the 1984 landmark Arthur Young case.[9]

> Corporate financial statements are one of the primary sources of information available to guide the decisions of the investing public. In an effort to control the accuracy of the financial data available to investors in the securities markets, various provisions of the federal securities laws require publicly held companies to file their financial statements with the Securities and Exchange Commission. Commission regulations stipulate that these financial reports must be audited by an independent CPA in accordance with generally accepted auditing standards. *By examining the corporation's books and records, the independent auditor determines whether the financial reports of the corporation have been prepared in accordance with generally accepted accounting principles. The auditor then issues an opinion as to whether the financial statements, taken as a whole, fairly present the financial position and operations of the corporation for the relevant period.* [Authors' italics.]

Burger puts the responsibility of the auditor clearly – to issue an opinion as to whether the financial statement *fairly* presents the financial position of the corporation. Performance of this role attesting that the financial positions and operations of the corporation are fairly presented requires the auditor to have as much integrity and honesty as possible. Further, to assure that an accurate picture has been presented it is essential that the integrity and honesty of the auditor not be imperiled by the presence of undue influence. To bolster integrity and honesty the auditor must have as much independence as possible. For the market to function efficiently those who need to make decisions about the company based on as true and accurate information as possible must be able to trust the accountants' pictures. But such trust is eroded if there is even an appearance of a conflict of interest. Mara Der Hovanesian puts it succinctly.

> The heat is on for Corporate America. In the wake of the Enron Corp. debacle, the quality of earnings is being questioned as never

before. . . . Earnings jitters may yet rock the markets. More shaky accounting practices could come to light. Some companies won't have registered the full impact of the downturn on their books, while others will still massage their numbers . . . Investors have every reason to be twitchy.[10]

▲ TRUST ▲

We can understand all this if we apply Immanuel Kant's first categorical imperative, the universalizability principle: "Act so you can will the maxim of your action to be a universal law." As we saw, the imperative demands that an action be capable of being universalized – i.e. we need to consider what would occur if everyone acted the same way for the same reason. Consider the reasons people have for not giving the most accurate picture possible of the financial status of a company. As we saw, one generally gives a false picture to get another party to act in a way other than they would act given full and truthful information. For example, a CFO misrepresents his company's profits to get a bank loan, thinking that if the bank had the true picture, no loan would be forthcoming. In the Enron case it was more complicated, the aim being to buoy up the price of the stock, which was then used as collateral to float loans to cover (bad?) debts. What would happen if such behavior were universalized, i.e. if everybody misrepresented the financial health of their company when it was to their advantage to lie?

In such a situation two things would happen. First, trust in business dealings that required information about the financial picture would be eroded. This certainly happens, as Der Hovanesian relates. Chaos would ensue, because financial markets cannot operate without trust. Cooperation is essential, and trust is a precondition of cooperation. We engage in hundreds of transactions daily, which demand that we trust other people with our money and our lives. If misrepresentation were to become a universal practice such trust, and consequently such cooperation, would be impossible.

Secondly, universalizing misrepresentation, besides leading to mistrust, chaos, and consequently inefficiencies in the market, would make the act of misrepresentation impossible. When universalizing misrepresentation makes trust impossible, it simultaneously makes the very act of misrepresenting impossible, because misrepresentation can only occur if the person lied to trusts the person lying. Since prudent people don't trust known liars, if everyone lied, no one would trust another and it would be impossible to lie. So universalized lying makes lying impossible. Do we trust the defendant in a murder case to tell the truth? Do we trust young children who are worried about being punished to tell the truth? Of course not. Once we recognize that certain people are unreliable or untrustworthy it becomes impossible for them to misrepresent things to us, because we don't believe a word they're saying. Hence the anomaly – if misrepresentation became universalized in certain situations, it would be impossible to misrepresent in those situations, since no one would trust what was being represented. This makes the universalizing of lying irrational or self-contradictory.

The contradiction here, according to Kant, is a will contradiction, and the irrationality lies in the fact that you are simultaneously willing the possibility of misrepresentation and the impossibility of misrepresentation, by willing out of existence the conditions (trust) necessary to perform the act you will to perform. Face it, people who lie don't want lying universalized. Liars are free riders. Liars want an unfair advantage. They don't want others to lie – to act like the liars are acting. Liars want others to tell the truth and be trusting so that the liars can lie to those trusting people. Liars want the world to work one way for them and differently for all others. In short, liars want a double standard. They want their cake and want to eat it too. But such a selfish self-serving attitude is the antithesis of the ethical. In this case auditing would become a useless function. As a matter of fact, in an issue of *Accounting Today*, Rick Teleberg thinks this has already happened: "CPA firms long ago became more like insurance companies – complete with their focus on assurances and risk-managed audits – than attesters." We won't risk telling the public what your financial state looks like; we'll just guarantee that your presentation won't be subject to charges of illegal behavior. They serve the client and not the public.

In this discussion we can see another important aspect of trust. Only a fool trusts someone who gives all the appearances of being a liar. Only a fool trusts someone who puts themselves in positions where they seem likely to have their integrity compromised. These are the reasons why people take precautions against getting involved with those who give even the appearance of being caught in a conflict of interest. Because trust is necessary, even the *appearance* of honesty and integrity of accountants becomes important. So the auditor must not only be trustworthy, he or she must also appear trustworthy, for the prudent manager as the prudent accountant has an obligation to be sufficiently skeptical in order to protect the legitimate claims of stakeholders. We will return to the arguments for avoiding even the appearance of independence later.

▲ THE AUDITOR'S RESPONSIBILITY ▲
TO THE PUBLIC

This role and the consequent duty to attest to the fairness of the financial statements gives the accountant special responsibilities to the public. As we saw in the chapters on codes of ethics, possessing these responsibilities puts the accountant in a different relationship with the client who hires him or her than the client relationships found in the other professions. Justice Burger mentions this in his classic statement of auditor responsibility.

> The auditor does not have the same relationship to his client that a private attorney who has a role as ". . . a confidential advisor and advocate, a loyal representative whose duty it is to present the client's case in the most favorable possible light. An independent CPA performs a different role. *By certifying the public reports that collectively depict a corporation's financial status, the independent auditor assumes a public responsibility transcending any employment relationship with the client* [authors' italics]. The independent public accountant performing this special function owes ultimate allegiance to the corporation's creditors and stockholders, as well as to the investing public. This 'public watchdog' function demands that the accountant maintain total independence from the client at all times and requires complete fidelity to the public trust. To insulate from disclosure a CPA's interpretations of the client's financial statements would be to ignore the significance of the accountant's role as a disinterested analyst charged with public obligations."[11]

Given the conflict of interests between the public and clients, it is clear that auditors face conflicting loyalties. To whom are they primarily responsible, the public or the client who pays the bill? We have seen that accountants are professionals and, consequently, should behave as professionals. Like most other professionals, they offer services to their clients. But the public accounting profession, because it includes operating as an independent auditor, has another function. The independent auditor acts not only as a recorder, but also as an evaluator of other accountants' records. The auditor has what Justice Burger calls "a public watchdog function."

As we have seen, over time, the evaluation of another accountant's records has developed into a necessary component of capitalist societies, particularly that part of society that deals in money markets and offers publicly traded stocks and securities. In such a system, it is imperative for potential purchasers of financial products to have an accurate picture of the companies in which they wish to invest, to whom they are willing to loan money, or with whom they wish to merge. In such a system there needs to be a procedure for verifying the accuracy of the financial picture of companies. The role of verifier fell to the public accountant – the auditor.[12]

Baker and Hayes reiterate the accountant's different kind of role.

> Other professionals, such as physicians and lawyers, are expected to perform their services at the maximum possible level of professional competence for the benefit of their clients. Public accountants may at times be expected by their clients to perform their professional services in a manner that differs from the interests of third parties who are the beneficiaries of the contractual arrangements between the public accountant and their clients. This unusual arrangement poses an ethical dilemma for public accountants.[13]

In short, while auditors' clients are the ones who pay the fees for the auditor's services, the auditor's primary responsibility is to look out for the interest of a third party, the public, and not to look out primarily for the interests of the one who employs the accountant.

Since the auditor is charged with public obligations, he or she should be a disinterested analyst. The auditor's obligations are to certify that the public reports depicting a corporation's financial status *fairly* present the financial position and operations of the corporation for the relevant period. In short, the fiduciary responsibility of the auditor is to the public trust, and "independence" from the client is demanded for that trust to be honored. The importance of this can be seen in the emphasis the Securities and Exchange Commission puts on the independence factor.

> In January of 2000, partners and employees at Pricewaterhouse-Coopers were found by the S.E.C. to have routinely violated rules forbidding their ownership of stock in companies they were auditing. The investigation found 8,064 violations at the firm, which then

dismissed five partners. Pricewaterhouse said at the time that it did not believe that the integrity of any audit had been compromised by the violations.[14]

The fact that the auditor's role requires "transcending any employment relationship with the client" quite often creates dilemmas for the auditor. Since dilemmas arise because of conflicts of responsibility, it will be helpful to specify the particular responsibilities of an auditor.

▲ THE AUDITOR'S BASIC ▲ RESPONSIBILITIES

While the first responsibility of the auditor is to certify or attest to the truth (as far as one is able) of financial statements, an auditor has other responsibilities specified in the AICPA's statements on auditing standards. In Statement of Auditing Standards No. 1, the *Codification of Auditing Standards and Procedures*, the Auditing Standards Board specifies the *generally accepted auditing standards* (the GAAS). These consist in three general standards, three standards of fieldwork and four standards of reporting. They call for: (1) proficiency on the part of the auditor; (2) independence in fact and in appearance; (3) due professional care which involves a sense of "professional skepticism;" (4) adequately planned and properly supervised field work; (5) a sufficient understanding of the internal control structure of the audited entity; (6) sufficient inspection, observation, and inquiries to afford a "reasonable basis" for an opinion; (7) a report stating whether the financial statements are in accord with GAAP; (8) identification of circumstances in which the principles have not been consistently observed; (9) disclosures (including notes and wordings) in the financial statements are to be regarded as reasonably adequate unless otherwise stated; and (10) a report shall contain either an opinion of the statement taken as a whole, or an assertion to the effect that an opinion cannot be expressed.[15]

Over the last 62 years, the AICPA has issued 93 Statements on Auditing Standards and a large number of Auditing Interpretations. The AICPA has also published audit and accounting industry guides, Auditing Statements of Position, and various other auditing publications. The intent behind this gargantuan collection of auditing literature is to provide guidance on how to conduct an audit of financial statements in accordance with generally accepted auditing standards (GAAS). Unfortunately, the immense size of this collection has left doubt in some auditors' minds about whether or not they are aware of all the publications that might apply to their audit engagements.[16]

It will help us understand the major areas of responsibility if we go back a quarter of a century to a document known as the Cohen Report.[17]

In 1974, the AICPA's Commission on Auditor's Responsibilities (The Cohen Commission) was established to develop conclusions and recommendations regarding the appropriate responsibilities of independent auditors, and to examine the gap between public expectations and needs and what auditors can reasonably accomplish. If gaps existed, the Commission was to determine how the disparity between the public's expectations and needs and the realistic capabilities of the accountant could be resolved.

The report defined the independent auditor's primary role in society as that of an intermediary between the financial statements and the users of those statements. Because the auditor is a third party between the client and the public, he or she has an accountability relationship between the issues covered in financial statements and users who rely on those statements. The Cohen Commission made it clear that the primary responsibility of auditors is to the user of the financial statements, not to their clients.

But the report did more than reiterate the primary responsibility of the auditor to attest to fair financial pictures. It examined the gap between public expectations of auditors and what auditors, given the restraints of time and business pressures, can reasonably be expected to accomplish. The report took pains to point out some areas that *are not* the responsibility of the independent auditor.

For example, there is an erroneous belief among some of the public that auditors are responsible for the actual preparation of the financial statements. Others erroneously believe that an audit report indicates that the business being audited is sound. Auditors are not responsible for attesting to the soundness of the business. In fact management, and not auditors, are responsible for the preparation of the financial statements. Indeed, in most cases, management accountants will prepare the financial statements, but that is a different role for the accountant which we will examine in the next chapter.

Auditors are responsible for forming an opinion about whether the financial statements are presented in accord with appropriately utilized accounting principles. This raises a controversial subject in the accounting ethics literature. The traditional attest statement stated that the financial statements were "presented fairly in accordance with generally accepted accounting principles." In the 1960s a committee of the AICPA had raised the following questions about the fairness claim.

> In the standard report of the auditor, he generally says that financial statements "present fairly" in conformity with generally accepted accounting principles – and so on. What does the auditor mean by the quoted words? Is he saying: (1) that the statements are fair *and* in accordance with GAAP; or (2) that they are fair *because* they are in accordance with GAAP; or (3) that they are fair only *to the extent* that GAAP are fair; or (4) that whatever GAAP may be, the *presentation* of them is fair? [Emphasis in original.][18]

The Cohen Report pointed out that "fairness" is an ambiguous word and hence it is imprudent to hold auditors accountable for the fairness of the report, if that means accuracy of material facts. Rather, the responsibility of the auditors is to determine whether the judgments of managers in the selection and application of accounting principles were appropriate or inappropriate for use in the matter at hand. Note that this differs from Justice Burger's notion that the auditor attests to the "fairness" of the picture.

The Cohen Report would find Burger's requirement is too rigid, for three reasons. In some situations there may be no detailed principles that are applicable, in others alternative accounting principles may be applicable, and at times there need to be evaluations of the cumulative effects of the use of a principle. The Report called for more guidance for auditors in these three areas. Still, that is hardly the end of the matter, for there seems to be a sense in which the notion of "fairly" presented means the report that is being audited will give the reasonable person a fairly good picture of the financial status of the entity being pictured. One can argue that the GAAP can be used by artful dodgers to hide the real health or sickness of a company. Indeed, many accountants have suggested that accounting is an art, and a truly proficient artist can by the skillful use of GAAP make the same company look to be dizzyingly successful or failing miserably.

Consider the opinion of a federal judge in *Herzfeld v. Laventhol.*

Compliance with generally accepted accounting principles is not necessarily sufficient for an accountant to discharge his public obligation. Fair presentation is the touchstone for determining the adequacy of disclosure and financial statements. While adherence to generally accepted accounting principles is a tool to help achieve that end, it is not necessarily a guarantee of fairness.

Too much attention to the question whether the financial statements formally complied with principles, practices and conventions accepted at the time should not be permitted to blind us to the basic question whether the financial statements performed the function of enlightenment, *which is their only reason for existence.*[19]

Finally, consider the words of former SEC Commissioner A. A. Sommer, Jr.

More disturbingly to the accounting profession . . . was the language in which Judge Henry J. Friendly, surely one of the most knowledgeable of federal judges in financial and accounting matters, scrapped the affirmance (in *Continental Vending*). He said in effect that the first law for accountants was not compliance with generally accepted accounting principles, but rather full and fair disclosure, fair presentation, and if the principles did not produce this brand of disclosure, accountants could not hide behind the principles but had to go beyond them and make whatever additional disclosures were necessary for full disclosure. In a word, "present fairly" was a concept separate from "generally accepted accounting principles," and the latter did not necessarily result in the former.[20]

Whatever the meaning of fairness, it seems to require that the picture presented be such that it gives as accurate a picture as possible to third parties that have a market interest in the financial statements. Thus whatever would fulfill the misrepresentation criteria that we suggested earlier in the chapter would determine what counted as "unfair."

Besides the difficulties the Cohen Report had with the ambiguity of the word "fairly" it went on to examine some further important responsibilities of auditors, responsibilities that have been reiterated in subsequent AICPA statements of auditing standards.

The evaluation of internal auditing control: The Cohen Report also insisted that it was a responsibility of the auditor to express an opinion on internal accounting control. The auditor is responsible for determining whether the internal auditing system and controls are adequate. Expressing an opinion on internal accounting control necessarily leads to a claim that auditors have an obligation to examine the internal workings of the company's accounting procedures, and the safeguards from risks that are in place. It is interesting to contemplate how Arthur Andersen, who served as both the internal and external auditor of Enron, could possibly in an objective manner fulfill the role of critiquing the internal auditing of the company.

But what specifically is an internal auditor to do? To discuss that will require an articulation of the obligations of the management accountants, to see if those are adhered to. We will examine those obligations in the next chapter, but the point here is that the auditor is responsible for evaluating whether the management accountant is living up to his or her obligations and whether the internal auditing controls are adequate and adhered to.

Responsibility to detect and report errors, irregularities, and/ or fraud: A further area that the Cohen Report claimed was an area of responsibility was the auditor's responsibility to report on significant uncertainties that were detected in the financial statements. Further, in a most important area, the Report went on to clarify the responsibility of auditors for the detection of fraud and the detection of errors and irregularities. The Report cited an important document, which lays out the specific obligations of the public watchdog function – Section 53 of the AICPA Statement on Auditing Standards, entitled "The Auditor's Responsibility To Detect And Report Errors And Irregularities." However, SAS 53 was superseded by SAS 82 in 1997 and SAS 82 was amended in February 2002. We have included a summary of the Exposure Draft of 2002 and some relevant passages in appendix III.

To more clearly ascertain auditors' responsibilities, let's consider the following situation:

> Lawyers for the Allegheny health system's creditors have sued Allegheny's longtime auditors, Pricewaterhouse-Coopers, asserting that the accounting firm "ignored the sure signs" of the system's collapse and failed to prevent its demise.

The suit called Pricewaterhouse-Coopers, "the one independent entity that was in a position to detect and expose" Allegheny's "financial manipulations." Yet the system's financial statements audited by the firm "consistently depicted a business conglomerate in sound financial condition," even after Allegheny's senior officials were fired in 1998.

A spokesman for Pricewaterhouse-Coopers, Steven Silber, said, "We believe this lawsuit to be totally without merit. We intend to defend ourselves vigorously and we're fully confident that we will prevail. Accounting firms are considered to be deep pockets and lawsuits happen to auditors with great frequency."[21]

What was Pricewaterhouse-Coopers' responsibility to detect and expose Allegheny's financial manipulations? How much time, effort and money needed to be expended to detect the signs of the system's collapse? Does the public have a right to expect that an audit should turn up such matters and, if it does, to report them when detected?

To report such errors and irregularities seems to be one of the most serious and perplexing responsibilities of an auditor. In the first place it seems prima facie to run counter to the accountant's responsibility of confidentiality that we examined in chapter 6.[22]

John E. Beach, in an article entitled "Code of Ethics: The Professional Catch 22,"[23] gives two examples showing how the accountant's responsibility to the public, when in conflict with the responsibility to keep the client's affairs confidential, can lead to accounting firms getting sued, and losing lawsuits. According to Beach:

In October of 1981, a jury in Ohio found an accountant guilty of negligence and breach of contract for violating the obligation of confidentiality mandated in the accountant's code of ethics, and awarded the plaintiffs approximately $1,000,000. At approximately the same time, a jury in New York awarded a plaintiff in excess of $80,000,000 based in part on the failure of an accountant to disclose confidential information.

Without wrestling with this complex issue, which involves deciding when it is permissible for auditors to report certain inappropriate activities of their clients as well as when it is required to report those activities,[24] suffice it to say there is legal opinion that the duty of confidentiality is not absolute and "overriding public interests may exist to which confidentiality must yield."[25]

But what about the auditor's responsibility to detect errors, irregularities, or fraud? What do the Statement of Auditing Standards No. 53 (published in 1988) and No. 82, which dropped the word "irregularities" in favor of "fraud" (published in 1997), indicate are the responsibilities of auditors?[26] These documents are particularly useful in evaluating the behavior of Arthur Andersen toward its client Enron, for there is documented evidence indicating that Sherron Watkins blew the whistle on Andersen's handling of Special Purpose Entities (SPEs) and found the accounting procedures suspect.[27] Subsequent memos coming out of Andersen indicated uneasiness with the procedures, but nothing was done about it. Did Andersen have a responsibility to act on those perceived irregularities? We think an examination of the audit standards will indicate clearly that it did. But to show this we need to look more carefully at these surprisingly little-known standards.

The standards documents do several things. Not only do they provide guidance for the responsibility to detect errors, irregularities, and fraud[28] in an audit, they also describe factors that influence the auditor's ability to detect them and explain how the exercise of due care should give appropriate consideration to the possibilities of those errors, irregularities, and/or fraud. Finally, they provide guidance concerning the auditor's responsibility to communicate those discovered errors, irregularities, and/or fraud, both within and without the organization whose financial statements are being audited.

As we mentioned, SAS 53 refers to "irregularities", a term that is dropped in SAS 82. But in essence what the auditor is looking for are material misstatements or misappropriations of assets or liabilities. If these misstatements or misappropriations are done intentionally, we have a case of fraud. If not intentionally, we have a case of error.

SAS 53 and SAS 82 require the auditor to assess the risk that errors and irregularities may cause the financial statements to contain a material misstatement. On the basis of that risk assessment the auditor should design the audit to provide "reasonable assurance" of detecting errors, irregularities, or fraudulent claims that are material to the financial statements. A material misstatement is simply one large enough to influence a user of the statement to act in a way he or she would not act if there were no misstatement (e.g. not buy a stock if he or she knew the truth). What are the risks that there are errors or fraud? The auditor must assess the risk.

This of course requires that the auditors understand "a number of factors, including management's characteristics and influence over the control environment, industry conditions and operating characteristics, and financial stability."[29]

An auditor may not be able to detect a material irregularity because generally accepted auditing standards do not require the authentication of documents, or there may be collusion and concealment. For example, because of forgery an auditor may not be able to detect a material irregularity. If a high-level manager is involved in a cover up it may go undetected because of a lack of a proper internal control structure. Nevertheless, the standards require that "The auditor should exercise (a) due care in planning, performing, and evaluating the results of audit procedures, and (b) the proper degree of professional skepticism to achieve reasonable assurance that material errors or irregularities will be detected."[30] The auditor is not an insurer; nor does his or her report constitute a guarantee. He or she needs give only reasonable assurance. The important concept here though is the proper degree of professional skepticism.

This concept of skepticism is illuminated by showing that to be properly skeptical the auditor needs to consider factors that influence audit risk, especially the internal control structure.

During planning the auditor should assess risk of material misstatements. "The auditor's understanding of the internal control structure should either heighten or mitigate the auditor's concern about the risk of material misstatements." Are there significant difficult-to-audit transactions? Are there significant and unusual related party transactions not in the ordinary course of business? Are there a significant number of known and likely misstatements detected in the audit of prior periods' financials from the predecessor auditor?

The standards require the auditor to review information about risk factors and the internal control structure by considering matters such as the following. Are there circumstances that may indicate a management predisposition to distort financial statements? Are there indications that management has failed to establish policies and procedures to assure reliable accounting estimates, by utilizing unqualified, careless or inexperienced personnel? Are there indications of lack of control, such as recurrent crises conditions, disorganized work areas, excessive back orders, shortages, delays or lack of documentation for major transactions? Are there indications of a lack of control over computer processing? Are there inadequate policies and procedures for security of data or assets?[31]

The auditor needs to consider the effects of these matters on the overall audit strategy. High risk ordinarily demands more experienced personnel and more extensive supervision. "Higher risk will also ordinarily cause the auditor to exercise a heightened degree of professional skepticism in conducting the audit."[32]

As the generally accepted auditing standards say about skepticism:

> Due professional care requires the auditor to exercise *professional skepticism* . . . an attitude that includes a questioning mind and a critical assessment of audit evidence. The auditor uses the knowledge, skill, and ability called for by the profession of public accounting to diligently perform, in good faith and with integrity, the gathering and objective evaluation of evidence.[33]
>
> An audit of financial statements in accordance with generally accepted auditing standards should be planned and performed with an attitude of professional skepticism. The auditor neither assumes that management is dishonest nor assumes unquestioned honesty. Rather, the auditor recognizes that conditions observed and evidential matter obtained, including information from prior audits, need to be objectively evaluated to determine whether the financial statements are free of material misrepresentation.[34]

The standards also emphasize that auditors need to be able to cope with illegalities and/or questionable acts within an agreed-upon framework. The accountant may have an obligation to blow the whistle, but that should not be laid upon him or her without some protections. The auditor "ought to be able to approach the detection and disclosure of illegal or questionable acts by management within a defined and agreed-on framework."[35] The framework should include a policy on corporate conduct, and a system to monitor compliance with the corporate conduct. The auditor should determine whether the operations of the company comply with the standards of corporate conduct. The auditor should also consider illegal or questionable acts without regard for their materiality.

So much for the responsibilities of the auditor as enumerated by the Cohen Report and further specified by auditing standards. At this point we turn to examine another important obligation of the auditor, the obligation to maintain independence.

▲ INDEPENDENCE ▲

Thus far we have looked at the responsibilities of the auditor. But to meet those responsibilities it is imperative that the auditor maintains independence. Let's recall Justice Burger's statement:

> The independent public accountant performing this special function owes ultimate allegiance to the corporation's creditors and stockholders, as well as to the investing public. *This 'public watchdog' function demands that the accountant maintain total independence from the client at all times and requires complete fidelity to the public trust.*

"Total independence" is the key phrase that Burger uses. But what does total independence require? Obviously an external auditor should be *independent* from the client. But must independence be *total*, as Justice Burger says? If so, what exactly does *total independence* require? What does "complete" fidelity to the public trust require? We need to examine whether total independence is a possibility or even a necessity. How much independence should an auditor maintain and how should the auditor determine that?

Let us suggest that what is usually meant by total independence is independence not only in fact, but also in appearance. As we have already noted, the AICPA code of ethics recognizes these two kinds of independence: independence in fact and independence in appearance. Independence in fact is applicable to all accountants, for if the function of the accountant is to render accurate pictures of the financial situation, then conflicts of interest that cause inaccurate pictures do a disservice to whomever is entitled to and in need of the accurate picture.

Whether independence in appearance need be applicable to all accountants or only to independent auditors is an open question. Some would claim[36] that independence in appearance is applicable only to independent auditors. Hence, it is clear that the appearance of independence is important for independent auditors, but whether it is necessary for all accountants is a discussion that can wait for a later time.

The most recent thinking about independence has been carried on by the Independence Standards Board, which has recently published *A Statement of Independence Concepts: A Conceptual Framework for Auditor Independence*. The Independence Standards Board (ISB) was established in 1997 by Securities and Exchange Commission Chairman Arthur Levitt in concert with the American Institute of Certified Public Accountants. "The ISB was given the responsibility of establishing independence standards applicable to the audits of public entities, in order to serve the public interest and to protect and promote investors' confidence in the securities markets." It acknowledges that "The various securities laws enacted by Congress and administered by the SEC recognize that the integrity and credibility of the financial reporting process for public companies depends, in large part, on auditors remaining independent from their audit clients."[37]

As the home page of the ISB states, "The ISB was developed from discussions between the American Institute of Certified Public Accountants ("AICPA"), other representatives of the accounting profession, and the U.S. Securities and Exchange Commission ("SEC")."[38] However, indicative of the pressure being put on the AICPA by the large accounting firms, for whom independence might mean surrendering their lucrative consulting contracts with firms they audited, the ISB was dissolved in August of 2001. In the fall, of course, the fallout from the Enron/Andersen debacle began, and in the winter of 2001–2, the Big Five began separating their auditing and consulting functions. But enough of the history. We have learned that independence is necessary.

John Bogle gives us an eloquent account of why.

> Our government, our regulators, our corporations, and our accountants have . . . properly placed the auditor's independence from his client at the keystone of our financial reporting system. And auditor independence has come to mean an absence of any and all relationships that could seriously jeopardize – either in fact or in appearance – the validity of the audit, and, therefore, of the client's financial statements. The auditor, in short, is the guardian of financial integrity. On the need to maintain, above all, this principle of independence, I hear not a single voice of dissent – not from the corporations, not from the profession, not from the regulators, not from the bar, not from the brokers and bankers (the financial market intermediaries) and not from the institutional investors who, as trustees, hold and manage the securities portfolios of their clients.[39]

But what did the proposed conceptual framework of the now-defunct ISB say about independence? The ISB defined auditor independence as "freedom from those pressures and other factors that compromise, or can reasonably be expected to compromise, an auditor's ability to make unbiased audit decisions." This, of course, does not mean freedom from all pressures, only those that are "so significant that they rise to a level where they compromise, or can reasonably be expected to compromise, the auditor's ability to make audit decisions without bias." By "reasonably be expected," the Report has in mind the rationally based beliefs of well-informed investors and other users of financial information. For example, if I stood to gain from a company to which I give a favorable attestation, because I am a shareholder in that company, or because the company is planning on hiring my firm to do extensive consulting work when it gets a loan from a bank which is contingent upon a favorable audit, the reasonable person would be somewhat skeptical of my ability to be unbiased in that case, not because I was a dishonorable person, but because human beings in general can be unduly influenced by such pressures.

But what sorts of pressures are there? To begin with, there are pressures that can come from relationships such as those with family, friends, acquaintances or business contacts. Standard-setting bodies issue rules that limit certain activities and relationships which they believe represent "potential sources of bias for auditors generally." As we noted, some auditors might be able to remain unbiased in such situations, but the rules apply to them also because "it is reasonable to expect audit decisions to be biased in those circumstances." "Accordingly, non-compliance with those rules might not preclude a particular auditor from being objective, but it would preclude the auditor from claiming to be independent," at least in appearance if not in reality.

Finally, not every situation can be identified or covered by a rule, so the absence of a rule covering a certain relationship does not mean the independence is not jeopardized by the relationship, if the audit decision could reasonably be expected to be compromised as a result of that relationship. "Compliance with the rules is a necessary, but not a sufficient, condition for independence."

The Report then turned to the goal of auditor independence, using that goal as the focal point to determine what the auditor needs to do to achieve that independence. That is what the Report meant by a conceptual framework. The goal is "to support user reliance on the financial reporting process and to enhance management efficiency." Hence, independence is an instrumental good while the main goal to keep in mind is management efficiency.

The Report next delineated four basic principles and four concepts that could be used as guidelines for deciding what interferes with or aids independence. In that context it discusses four concepts that relate to independence: (1) threats, (2) safeguards, (3) independence risk, and (4) significance of threats/effectiveness of safeguards. On the first of these, it says: "Threats to auditor independence are sources of potential bias that may compromise or may reasonably be expected to compromise an auditor's ability to make unbiased audit decisions."

There are five types of threats to independence:

1. Self-interest threats
2. Self-review threats
3. Advocacy threats
4. Familiarity threats
5. Intimidation threats

Gordon Cohn, in an article entitled "Auditing and Ethical Sensitivity,"[40] discusses several other factors jeopardizing auditor independence. He begins by considering how family and financial relations affect independence. Obviously, if the auditor is a relative of a client or maintains financial interests with clients, this could create a conflict of interest and affect the independence of the auditor. Hence, the AICPA's rule of independence prevents one being an auditor where such relationships exist. Even if the auditor could overcome the conflict of interest and was impeccably honest in his or her evaluation and attestations, the public would be suspicious of the auditor's findings. In such a case, then, one needs to avoid even the appearance of a conflict.

But there are a number of other possible areas of conflict of interest where independence is challenged. As Cohn says, "it is obvious that auditing firms' aspirations to maximize the number of well-paying clients provides them considerable interest in their clients' financial success."

The problems with an auditor's independence, according to Cohn, came from two places: first, an actual or apparent lack of independence, and, second, the inefficient functioning of accounting firms. We will review these one at a time.

Concerning lack of independence it is important to note the following. As is clear in the Enron/Andersen case, among others, auditing firms have a strong stake in client retention and financial solvency so a claim can be made that an "accountant's dependence on compensation from and gratitude to the client limits independence."[41]

Having "other financial relationships" with the client firm puts a strain on the auditor's independence. For example, auditing and consulting services for the same firm "increases already extensive financial dependency." The fact that *opinion shopping* goes on is an indication of how far we are from desired independence. Opinion shopping is, prima facie, bad. It is simply the case of someone wanting to come up with a positive attestation, and showing he or she is willing to pay for it. Any accountant or accounting firm that succumbs to that should be immediately ethically suspect.

On the other hand, defenders of the claim that auditors can remain independent, even when they are performing consulting or other services for a company, maintain, "the synergy between two functions assists the accounting firm to produce improved services in both areas." Indeed, there are studies[42] that claim that after 15 years of research not one instance has been found to show that management advisory services by an accounting firm have caused the auditing department of that accounting firm to compromise values. However, those studies have been challenged by Bartlett (1991)[43] on the grounds that the AICPA's definition of independence is ambiguous, and that some of the cases where this might show up are settled out of court, and hence don't show up as evidence of the compromising of the integrity of the accounting firm. Finally, the recent scandals seem to weaken that argument, along with the decision of the Big Five to limit their consulting roles for firms they are auditing.[44]

But there is a second threat to auditor independence – *shortcomings in firm structure*. Lest we forget, being skeptical takes time. Consider a teacher who suspects plagiarism. Think of the expenditure of time in tracing the possible sources from which the material was plagiarized. So, a pertinent question arises: how much time and effort can and should be spent to determine the accuracy of presented data?

As Keller and Mangheim[45] point out, *audit firms use strict time budgets*. This leads to several problems. First, the use of time is largely unobserved and not easily monitored. Second, "there is an alarming increase in underreporting of audit time and audit quality reductions are occurring in practice." Auditors prematurely sign off, reduce work and investigations below reasonable levels, and accept weak client explanations.

Schlacter (1990, cited in Cohn) reports that "disregard of ethical standards jeopardizes career opportunities," while a reputation for high ethical behavior does not enhance advancement. Further, according to Montagna (1974, as quoted by Cohn), overly individualistic behavior would be "a handicap in terms of audit firm promotion." Thus, a person like Nancy in our opening scenario, who made a fuss about the work of the MAS department, would jeopardize her chances for promotion.

We need to return to the ISB Report. After examining the threats, the Report turns to examine safeguards and factors that enhance independence, which are defined as "controls that mitigate or eliminate threats to auditors' independence." These include "prohibitions, restrictions, disclosures, policies, procedures, practices, standards, rules, institutional arrangements, and environmental conditions."

A third and quite important concept is that of independence risk, which is "the risk that threats to auditor independence, to the extent that they are not mitigated by safeguards, compromise, or can reasonably be expected to compromise, an auditor's ability to make unbiased audit decisions. Simply, risk to independence increases with the presence of threats and decreases with the presence of safeguards."

A fourth and final area of examination in the Report is that which deals with the significance of threats and effectiveness of safeguards. "The significance of a threat to auditor independence is the extent to which the threat increases independence risk." Both the third and fourth concepts set up a conceptual framework that will allow for some sort of evaluation of the amount of risk. Since there will always be some bias and interest, *pace* Justice Burger, and since no independence is absolute or "total," it is important to begin to evaluate the different levels of risk. For example, given the development of mutual fund investing and the sudden mergers that occur, such as that of Pricewaterhouse-Coopers, there are going to be family members who hold stocks in companies being audited, or stock holdings in companies audited by a firm with which one's own firm has recently merged. There need to be ways to judge the seriousness and significance of the threats.

The ISB Report's notions of independence risk and significance of threats gives a kind of calculus for determining the amount of risk to independence.

After setting out the four concepts, the framework turns to four basic activities necessary to evaluate auditor independence, which are called principles.

Principle 1. Assessing the level of independence risk: *Independence decision makers should assess the level of independence risk by considering the types and significance of threats to auditor independence and the types and effectiveness of safeguards.*
To help with this assessment, the Report suggests auditors can examine five levels of independence risk. There is the level of *no independence risk*, where compromised objectivity is *virtually impossible*. There is a level of *remote independence risk*, where compromised objectivity is *very unlikely*. There is a level of *some independence risk*, where compromised objectivity is *possible*. There is the level of *high independence risk*, where compromised objectivity is *probable*. Finally, there is the level of *maximum independence risk*, where compromised objectivity is *virtually certain*.

While none of these levels can be measured precisely, there is the opportunity to describe a specific threat as belonging to one of the segments or at one of the "end points of the continuum." Thus the continuum offers a tool that enables an auditor to fulfill the obligation to assess the risk to independence.

Principle 2. Determining the acceptability of the level of independence risk: *After assessing the level of risk the auditor needs to determine "whether the level of independence is at an acceptable position on the independence risk continuum."*

Principle 3. Considering benefits and costs: *Independence decision makers should ensure that the benefits resulting from reducing independence risk by imposing additional safeguards exceed the costs of those safeguards.*

Principle 4. Considering interested parties' views in addressing auditor independence issues: *Independence decision makers should consider the views of investors, other users and others with an interest in the integrity of financial reporting when addressing issues related to auditor independence and should resolve those issues based on the decision makers' judgment about how best to meet the goal of auditor independence.*

Recognizing that there is no such thing as total independence, the Report provides auditors with a framework that can be used in judging whether the amount of independence they have is sufficient for allowing them to avoid the risks to independence that would jeopardize their judgment or audit.

To protect independence, the SEC released a "Revision of the Commission's Auditor Independence Requirements," effective February 5, 2001. The revised rule identified certain non-audit services that impair auditor independence. It met with resistance from the accounting profession, but it was seen as necessary by Levitt of the SEC and those sympathetic with his position, a position that seemed prophetic in the light of subsequent events. As a matter of fact, since the Enron/Andersen debacle, Levitt has called for tighter controls.[46]

It is worth reviewing in some depth John C. Bogle's defense of the Commission's recommendations. According to Bogle the independence requirements recommended by the Commission ban "only those services which involve either a mutual or conflicting interest with the client; the auditing of one's own work; functioning as management or an employee of the client; or acting as the client's advocate."

Bogle rightly asserts that,

> . . . it is unimaginable . . . that any reasonable person could disagree *in the abstract* that such roles would threaten – or, at the very least, be perceived to threaten – the auditor's independence.
>
> It must also be clear that, whether or not the auditor has the backbone to maintain its independence under these circumstances, many management and consulting arrangements could easily be perceived as representing a new element in the relationship between auditor and corporation – a *business* relationship with a *customer* rather than a professional relationship with a client. Surely this issue goes to the very core of the central issue of philosophy that I expressed earlier: The movement of auditing from profession to business, with all the potential conflicts of interest that entails. So I come down with a firm endorsement of the *substance* of the proposed SEC rule, which would in effect bar such relationships.

Bogle goes on to recognize that there is some merit to some of the objections raised to the Commission's recommendations.

> Of course, I have read extensive material from the opponents of that rule making the opposite case. Some arguments seem entirely worthy of consideration, especially those relating to technical – but nonetheless real – issues that engender unnecessary constraints on an auditor's entering into *any* strategic alliances or joint ventures, or that relate to the complexity in clearly defining "material direct investment" or "affiliate of the audit client" and so on. Personally, I would hope and expect that this bevy of issues will be resolved by the profession and the Commission meeting and reasoning together.

Still, there are objections he thinks are knee-jerk, and without merit. Again, in the light of subsequent events like the Enron/Andersen situation, Bogle's insights are remarkably astute.

> But other opposition seemed to me to be rather knee-jerk and strident (rather like those debates I mentioned at the outset). No, I for one don't believe the SEC proposals represent "an unwarranted and intrusive regulation" of the accounting profession. And, no, I for one do not believe that the new rules "strait-jacket" the profession. And, yes, I do believe that the growing multiplicity of interrelationships between auditor and client is a serious threat to the concept of independence, the rock foundation of sound financial statements and fair financial markets alike. In this context, I was stunned to see this recent statement from one of the senior officers of the investment company industry group for one of the Big Five firms. "Fund companies have increasingly looked to . . . big accounting firms to help them with operational, regulatory, strategic and international decisions." If that isn't functioning as management, I'm not sure what would be.[47]

In short, the threat to independence of the auditor was known well before the Enron/Andersen case, and rather than this being an isolated case it was simply the one that erupted with the most notoriety. In May of 2000, Gretchen Morgenson, in an article in the *New York Times*, caught the threats to independence. She stated that,

> The issue of auditor independence has grown thornier in recent years as accounting firms have remade themselves into full-service operations, in which auditing takes a back seat to more profitable consulting services. According to the S.E.C., auditing now represents 30 percent of accounting firms' revenue, down from 70 percent in 1977, while consulting and other advisory services represent more than half of revenue, up from 12 percent.[48]

The face of the accounting profession has changed. Whereas it was natural 25 years ago to think of an accountant as a CPA who did auditing, auditing is no longer the chief occupation of the accountant. Auditing is no longer the great money-maker that it once was, forcing at least the Big Five firms to expend more and more energy on other money-making enterprises. But such enterprises, including financial advising, tax accounting, and management consulting, have the potential to create serious conflicts of interest or at very least the serious appearance of conflicts of interest.

The potential for conflict is that an auditor, eager to get consulting fees from a corporate customer, would not be as aggressive on its audit as he might otherwise be. John H. Biggs, chairman of TIAA-CREF, the pension fund management group, said that his organization makes it a rule to hire separate firms for audits and for consulting services. "When you're paying the auditor $3 million to do an audit and paying them $17 million to do management consulting, it's way out of balance," he said.[49]

Thus, we can conclude that because of the financial pressures on accounting firms to gain revenue from other sources, there has been a move in the profession to be less stringent about the appearance of independence. But that did not sit well with Arthur Levitt, the head of the SEC, who in a speech at New York University on May 10, 2000, stated quite clearly that auditors must not only avoid conflicts of interest, but must avoid even the appearance of such conflicts that could be seen as sacrificing their independence. According to Levitt, "It is not enough that the accountant on an engagement act independently . . . For investors to have confidence in the quality of the audit, the public must perceive the accountant as independent."[50]

But even in the light of the Enron/Andersen debacle, is it all that clear that the *mere* appearance of independence is so important? After all, couldn't one argue that even though it appears an accountant has a conflict, he or she might have resolved it and/or avoided it? Is it not simply the case that people can set aside conflicts of interest and do the right thing?

Lynn Turner, former chief accountant at the SEC, weighed in with an extensive argument for the importance of appearing independent. He cited four different authors who emphasize the importance of the appearance of independence, beginning with Justice Burger's Supreme Court opinion that we have already mentioned.

The SEC requires the filing of audited financial statements to obviate the fear of loss from reliance on inaccurate information, thereby encouraging public investment in the Nation's industries. It is therefore not enough that financial statements *be* accurate; the public must also *perceive* them as being accurate. Public faith in the reliability of a corporation's financial statements depends on the public perception of the outside auditor as an independent professional. . . . If investors were to view the auditor as an advocate for the corporate client, the value of the audit function itself might well be lost.

The accounting profession has long embraced the need for auditors to not only be, but also to appear to be, independent. Statement on Auditing Standards No. 1 states, "Public confidence would be impaired by evidence that independence was actually lacking, and it might also be impaired by the existence of circumstances which reasonable people might believe likely to influence independence . . . Independent auditors should not only be independent in fact, they should avoid situations that may lead outsiders to doubt their independence."

Witnesses at the Commission's hearings on the auditor independence rule strongly endorsed the need for auditors to maintain the appearance of independence from audit clients. Paul Volcker, former Chairman of the Federal Reserve Board, in response to a question about investors' perceptions of a conflict of interest when auditors provide non-audit services, said, "The perception is there because there is a real conflict of interest. You cannot avoid all conflicts of interest, but this is a clear, evident, growing conflict of interest. . . ."

John Whitehead, former co-chairman of Goldman Sachs and a member of numerous audit committees testified, "Financial statements are at the very heart of our capital markets. They're the basis for analyzing investments. Investors have every right to be able to depend absolutely on the integrity of the financial statements that are available to them, and if that integrity in any way falls under suspicion, then the capital markets will surely suffer if investors feel they cannot rely absolutely on the integrity of those financial statements."[51]

Thus, in summary, the reasons for avoiding even the appearance of having a conflict of interest, which might affect one's independence, are obvious. In order for people to make their best judgments they need faith in the representations upon which they make those judgments. And representations made by those who have – or even appear to have – conflicting interests do not inspire such faith. Reasonable people, taking a commonsense approach to human behavior, would think that certain relationships would affect one's behavior. A skepticism that believes where there's smoke, there's fire, serves one well. It may be that where there appears to be a conflict, there is none, but there may also be self-delusion, and where the appearance of conflict is the only thing to exist, such a situation presents a temptation, that while currently is being resisted, sooner or later will probably prevail.

People respond on the basis of what they think. If we think someone is angry, we will respond differently to him or her than if we think they are in pain. Similarly, if we trust someone, we will respond differently than if we suspect him or her. Contrast the perceptions we have of an independent prosecutor with those we have of one appointed by the justice department. Whom do we trust more? Compare the perceptions we have of a police department report clearing officers of illicit behavior with a report of an independent panel of judges clearing those same officers. The appearance of dependence will have major effects on the estimation of the worth of all sorts of financial entities.

To bolster the emphasis on independence, the SEC, with its revision of Rule 201 and because of Arthur Levitt's speech, used pressures that the SEC could bring to bear to help provoke change in the profession. Mr. Levitt addressed the rapid growth in the past two decades in management consulting work to audit clients. In a section entitled "Serving Two Masters," Mr. Levitt decribed how this diversification could lead an auditor too close to its client's management. "In this dual role, the auditor . . . now both oversees and answers to management." After the Enron/Andersen failure, the accounting profession, the SEC, and the government are all addressing anew the issue of auditor independence.

We will return in the final chapter to an examination of the crisis of independence being faced by the accounting firms and look at some suggestions that are made to resolve the issue. For now, suffice it to say that the prerequisite for an auditor to do his or her job effectively is the maintaining of both the appearance of independence and the fact of independence.

This concludes our discussion of the function and responsibilities of the auditor. We turn now to an examination of the role and responsibilities of the management accountant.

▲ NOTES ▲

1. Jonathan Weil, "Arthur Andersen's 'Double Duty' Work Raises Questions About Its Independence," *Wall Street Journal*, Money and Investing, December 14, 2001.
2. This case is adapted from a similar case in Philip G. Cottell, Jr. and Terry M. Perlin, *Accounting Ethics: A Practical Guide for Professionals* (Quorum Books, 1990), p. 42.
3. Michael Schroeder, "Former SEC Chairman Says Enron Case Shows Need for Tighter Accounting Curbs," *Wall Street Journal*, January 11, 2002.

4. Steven Silber, as quoted in Karl Stark, "Lawsuit is filed against auditors for Allegheny," *Philadelphia Inquirer*, Thursday, April 13, 2000, section D, p. 1.
5. William F. Hamilton and William D. Callahan, "The Accountant as a Public Professional," in T. Beauchamp and N. Bowie, *Ethical Theory and Business*, 3rd edn (Prentice Hall, 1988), pp. 487ff.
6. *Encyclopedia Britannica Micropaedia*, "Accounting."
7. John C. Bogle, "Public Accounting: Profession or Business?" presentation at NYU, October 16, 2000. Available online at www. cpaindependence.org.
8. Nanette Byrnes et al., "Accounting in Crisis," *Business Week*, January 28, 2002, p. 46.
9. *United States v. Arthur Young and Co. et al.*, 104 S.Ct, 465 US 805, 1984.
10. Mara Der Hovanesian, "Brutal Honesty Could Force a Market Correction," *Business Week*, February 4, 2002, p. 44.
11. As quoted in Abraham J. Briloff, "The 'Is' and the 'Ought'," *Accounting Today*, September 26, 1999, pp. 6ff.
12. Interestingly enough, in Germany, where most capitalization is done through a bank and not through securities, the role of this public auditor is not as essential. The verification function is handled by the bank.
13. C. Richard Baker and Rick Stephan Hayes, "Regulating the Public Accounting Profession: An International Perspective," from http:// les.man.ac.uk/cpa96/papers.htm/baker2.htm, p. 9.
14. Gretchen Morgenson, "S.E.C. Seeks Increased Scrutiny And New Rules for Accountants," *New York Times*, May 11, 2000, Thursday, late edition, section C Business/Financial Desk, p. 1, column 2.
15. AICPA, Professional Standards, Volume 1.
16. Ahmed Riahi-Belkaoui, *Morality in Accounting* (Quorum Books, 1992), p. 35.
17. The Commission on Auditors' Responsibilities, "Report, Conclusion and Recommendations" (New York: Commission on Auditors' Responsibilities, 1978), p. 3.
18. Quoted in Abraham J. Briloff, *The Truth About Corporate Accounting* (Harper & Row, 1980), p. 6.
19. Quoted in Briloff, ibid., p. 5.
20. Quoted in Briloff, ibid., pp. 4–5.
21. Karl Stark, "Lawsuit is filed against auditors for Allegheny," *Philadelphia Inquirer*, Thursday, April 13, 2000, section D, p. 1.
22. See AICPA Code, Rule 301: Confidential client information.
23. John E. Beach, "Code of Ethics: The Professional Catch 22," *Journal of Accounting and Public Policy*, 3 (1984), pp. 311–23.

24. See appendix III, note 4, Communicating about possible fraud to management, the audit committee, and others.

25. Appellate *Wagenheim, J.S. (Consolidated Services, Inc.) v. Alexander Grant & Co.*, 1983. 10th District, Court of Appeals, Ohio 3393.*l*.

26. Cf. the AICPA Statements on Auditing Standards No. 55, SAS 53 entitled "The Auditor's Responsibility To Detect And Report Errors And Irregularities."

27. Whether they contained irregularities or constituted fraud would make for an interesting discussion but is beyond the scope of the book.

28. We reiterate: Standard 82 which superseded SAS 53 eliminated the words "responsibility" and "irregularities." We are not clear why the Auditing Standards Board took this approach, but we will view it as a minor technical move. In this book we will continue to refer to "errors, irregularities and/or fraud."

29. SAS 82.16.

30. SAS 53.08.

31. SAS 53.12.

32. See SAS 53.16 to .21, SAS 82.27, and SAS No. 1 AU section 230, paragraphs 7–9.

33. SAS No. 1, section 230.

34. SAS 53.16.

35. Ahmed Riahi-Belkaoui, *Morality in Accounting* (Quorum Books, 1992), p. 37.

36. Cf. Philip G. Cottell, Jr. and Terry M. Perlin, *Accounting Ethics: A Practical Guide for Professionals* (Quorum Books, 1990), pp. 30ff.

37. John C. Bogle, "Public Accounting: Profession or Business," presentation at NYU, October 16, 2000. Available online at www. cpaindependence.org.

38. Home page of cpaindependence.org.

39. John C. Bogle, "Public Accounting: Profession or Business," presentation at NYU, October 16, 2000. Available online at www. cpaindependence.org.

40. Gordon Cohn, "Auditing and Ethical Sensitivity," forthcoming in *Outlook*. Available on the web at http://academic.Brooklyn.cuny.edu/economnic/cohn/ind.htm.

41. Cohn, ibid., p. 2.

42. Cited in Cohn, ibid.

43. Cited in Cohn, ibid.

44. Jonathan D. Glatern, "Audit Firms are set to Alter Some Practices," *Wall Street Journal*, February 1, 2002.

45. Cited in Cohn, "Auditing and Ethical Sensitivity," forthcoming in *Outlook*. Available on the web at http://academic.Brooklyn.cuny.edu/economnic/cohn/ind.htm.

46. Mr. Levitt, who led a campaign to clean up accounting-industry

conflicts of interest during his eight-year SEC tenure, said Arthur Andersen's disclosure that it destroyed documents related to its Enron accounting work adds urgency to the need for outside auditors to accept tough oversight through a new government-sponsored self-regulatory organization.

He has complained about the inadequacy of the American Institute of Certified Public Accountants, the primary accounting oversight organization. "It's time for the industry to discount the AICPA as an oversight mechanism and put in place something new," he said.

47. John C. Bogle, "Public Accounting: Profession or Business," presentation at NYU, October 16, 2000. Available online at www.cpaindependence.org.

48. Gretchen Morgenson, "S.E.C. Seeks Increased Scrutiny And New Rules for Accountants," *New York Times*, May 11, 2000, Thursday, late edition, section C Business/Financial Desk, p. 1, column 2.

49. Gretchen Morgenson, ibid.

50. Adrian Michaels, *Financial Times* (London), May 11, 2000, Companies and Finance: International section, p. 44.

51. Lynn E. Turner, "Current SEC Developments: Independence Matters," Chief Accountant, Office of the Chief Accountant, US Securities and Exchange Commission, 28th Annual National Conference on Current SEC Developments, December 6, 2000.

chapter eight

The Ethics of Managerial and Financial Accounting

Don't cook the books. Many companies manipulate their numbers so that profits grow steadily. The creativity of some accountants has no bounds. Example: Chainsaw Al Dunlap (Sunbeam) – total loss of credibility. Waste Management.[1]

To make a play on words, the Securities and Exchange Commission announced in mid-December that it initiated litigation against the management of W. R. Grace for disgracefully reporting the company's operating results. The case merits attention because it appears to offer perfect examples of cookie jar reserves and abuse of materiality.

In Litigation Release No. 16008, the SEC asserts that the numbers for Grace's Health Care Group for 1991 through 1995 were put together with the goal of misleading capital market participants. Specifically, it alleges that Grace's managers tucked some of the division's unanticipated earnings away in a cookie jar for later. They then dipped into the jar for 1995's fourth quarter to get reported earnings closer to their target.

What they did was clearly wrong, even if the amounts were immaterial. Under GAAP, revenue is recognized when the earnings process is essentially complete and when the amount is reasonably determinable. There is no provision for allowing managers to accelerate or delay recognition just because they want to. If both conditions are met, then the revenue should be booked – all of it. If either condition is not met, then none should be recognized, not a single penny.[2]

How much is a company worth? What are its assets? What are its liabilities? What sorts of internal auditing procedures are in place? How is one to know? It is the task of the financial accountant or the management accountant to determine those matters.

In discussing the management accountant or the financial accountant, we have in mind the accountant who works for a particular company, either as the chief financial officer or controller, as a line accountant doing any number of possible tasks, or even as a consultant doing specific tasks that input into the company's financial picture, usually someone who is an employee of the firm. Management accountants can operate as financial managers, accountants, or internal auditors, depending on their position in the firm and the size and nature of the firm or organization. Accountants who work for a firm have many of the same obligations as other accountants, but their relationship to the firm gives them a different set of responsibilities from those of the auditor. The contrast between outside auditors and internal management, including internal management accountants, is stated clearly by the Independence Standards Board:

> Management is responsible for the financial statements, and responsibility for the choices and judgments inherent in the preparation of those financial statements cannot be delegated to the auditor or to anyone else. Whatever the service being provided, the auditor must understand the level of management's expertise and must be satisfied that management has taken responsibility for the assumptions and judgments made during the course of the work, and for the results produced.[3]

The accountants within the firm – who work for the firm whether as financial officers, valuations experts, or bookkeepers – have the responsibility for the picture of the firm's financial situation that is portrayed. This chapter will show that there is the obligation to portray the picture of the firm as accurately and truthfully as possible, even if that may be detrimental to the company. One could say that while the management accountant has a responsibility to the firm, which is the accountant's employer, the management accountant has an overriding obligation to disseminating the truth.

The Standards of Ethical Conduct for Practitioners of Management Accounting and Financial Management, which is *the* code of ethics for management accountants, lays out the scope of the obligations of management accountants: "Practitioners of management accounting and financial management have an obligation to the public, their profession, the organization they serve, and themselves, to maintain the highest standards of ethical conduct."[4] Thus, according to their ethics code, management accountants have obligations to at least four stakeholders – the general public, the members of their profession, the organization they serve, and them-

142 ETHICS OF MANAGEMENT ACCOUNTING

selves. In accord with the primary principle of this book, the primary obligation of any accountant is to do their job, which, in the case of the management accountant, is to aid in whatever way they are designated to present as accurate a picture as possible of the financial situation of the company, including assets and liabilities, or as good advice as possible to all those entitled based on that picture.

It takes little imagination to see how such activity can be influenced by factors other than accurate reporting. Consider the following typical situation.

A new controller at a farm machinery company notices the high inventory of old, high ticket items. She is concerned about how accurately the inventory of the books reflects its fair market value. The company president asks her to wait and see if the auditors noticed the old inventory and, if so, to be able to "show them" that the items are turning over.[5]

It's obvious why presidents of companies act this way. If the president has a favorable fourth-quarter retained earnings report, the value of the company stock goes up, the board is pleased, the bank which is considering a loan is more likely to grant it, prospective investors are attracted to the company, and last but not least, the president's year-end bonus is positively affected. In short, painting such a favorable picture has many benefits.

However, if the picture is a deliberate distortion, doesn't creating such a picture constitute unethical behavior? Isn't the accountant either lying or being complicitous in telling a lie? Even if such behavior benefits the company, a big if, isn't it still unethical? Clearly such behavior is unfair to those, such as prospective investors, stockholders or board members, who need to make decisions about the company and are entitled to know the true financial picture of the company.

Suppose the president wants the accountant to paint as rosy a picture as possible to impress the board of directors who are considering renewing the tenure of the president. Obviously if the accountant does not comply with the president's request, he or she will put themselves and their position in the company in jeopardy. So in such a situation there is a great temptation to act in accordance with the president's request. But, it is fairly clear that to act in accord with the president's wishes would violate ethical principles, and specifically one of the principles cited in the code of ethics for managerial accounting – the responsibility to be objective.

The section on objectivity of the code claims that practitioners of management accounting have the responsibility to communicate information fairly and objectively. Of course, one does not need a code of ethics to point out such a responsibility. As we have seen, lying involves using another as a means to one's ends. Nevertheless, the code requires that managerial accountants, "Disclose fully all relevant information that could reasonably be expected to influence an intended user's understanding of the records, comments, and recommendations presented."[6]

Did the accountant "communicate the information fairly and objectively"? We have already discussed the notion of fair in the chapter on auditing, but it is helpful to remind ourselves of the problem. If we use the common and approved usage of "fair" found in *Black's Law Dictionary* as: "having the qualities of impartiality and honesty: free from prejudice, favoritism, and self-interest; just; equitable; even-handed; equal as between conflicting interests," we can conclude the information would not be communicated fairly and objectively if it is presented as the president wished. It would not be even-handed; it would not be free from favoritism; it would not be impartial; it would not be free of self-interest; nor would it be honest. It fails on all counts to be fair. It also fails to disclose fully relevant information that could reasonably be expected to influence an intended user's understanding of the reports, comments, and recommendations presented.

We have repeatedly insisted that in a market economy appropriate full disclosure is required for informed consent. If the distorted report is meant to impress the members of the board of trustees, it will lead them to make a recommendation on the president's tenure on the basis of that distorted information, a recommendation that it might not otherwise make. If it is meant to impress the stock market, it again succeeds in bringing about activity that probably would not have been engaged in had the report been more accurate. There is, of course, the conflict of interest here between the management accountant's self-interest and the interests of others, including the interests of the president. But what the discussion of this case should cause us to reflect on are the various constituencies, other than the president or the company, to which the management accountant is responsible.

But let us address the provisions of the code more specifically.

The code lays out four standards of ethical conduct: *competence, confidentiality, integrity,* and *objectivity.* Finally, it lays out provisions for resolving ethical conflict, which lead to the possibility of "blowing the whistle."

Under competence, the Standards expect the management accountant to be competent: meaning he or she should maintain an appropriate level of knowledge and skill; follow the laws, rules and technical standards; and prepare reports that are clear and complete, based on reliable and relevant information after appropriate analysis.

Under confidentiality, the requirements are the usual ones of refraining from disclosure of confidential information except when authorized and legally obligated to do so.

The integrity requirements require avoidance of "actual or apparent conflicts of interest," refraining from activities that would prejudice their ability to carry out ethical duties. They also need to refuse gifts and favors that could influence their actions. They should not subvert the organization's legitimate objectives, but should admit to their professional limitations, communicate favorable and unfavorable information, and refrain from behavior that would discredit the profession.

The central standard is objectivity, which requires management accountants to "communicate information fairly and objectively" and, as we have seen, "disclose fully all relevant information that could reasonably be expected to influence an intended user's understanding of the reports, comments, and recommendations presented."[7]

So, we see, looking at the ethical requirements laid down by the Standards, that the basic function of accountants does not change from auditor to managerial accountants. The following comment by Bill Vatter in his introduction to *Managerial Accounting,* published in 1950, succinctly articulates that point.

> One of the basic functions of accounting is to report independently on the activities of others, so that information concerning what has happened may be relevant and unbiased. The major function *served by both public and managerial accountants* is to use their independent judgment with complete freedom; thus they may observe and evaluate objectively, the fortunes and results of enterprise operations . . . This is a highly important aspect of accounting, and it is one of the reasons for the separation of the accounting function from the rest of the management process. The detached and independent viewpoint of the accountant must be kept in mind.[8]

Because of the management accountant's obligation to fair reporting, the accounting function should be kept separate from the rest of the management process. This is not only ethically sound, it is also managerially wise. In order to make decisions about a company it is important, even for those within the company, to have as accurate a picture as possible of the company's financial condition. In the scenario above, it is in the president's interests (misguided though they may be) to present books that are cooked, but it is not in the best interest of the company or the stockholders or any one else, that the true picture of the company's worth not come out. Hence, the accountant has a responsibility to the company and its stakeholders that should override his or her responsibility to do what the president asks.

We are all aware of the business equivalent of the story of the emperor with no clothes. All the surrounding sycophants admired the clothes of the naked emperor, afraid to tell him the truth. Now the health of the business enterprise depends on decisions being made on the basis of fact and true information. If the business is naked, it is best to know. That is the accountant's task. However, needless to say, it is also a responsibility, the meeting of which may not win him or her too many friends. It is fairly obvious that, in the long run, the management accountant does no one a favor by cooking the books. Still it is interesting to speculate a bit more deeply about why an internal accountant would misstate the financial picture.

A remarkable article by Saul W. Gellerman[9] indicates four rationalizations that managers use to justify suspect behavior. They are instructive in the case of the managerial accountant and can be used as helpful guides to warn against misrepresenting financial statements.

The first reason (rationalization?) given for unethical behavior is "a belief that the activity is within reasonable ethical and legal limits – i.e. that it is not 'really' illegal or immoral." Ambiguous situations allow a great deal of discretion in operating. In a recent article in *Newsweek*, "The Sherlocks of Finance," Daniel McGinn points out that a forensic accountant like Howard Schilit discovered that companies such as United Health Care, 3M, and Oxford Health Plans used "aggressive accounting moves that might camouflage a sagging business." Schilit points out that "aggressive accounting policies may distort the true financial condition of the company," while remaining legal.

Schilit specializes in flagging the frequent – and perfectly legal – gambit of "window dressing," which puffs up profits and revenues. He is not alleging fraud; indeed the accounting techniques he highlights are allowed under generally accepted accounting principles (GAAP). But GAAP rules are subject to wide interpretation – and companies have great leeway in choosing how conservatively or aggressively they account for financial transactions.[10]

The application of GAAP is more an art than a science, and there are clearly many opportunities to present financial statements in favorable rather than unfavorable lights, even in accord with GAAP. However, in those cases it may be that while the behavior is within the letter of the law, it violates the spirit of the law. Keeping within the letter of the law was also the modus operandi of the accountants at Enron. Douglas Carmichael, an accounting professor at Baruch College in Manhattan, described Enron's behavior in the following way: "It's like somebody sat down with the rules and said, 'How can we get around them?' They structured these things [special purpose entities] to comply with the letter of the law but totally violated the spirit."[11]

If one is operating within the letter of the law, and avoiding the spirit of the law, one should ask why one is doing that. It is usually to take advantage of someone else. The utilization of the letter of the law to say "but it's legal" already indicates that one is hesitant about performing an activity, and if one hesitates to do something, it is usually because one has doubts about the probity of doing it. One should be willing to seriously ask oneself, "Why do I hesitate to do this?" At that point, one should utilize what is often called the "sniff test" – "something just doesn't smell right." In such situations, perhaps the best ethical advice is, "When in doubt, don't do it."

A second reason, according to Gellerman, for a bad ethical choice is "a belief that the activity is in the individual's or the corporation's best interests – that the individual would somehow be expected to undertake the activity." The management accountant is, of course, an employee of a company; he or she does not work for an accounting firm. Consequently he or she is expected to be loyal to the company paying their salary. This loyalty seems to require doing things for the good of the company that one would not do if they were an objective outsider. While the managerial accountant's code of ethics requires objectivity and an obligation to the public, it is natural for the managerial accountants to give their first loyalty to the firm.

According to Andy Serwer, GE has produced 101 straight quarters of earnings growth by using accounting tactics that obfuscate its true performance. "GE uses gains and losses from certain businesses – particularly its financial services area, GE Capital – to offset gains and losses in other divisions, whether they ought to belong in that quarter or not . . . The problem: If GE ever stumbled and chose to hide a shortfall, some critics say, it could take many quarters for investors to find out. This kind of earnings management isn't illegal, maybe not even immoral. The concern, rather, is that it's not transparent."[12] Enron, of course, used the tactic of creating special purpose entities to hide losses, a perfectly legal but dubious maneuver. Thus there are cases where the firm is skirting the ethical territory, a tactic which can lead to unethical behavior justified in the name of firm loyalty. It is behavior that might be incentivized by the payment of a large bonus for making the figures come out right.

There are two things wrong with this kind of reasoning. First, acting unethically may not be in the company's long-term best interest. Stories abound that show that firms which lied or withheld information or defrauded the consumer, thinking it was necessary for the benefit of the company, are often discovered in the long run. Second, acting in such a way uses other people for the sake of the company's ends and in many cases flat-out hurts those other people. In short, such behavior is often unfair or harmful, or both.

A third reason for trying to justify a bad choice is "the belief that the activity is 'safe' because it will never be found out or publicized; the classic crime-and-punishment issue of discovery." If one looks at Cendant, Livent, Rite Aid, and Sunbeam, it is obvious that the books were cooked because of the belief the operation would never be detected. In *Business Week*, Michael Schroeder credits the investigations of Schilit with showing that Kendall Square Research Corp. was claiming revenue from computer sales to universities that had not paid for the equipment.[13] The literature is full of stories of firms that did something nefarious only to get caught in the long run: for example, Micro Strategy being accused by the SEC of fraud.[14] Schilit uncovers many other cases of accounting irregularities that were eventually found out.

If one recalls the W. R. Grace fiasco, one sees the same thing.

The plot seems to have thickened when the auditors decided that too many cookies were in the jar and that it was time to get rid of them. The critical issue was how to let them go. The managers [at W. R.

Grace] faced three choices, one of which was to admit the prior error and retroactively restate. Alternatively, the managers could assert a change of estimate by dumping all the revenue into reported earnings at once as a catch-up adjustment or by dribbling relatively small amounts into future reported earnings. Keep in mind that all we're talking about are book entries, not real money. The real income was unaffected by any of these belated financial representations of past events.

If the allegations are true, Grace and PW should have simply owned up to the misdeed and restated. Catching up all at once would only compound the problem by putting out another bad financial statement. Of course, dribbling would have messed up a great many more financial statements and would have been especially egregious because, at its heart, it would have been designed to cover up the first deceptions with more deceit. Instead, management's goal should have been to eliminate noise that makes investors work harder to evaluate the firm.

It's no surprise to us that Grace's managers seem to have taken the low road of dribbling. By claiming there was a change in estimate, they used some of the cookie jar revenues to meet earnings forecasts. They may have thought that they had a perfect solution to their little short-run business problem. The piper has now presented the bill for their mistakes.

Our biggest point is that the materiality principle is there to help management avoid needless costs, not to protect the guilty. It certainly is not there to make it possible for auditors to aid and abet deception. If a bookkeeping shortcut will produce essentially the same result as the best accounting (such as writing off the cost of inexpensive assets instead of capitalizing and depreciating them), the lack of materiality justifies a departure from GAAP.

The lack of materiality also might justify failing to correct inadvertent errors that really did not affect the financial statements that much. However, the lack of materiality cannot justify failing to rectify deliberate departures created expressly to deceive statement users. If the Grace managers and the auditors convinced themselves that a little fraud was immaterial, they were disgracefully wrong![15]

Notice, though, that in this third rationalization, the action is not justified. The managers know what they are doing is wrong; it's just that they expect it to help the firm and be good for the firm as long as it does not get detected. In the first rationalization, we are not sure whether the behavior is right or wrong, or at least if we suspect it is wrong we try to convince ourselves that it is legal. In the second rationalization the behavior is at least suspect behavior, but it is performed for the seemingly good motive of loyalty and the thought that it will benefit the company. In this third case, the action is clearly wrong, or at least very fishy, and is performed, probably for reasons one and two, but with the belief that the action will remain undetected.

A final reason for managers to make a bad ethical choice is "a belief that because the activity helps the company, the company will condone it and even protect the person who engages in it." Again the good side of the activity is that it at least "seems" to help the company, even while it is unethical. But that aside the belief that the company will condone it depends for its validity to a large extent on the integrity of the company's leaders. If they are the type of leaders who condone illegal or unethical activity, they will condone the loyalty. However, one would be advised that this condoning lasts only as long as the unethical or illegal activity remains undiscovered. After that the rats will desert the sinking ship, and the person who performed the unethical or illegal activity will be sunk, so to speak. It is important to recognize that if one is operating as an accountant in a culture that expects, promotes, or encourages unethical cutting of corners, up to even silently condoning illegal activity, to stay on would put one's integrity in mortal danger. The best course of action is never to condone such activity, and when it is encouraged, to refuse to do it, even if it means losing one's job. Accountants have been fired, many times. Fortunately it is a profession with many opportunities.

The case of management accounting brings up a further issue: that of *whistle blowing*. The code offers the following suggestion in the face of significant ethical conflict, where the established policies of the company do not provide an outlet to report such conflicts.

> "Discuss such problems with the immediate superior except when it appears that the superior is involved, in which case the problem should be presented initially to the next higher managerial level." If it is not resolved there, then to the next level. "Except where legally prescribed, communication of such problems to authorities or individuals not employed or engaged by the organization is not considered appropriate."
>
> "Clarify relevant ethical issues by confidential discussion with an objective advisor (e.g. IMA Ethics Counseling service) to obtain a better understanding of possible courses of action. Consult your own attorney as to legal obligations and rights concerning the ethical conflict."

"If the ethical conflict still exists after exhausting all levels of internal review, there may be no other recourse on significant matters than to resign from the organization and to submit an informative memorandum to an appropriate representative of the organization. After resignation, depending on the nature of the ethical conflict, it may also be appropriate to notify other parties."[16]

But aside from what the code said, two questions remain. When is it permissible to blow the whistle and when is it an ethical obligation to blow the whistle?

In a recent episode of *Chicago Hope*, the TV show about doctors at a Chicago hospital, a patient died in the recovery room after undergoing liposuction from a particularly greedy doctor, who would schedule two or three surgeries simultaneously. One of the ethical issues raised was what fellow doctors should do to prevent him from acting in that way again. Doctors are professionals, and one of the ethical obligations of professionals is to police their professions.

Although not as dramatic, there is an analogous problem among accountants. Consider the following scenario. You are an accountant for a large insurance company. As you begin an internal audit of the company books you discover that a particular manager was replacing virtually every policy that he had sold with his previous carrier, with no analysis, no 1035 exchanges and no filling out of replacement forms, as well as writing smokers as non-smokers. What should you do? Are you obliged to blow the whistle? Suppose after you go up the chain of command the company officials refuse to do anything about their shady practices? Do you need to go further?

As we saw in our discussion of professionalism, one of the necessary characteristics is the following: "The practitioner should possess a spirit of loyalty to fellow practitioners, of helpfulness to the common cause they all profess, and should not allow any unprofessional acts to bring shame upon the entire profession." If a professional "should not allow unprofessional acts to bring shame on the profession," it follows there may be a time when he or she is obliged to set aside loyalty to a fellow practitioner or a company and blow the whistle.

In the context of business ethics, whistle blowing refers to a practice in which employees who know that their company or a colleague is engaged in activities that (a) cause unnecessary harm, (b) violate human rights, (c) are illegal, (d) run counter to the defined purpose of the institution or the profession, or (e) are otherwise immoral *inform* superiors, professional organizations, the public, or some governmental agency of those activities. However, it is important to consider two issues: first, when, if ever, is whistle blowing acceptable; and second, when, if ever, is it ethically required?

First off, there is a strong presumption against whistle blowing. Early on in life we learn not to "tell on others." Such behavior is characterized by words such as "finking," "tattling," "ratting," "stooling," or some such pejorative term. So people not only hesitate to blow the whistle, they think it's wrong. Note that in sports, from which the term derives, "whistle blowing" is the function of a neutral detached referee who is supposed to detect and penalize the illicit behavior of players of both teams. In competitive team sports, it is neither acceptable nor ethically obligatory for a player to call a foul on his team mates. Because of these considerations, whistle blowing is viewed as an act of disloyalty and there is a presumption against it. If the analogy holds, what is unacceptable in sports is also unacceptable in business and whistle blowing is considered wrong.

In spite of our early training, though, there seem to be times when whistle blowing is acceptable. There is an ethical obligation for human beings to prevent harm in certain circumstances. If the only way to prevent harm in those circumstances is to blow the whistle, then not only is whistle blowing not wrong, it is an obligation. So, a countervailing obligation to the public to prevent harm is a justification for overriding the obligation of loyalty to one's profession or company, and blowing the whistle.

When do such times occur? The whistle blowing should be done for the purpose of preventing unnecessary harm, which includes violations of human rights, illegal activity, or conduct counter to the defined purpose of the profession. But the following conditions should be met.

1. **The proper motivation:** The whistle blowing should be done from the appropriate moral motive – i.e. not from a desire to get ahead, or out of spite or similar motivation. Unfortunately, in business, people quite often blow the whistle on another person simply because they think the other has "stolen" some business away. Nevertheless, whether whistle blowing is called for is not determined by the whistle blower's motive, but by the fact that there is illegal or immoral action.
2. **The proper evidence:** The whistle blower should make certain

that his or her belief that inappropriate actions are ordered or have occurred is based on evidence that would persuade a reasonable person.

3. **The proper analysis:** The whistle blower should have acted only after a careful analysis of the harm being done or that can be done. Questions to ask oneself include: (a) how serious is the moral violation? (Minor moral matters need not be reported.) (b) How immediate is the moral violation? (The greater the time before the violation occurs the greater the chances that internal mechanisms will prevent the anticipated violation.) (c) Is the moral violation one that can be specified? (General claims about a rapacious agent, obscene commissions, and actions contrary to public interest simply will not do.)

4. **The proper channels:** Except in special circumstances, the whistle blower should have exhausted all internal channels for dissent before informing the public. The whistle blower's action should be commensurate with one's responsibility for avoiding and/or exposing moral violations. If there are personnel in the company whose obligation it is to monitor and respond to immoral and/or illegal activities, it is their responsibility to address those issues. Thus, the first obligation of the potential whistle blower is to report the unethical activities to those persons, and only if they do not act to inform the general public.

But these conditions speak to the acceptability or permissibility of blowing the whistle – when is it all right to override the taboo against reporting others? A further question is: "When is it morally required (obligatory), if ever, for a professional to blow the whistle on a fellow professional?" As we stated, there is tacit agreement in our society – some sort of Good Samaritan principle – that under certain circumstances there is a moral obligation to prevent harm. For example, if we see a small child drowning in a wading pool, and no one helping him or her, we have a moral obligation to prevent the child from drowning. We can use the example to specify four general conditions, developed by Simon, Powers, and Gunneman, for this obligation, all of which must be met to have the obligation: *need, capability, proximity,* and *last resort.*[17]

1. **Need:** The child will drown without help. There is a need. If there is no harm occurring or about to occur, there is no ethical obligation.

2. **Capability:** There is a condition of capability. If the child is drowning in a wading pool, most people are capable of pulling the child out. If the child is drowning in a deep lake, a person who cannot swim lacks the capability to prevent harm in that situation and so is not obliged to save the child. As we saw, in morality "ought" implies "can." In whistle blowing, capability also includes the likelihood of success. If no one will listen when you blow the whistle, you are not capable of preventing the harm, and so have no obligation.

3. **Proximity:** Even though you did not cause the child to be in the wading pool, you have an obligation simply because you happen to be there. You are in a position to help because you are close by. You are not obligated to help everybody in the world. That is because of the last resort condition.

4. **Last resort:** If the parents of the child are there and functioning, saving the child is their responsibility. That is the division of responsibility that society sets up. Unless the parents panic and become frozen into inaction, you are not responsible for the child. If, however, everyone around freezes and cannot act, you become the last resort. In your professional capacity, if you are the only one who knows of an unethical activity on the part of a colleague, you are the last resort for blowing the whistle. If a superior of the colleague knows of the activity, it is his or her responsibility to stop the unethical activity. If, however, they do not act on it, from whatever motive, be it dereliction or inability to act, you become the last resort and the responsibility falls to you.

We need to add to these conditions a further consideration, which Simon, Powers, and Gunneman do not consider: *the likelihood of success.* The whistle blower should have some chance of success. If there is no hope in arousing societal, institutional, or governmental pressure, then one needlessly exposes oneself, and others one is related to, to hardship for no conceivable moral gain. The obligation arises from the duty to prevent harm. If no harm will be prevented, and there is no other ground for the obligation, there is no obligation. If nothing gets accomplished except bad feelings toward the whistle blower, there is hardly an obligation to blow the whistle.

Hence, the responsibility to blow the whistle can be summed up in the following way. If you are in a proximate position and capable of preventing harm (the need) without sacrificing something of comparable moral worth, and if you are the last resort, it is not only acceptable to blow the whistle, you have an *obligation* to blow the whistle to prevent such harm.[18]

In the business world, companies and fellow practitioners are seen as a team; loyalty is expected, and rewarded. Forsaking the team to function like a detached referee and blow the whistle is seen as disloyal and cause for punitive action. Because of that, whistle blowing requires a certain moral heroism. It will not be easy, and the consequences can be dire. Nevertheless, given the fact that society depends on whistle blowers to protect it from unscrupulous operators, it is sometimes called for. Because of this, Sherron Watkins, a vice president for corporate development at Enron, who sent a letter to Kenneth Lay, Enron's chairman, in August of 2001, questioning Enron's financial activities and questionable reporting behaviors, and warning that improper accounting practices threatened to destroy the company, has emerged as a hero in the Enron debacle.

Professionals need to realize that, at times, upholding the standards of one's profession may require blowing the whistle. Professionals such as accountants have a fiduciary responsibility to report certain illegal or potentially harmful activities if they encounter them in the course of their auditing or accounting. These obligations come from the professional status of the accountants, and from the human duty to prevent harm under conditions of need, proximity, capability, and last resort. If accountants are to be true professionals, there will be times, when, as difficult as it is, they will be obliged to blow the whistle.

Let us summarize what responsibilities a management accountant has. The first responsibility is to do one's job, which would be to carry out whatever accounting function the person was hired to perform. The second would be to do that with objectivity, honesty, and integrity, overcoming temptations from business pressures and pressures of leaders to "cook the books." Finally, there may come the unfortunate and difficult obligation to blow the whistle on wrongdoing, but that should be done only under the circumstances described.

With that, we turn to an examination of the role of the tax accountant.

◢ NOTES ◣

1. Lawrence D. Ackman, "The 10 Commandments of Good Business Ethics." A speech given at the New York University Stern School of Business, on March 7, 2000.
2. J. Edward Ketz and Paul B.W. Miller, "W. R. Grace's disgraceful abuse of materiality," *Accounting Today*, May 24, 1999–June 6, 1999.
3. ISB Interpretation 99–1, "Impact on Auditor Independence of Assisting Clients in the Implementation of FAS 133 (Derivatives)."
4. Rena A. Gorlin, ed., "The Standards of Ethical Conduct for Practitioners of Management Accounting and Financial Management," *Codes of Professional Responsibility*, 4th edn (Washington, DC: BNA Books, 1997), pp. 20–24.
5. Arthur Andersen and Co., Business Ethics Program: Minicase Index, 1.
6. Rena A. Gorlin, ed., "The Standards of Ethical Conduct for Practitioners of Management Accounting and Financial Management," *Codes of Professional Responsibility*, 4th edn (Washington, DC: BNA Books, 1997), p. 23.
7. Gorlin, ibid., p. 23.
8. Vatter, William J., *Managerial Accounting* (New York: Prentice Hall, 1950), p. 8.
9. Saul W. Gellerman, "Why 'Good' Managers Make Bad Ethical Choices," *Harvard Business Review*, July–August 1986, p. 88.
10. Daniel McGinn, "The Sherlocks of Finance," *Newsweek*, 132, 8, pp. 38–9.
11. Douglas Carmichael, as quoted in "Shell Game: How Enron concealed losses, inflated earnings – and hid secret deals from the authorities," by Daniel Fisher in *Forbes*, January 7, 2002, p. 52.
12. Andy Serwer, "A Rare Skeptic Takes on the Cult of GE," *Fortune*, Monday, February 19, 2001.
13. Michael Schroeder in *Business Week*, September 5, 1994.
14. *New York Times*, April 26, 1999.
15. J. Edward Ketz and Paul B.W. Miller, "W. R. Grace's disgraceful abuse of materiality," *Accounting Today*, May 24, 1999–June 6, 1999.
16. Rena A. Gorlin, ed., "The Standards of Ethical Conduct for Practitioners of Management Accounting and Financial Management," *Codes of Professional Responsibility*, 4th edn (Washington, DC: BNA Books, 1997), p. 24.
17. Cf. John G. Simon, Charles W. Powers, and Jon P. Gunneman, *The Ethical Investor* (New Haven: Yale University Press, 1972).
18. Ibid.

chapter nine

The Ethics of
Tax Accounting

One of your most important clients has strongly suggested that you
change the treatment of an item on his income tax return. You believe
that the treatment of the item suggested by the client will materially
understate the client's correct tax liability. Further, there is no reasonable basis for the change. You have basically two choices: (1) You
could refuse to change the item; (2) You could agree to change the
item as suggested by the client. Would you agree to change the item?[1]

The AICPA's *Statements on Responsibilities in Tax Practice* deal with
the accountant's "dual role as advisor to clients and attestor to the
government." This dual role is important from an ethical perspective
because, though a lesser known dual role than that of the auditor,
the role of the tax accountant has a similar twofold responsibility, to
the client as well as to the public.

The tax accountant has several responsibilities to the public,
through the government. First, the tax accountant has an obligation
not to lie or be party to a lie on a tax return. Second, as an attestor,
the signature on a tax return is a declaration under penalties of
perjury that, to the best of the preparer's knowledge, the return and
accompanying schedules and statements are "true, correct, and
complete."[2] Consequently, there is a responsibility to both the client
and the public to be forthright and not to be complicitous in a
client's attempt to deceive, even if that means breaking off the
relationship with the client.

Why that is the case is clearly laid out in the AICPA's Statement
of the Responsibility of Tax Preparers (SRTP)[3] in Tax Return
Positions 5.05 and 5.06:

.05 "Our self-assessment tax system can only function effectively if
taxpayers report their income on a tax return that is true, correct, and
complete. A tax return is primarily a taxpayer's representation of facts,

and the taxpayer has the final responsibility for positions taken on the return."

.06 "CPAs have a duty to the tax system as well as to their clients. However it is well-established that the taxpayer has no obligation to pay more taxes than are legally owed, and the CPA has a duty to the client to assist in achieving that result."

Position .06 clearly spells out the fact that tax accountants have a duty not only to their clients but also to the system. The client's duty is to pay the taxes they legally owe – no more, no less. The taxpayer has the final responsibility for the representation of the facts and for the positions taken on the return, but the accountant has the responsibility to point out to the client what is legally owed and not owed, and the responsibility not to go along with a client who wants to take advantage of the tax system.

These responsibilities flow from the nature of the tax system. The tax system, which depends on self-assessment to function effectively, needs everyone to give honest assessments and pay their fair share of taxes.

Some might object that such a position is naïve, since certain taxes are unfair. Didn't the founding fathers of the United States refuse to pay taxes, which they deemed unfair because they were taxes established without representation in an undemocratic fashion? One could adopt such a position to rationalize cheating the government of taxes. However, in spite of the fact that the founding fathers made such an argument, to do so in a modern democratic society is a perilous move. Fairness is a notoriously ambiguous concept and in applying it to the evaluation of tax burdens the most prudent course is probably that of adhering to what the society, following its due process of passing determining legislation, decides is fair. The founding fathers of the United States did not rail against taxes so much as taxation without representation. If everyone decided not to pay what is owed there would be chaos in the government. Hence, there should be general agreement to go with what are current tax demands and, if one thinks such demands are unfair, to work through the proper procedures to change them.

Not only is working within the system called for, we would claim also that the tax accountant should be ruled by the spirit of the law and not just the letter of the law. Still, we recognize that this goes against what may be the prevailing business culture, namely to get away with paying as little tax as possible. Consider the following:

> In 1993, Goldman Sachs & Co. invented a security that offered Enron Corp. and other companies an irresistible combination.
> It was designed in such a way that it could be called debt or equity, as needed. For the tax man, it resembled a loan, so that interest payments could be deducted from taxable income. For shareholders and rating agencies, who look askance at overleveraged companies, it resembled equity.
> To top officials at the Clinton Treasury Department, the so-called Monthly Income Preferred Shares, or MIPS, looked like a charade – a way for companies to mask the size of their debt while cutting their federal tax bill.
> Treasury made repeated attempts to curtail their use. In 1994, it scolded Wall Street firms and asked the Securities and Exchange Commission to intervene. The next year, the department sent legislative proposals to Congress aimed at closing loopholes and punishing offenders. In 1998, the Internal Revenue Service tried to disallow Enron's tax deductions. Each move was beaten back by a coalition of investment banks, law firms and corporate borrowers, all of whom had a financial stake in the double-edged accounting maneuver.
> The MIPS saga shows how moneyed interests, with armies of well-connected lobbyists and wads of campaign contributions to both parties, defeated the Treasury's efforts to force straightforward corporate accounting. With corporate bookkeeping now under scrutiny, the story of this flexible financial instrument shows how such accounting gimmickry gained acceptance.[4]

We want to argue that such an approach goes against the general tenor of the code of ethics of the accounting practice, and goes against the spirit of the laws that are behind the tax structure of the market economy. The tax laws were developed with certain purposes in mind, certain objectives that were deemed desirable by duly elected officials.

In any law there are loopholes that can be exploited, but applying the Kantian universalizability principle we see that if everyone exploited those loopholes the system would not accomplish what duly elected officials thought we needed to accomplish, and indeed might collapse. It is only because most people abide by the spirit of the law and don't exploit the loopholes that the laws continue to function. Those who exploit the loopholes are *free riders* who take advantage of the others. That is patently unfair. (As an aside here, one of the scandals of the Enron debacle was the fact that Enron paid no corporate taxes for four out of five years. If every corporation found loopholes to avoid such taxes, it would have the effect of undermining the goodwill of those who do not dodge tax burdens by utilizing loopholes that may adhere to the letter of the law, but avoid the spirit of the law.)

Those would seem to be the general ethical considerations that underlie standards put forward by the Tax Executive Committee of the AICPA in a pamphlet titled *Statements on Standards for Tax Services*. These statements, referred to as the SSTSs, and their interpretation "superseded and replaced the SRTPs and their interpretations on October 1, 2000."[5] It is interesting to note the opening paragraph of the work: "Practice standards are the hallmark of calling one's self a professional. Members should fulfill their responsibilities as professionals by instituting and maintaining standards against which their professional performance can be measured."[6] In that case perhaps the best indication of the ethical standards that should be met by a tax accountant is found in these standards.

There are six standards presented in the SSTSs, the last two being the most noteworthy for our purposes. Nevertheless we will discuss all six.

1. A tax accountant should not recommend a position unless it has a realistic possibility of being sustained on its merits.
2. A tax accountant should not prepare or sign a return if it takes a position one could not recommend under 1 above.
3. A tax accountant can recommend a position that he or she concludes is not frivolous so long as it is adequately disclosed.
4. A tax accountant has an obligation to advise the client about potential penalties on some positions, and recommend disclosure.
5. A tax accountant should not recommend a position that "exploits" the IRS audit selection process or:
6. Serves as a mere "arguing" position.

Let's return to the scenario with which we started this chapter. According to the standards, it would be unethical to capitulate to the client's request to materially understate the client's correct tax liability, since in signing a return you are attesting that the return is true, correct, and complete. To sign it would be to engage in lying, and that is a clear-cut ethical violation.

But there is an area of tax accounting that is not so clear-cut, and is therefore problematic. This is the area where there is exploitation of the tax system. Standard five states that "A tax accountant should not recommend a position that 'exploits' the IRS audit selection process." But what exactly counts as exploiting? For example, what is the ethics of engaging in tax-dodge schemes, and are there other areas where the accountant can help the client exploit the tax system and avoid paying his or her fair share of the tax burden?

Consider the following scenarios:

1. You assured your client that a particular expenditure was deductible only to find out later that it was not. However, it is unlikely the item will be detected by the IRS. Do you tell your client about your mistake and change the form, or do you let it stand as it is?

2. You discover that the client's previous year's return, which someone else prepared, listed a deduction $3000 in excess of the actual expenditure. The mistake was not intentional and the IRS will probably not detect the error. Should you correct the error, costing your client additional liability? What if you prepared the return the previous year so that the mistake was yours?

3. You are preparing a tax return for a very wealthy client, who can provide you with excellent referrals. You have reason to think the client is presenting information that will reduce his tax liability inappropriately. Should you inquire about the veracity of this information or just prepare the tax form with the information as given?[7]

4. The accounting firm you work for sells tax-savings strategies to clients, demanding a 30% contingency fee of the tax savings plus out of pocket expenses. The company will defend its "strategy" in an IRS audit, but not in court, and refund a piece of the fee if back taxes come due.[8] Is what your company is doing acceptable? What obligation do you have?

What do you do in these cases? In making a decision about the appropriateness of these activities, particularly the fourth case, it is important to keep in mind the STRP statement, "Our self-assessment tax system can only function effectively if taxpayers report their income on a tax return that is true, correct, and complete." This position is eloquently stated in Justice Burger's opinion in the landmark Arthur Young case.[9]

Our complex and comprehensive system of federal taxation, relying as it does upon self-assessment and reporting, demands that all taxpayers be forthright in the disclosure of relevant information to the taxing authorities. Without such disclosure, and the concomitant power of the government to compel disclosure, our national tax burden would not be fairly and equitably distributed.

A system that depends on self-assessment and reporting puts one in mind of the type of operation which makes golf such an honorable game. The rules of golf exist such that if something happens – for example, if a ball moves upon address – it is incumbent on the golfer to penalize him- or herself one stroke. Taxation is similar. It depends largely on self-assessment and reporting. In that context the fair thing for everyone to do is to police themselves. Our society is based on a large honor system and will work best when most people abide by that honor system. As we noted, those who take advantage of the system are free riders.

There are those who would like to insist that Justice Burger rightly indicates that the success of the scheme rests not so much on honor as on the concomitant power of the government to compel disclosure. But this does not mean that because the government does not apprehend people it is acceptable to try to ignore elementary fairness in meeting one's tax burden. That is why as standard five states, "A tax accountant should not recommend a position that 'exploits' the IRS audit selection process" and standard six adds, "or serves as a mere 'arguing' position." Even though some insist that from Justice Burger's perspective, such schemes as the last may be within the letter of the law, they are certainly not within the spirit of the law, which necessarily requires our national tax burden be fairly and equitably distributed.

What we may have here is a continuum between clearly unethical and illegal practices, practices which may be legal but are unethical, and practices which are ethically acceptable as well as legal.

Such activity is dubbed "hustling" by respected critics of the practices. *Forbes Magazine* reported that Deloitte and Touche was engaged in selling strategies labeled as "The Hustling of Rated Shelters."[10] The hustling consists, according to Abraham J. Briloff, of "the ways respectable tax professionals and respectable corporate clients are exploiting the exotica of modern corporate finance to indulge in extravagant tax-dodging schemes." Rep. Lloyd Daggett (D-Tex.), who has an anti-tax shelter measure pending in the house of representatives, in a *Washington Post* article is quoted as referring to these operations as "The literal hustling of improper tax shelters." Daggett quotes Yale law professor Michael J. Graetz, who defines a tax shelter as "a deal done by very smart people that, absent tax considerations, would be very stupid," and Daggett bemoans the inattention of Congress to "the rapid spread of abusive corporate tax shelters."[11]

If one takes the characterization of these moves by accounting firms as "hustling" and "improper," and the "schemes" as "abusive," it is clear that at least from some perspectives the accounting firms are doing something ethically questionable if not downright unethical.

Of course, defenders of such practices will argue that these activities are necessary given the competition of the marketplace. Some will refer to Oliver Wendell Holmes' view about paying taxes, namely that we should not pay one iota more than the law allows. Still, every law, being composed by human beings, will probably have a loophole that can be exploited. We would argue that there is something contrary to fairness and the public welfare in attempting to circumvent the obvious purpose of a specific law to give one's client an edge in getting out of paying one's fair share of the taxes.

Indeed it can be objected that many taxes are not ethically proper. Nevertheless, many are, and their spirit should be met in the interest of fair play. For those that can be shown to be unfair, the answer is not to circumvent the law, but to change it. Taxation, as much as one does not like it, is the human invention that centralizes the sharing of the expense of performing government functions in a fair and equitable manner. To view accounting as a profession best employed in dodging those expenses is a distortion of the role of the accountant.

David A. Lifson, who chairs the Tax Executive Committee of the American Institute of Certified Public Accountants, made the following statement in testifying to congress.[12] It indicates the AICPA view of the ethics of tax shelters.

> We [the AICPA] strongly oppose the undermining of our tax system by convoluted and confusing tax sophistry. Clearly, *there are abuses* and they must be dealt with effectively. However, we have a complex tax system and believe that taxpayers should be entitled to structure transactions to *take advantage of intended incentives* and to pay no more tax than is required by the law. Drawing this delicate balance is at the heart of the issue we are addressing today.

Clearly this is a call to determine the "spirit of the law" by referring to the "intended incentives" that the legislature has provided. But to abuse the law by seeking out loopholes eventually undermines the essential system of taxation.

It is imperative to strike a balance in distinguishing between those individual accountants or accounting firms taking advantage of intended incentives and those abusing loopholes to take advantage of the system itself. Such operating may be legal, but it is hardly ethical. It may strictly comply with the law, but for an organization, including the government, to run efficiently, more than minimal compliance is required.

Let's call this the Lifson Principle, and see what implications it has for accountants and their clients. "Taxpayers should be entitled to structure transactions to *take advantage of intended incentives* and to pay no more tax than is required by the law." The presence of the words "should" and "entitled" in the principle clearly make it an ethical principle. According to the principle, taxpayers have the ethical right to take advantage of *intended* incentives, and one could add that their accountants or accounting firms would be remiss in their responsibility to their clients if they did not take full advantage of the intended incentives. But, by implication, Lifson is suggesting that there is something ethically problematic about taking account of *unintended* incentives, and this is precisely the kind of operation that Burger and Briloff are objecting to on the part of individual accountants and accounting firms.

As Lifson says, "We strongly oppose the undermining of our tax system by convoluted and confusing tax sophistry. Clearly, *there are abuses* and they must be dealt with effectively." The tax system can be and is abused by accountants and accounting firms using tax-dodge schemes.

No one is sure how much revenue the government is losing as a result of corporate tax shelters, but estimates range into billions of dollars a year. And the broad data are suggestive. Corporate tax receipts for fiscal 1999 actually declined by 2 percent – or $4 billion. The last time corporate tax receipts declined was in fiscal 1990, when the economy was heading into recession, the taxation committee noted. Promoters make use of such devices as foreign tax credits, interest deductions, depreciation and insurance benefits to devise deals that accomplish little other than to generate deductions and credits.[13]

Implicit in all of this is a recognition of the responsibility of the accountant and firms to uphold the soundness of our tax system – to draw the delicate balance between intended tax advantages and loopholes which undermine the system.

But we have a cultural problem. Will such an interpretation of the responsibility of tax preparers fly? If you hire a tax accountant, what sort do you want – one who finds the loopholes or one who, having found them, tries to convince you it would be ethically unwarranted to take advantage of them? No one likes taxes, yet if no one pays taxes government cannot run.

> The Treasury Department, the ABA and others say shelters cause harm far beyond the initial loss of revenue. When one firm uses a shelter successfully, its competitors will feel pressure to try it, too, or be left at a disadvantage.
>
> In addition, individual taxpayers, who have to pay more as others succeed in paying less, become contemptuous of the tax system and more inclined to try tax avoidance maneuvers of their own. "If unabated, this will have long-term consequences to our voluntary tax system far more important than the revenue losses we currently are experiencing in the corporate tax base," Talisman told the Ways and Means panel.[14]

Obviously what is needed in the popular culture is a sea shift in attitude, where the ethical responsibility to support the legitimate purposes of government overrides the individual interest of paying as little support as possible, even less than one's "fair share." Accountants and accounting firms need to recognize their responsibility to the society at large, even where this might be at the expense of their client. But, of course, this will probably damage them in the competitive race for clients. Who will pay for an accountant who up-front indicates they may not take all the deductions "you can get away with"?

To think this would be voluntarily practiced is naïve in the extreme. If it were, we would need no sanctions by the IRS to compel compliance with the tax code, not to mention the spirit of the tax code. Nevertheless, absent the threat of the IRS, one could argue that the accountant has an ethical obligation to temper his aggressive tax scheming on behalf of his client for the sake of the general welfare.

But why would a client, who is solely self-interested, hire an accountant or firm who he knew would not save him every penny possible? Such a client would not: "I want my tax accountant to save me as much money as possible." Nevertheless, there are people who put a constraint on that imperative, "as long as it is no more or less than my fair share." If we assume the client shares the same ethical values as the accountant or the firm there will be a happy marriage of honorable people not taking unfair advantage.

Perhaps the way to convince skeptics that such a constraint is necessary is to imagine what would happen if waste disposal firms operated in the same solely self-interested way: "I will dispose of your industrial waste in the cheapest way possible, even if it means harming the environment, as long as it is within the letter, but not the spirit, of the law." The quest for profit forces all sorts of ethical shortcuts, but if such harming is not acceptable for waste disposal firms, why is it acceptable for accounting firms to harm people by taking their money?

Clearly accountants and their companies need to insist, because of their professionalism, on following the ethical path. In an interesting article in *The Tax Adviser*, Yetmar, Cooper, and Frank address two questions: what helps tax advisers to be ethical, and what challenges their ethics?

The leading helps are personal moral values and standards plus a culture in the firm which does not encourage compromising ethical values to achieve organizational goals – a strong management philosophy that emphasizes ethical conduct and clear communication that such ethical behavior is expected. In the situations described above, even in the face of a loss of a client, the accountant would do what's right. Threats of losing one's license for unethical conduct is a factor, but it is not ranked as the primary factor.

As to what challenges ethical conduct, the following were mentioned high on the list: the complexity and constantly changing nature of the tax laws; scarcity of time to practice due diligence; keeping current with increasingly complex tax laws; pressure from clients to reduce their tax liability; and clients' lack of understanding regarding accountants' professional responsibilities and potential penalties for both the tax practitioner and the taxpayer. So, complex tax laws and unethical demands of clients are the biggest potential challenges to ethical behavior on the part of tax accountants.

The authors conclude their study by stating the following:

First, business can encourage ethical behavior by refraining from pressuring managers and employees to compromise their personal values. Second, businesses should ensure that managers are equipped not only to deal with their own ethical dilemmas, but also those encountered by their subordinates. Professional associations have an opportunity to help prepare their members holding managerial positions in business to meet these responsibilities.[15]

As already noted, defenders of such practices as hustling tax shelters will argue that these activities are necessary given the competition of the marketplace, but as Rick Telberg suggests, if accountants are willing to go along with such pressures, "then the profession's entire system and philosophy of independence will need re-thinking."

But why if the government makes the tax laws can't they plug the loopholes? Why should it be the responsibility of the accountants and accounting firms?

Acting Assistant Treasury Secretary Jonathan Talisman noted that the government administration has already shut down a number of shelter schemes through administrative action and that it will make anti-shelter legislation a priority. [But] unlike shelters for individual taxpayers, which were shut down several years ago, no single approach will suffice because corporate shelters evolve so quickly.

"It's like a hydra," he said. "You cut off its head in one place and it just grows another someplace else." Thus, a multi-pronged approach of administrative, legislative and enforcement actions is required, he said.

In the past two years, the courts have backed the IRS in attacks on three major shelters, including some used by Winn-Dixie Stores Inc. and Compaq Computer Corp.

The Joint Committee on Taxation's staff director, Lindy Paull, noted that those three cases alone involved tax revenue of more than $7 billion over a number of years, and many other companies have tried strategies similar to those the court knocked down.

She said her committee understands that there are as many as 100 other cases similar to Winn-Dixie's, which involved the company's purchase of life insurance on its employees in a deal that allowed Winn-Dixie to borrow against the insurance and realize more in tax savings than the cost of the plan.

Crenshaw in his article cites four reasons why these tax shelters appeal.

1. Corporate management's search for new ways of maximizing profits and cash flow. Having squeezed production and other

business costs, and unable to raise prices much, companies have begun looking at their taxes as a cost to be cut.

2. Increasing complexity in both the tax code and the world of finance make it easier to obscure economic reality – or lack of it – in a series of transactions.

3. The perception among investment banks and others that dreaming up and packaging tax products "could be a successful business line," as William J. Wilkins, of Wilmer, Cutler & Pickering and a member of the American Bar Association tax section, put it. (The tax section, which does not speak for the full ABA, is made up of lawyers who specialize in taxes.)

4. Low risk. Not only is it difficult for the IRS to detect a shelter, but penalties are modest and not always imposed. If a shelter is discovered and disallowed, the company will likely owe only the taxes it would have owed anyway, plus interest. "So it's a pretty good financial deal," said John E. Chapoton, a former Assistant Treasury Secretary and member of the ABA's tax section, which has been pushing for increased disclosure by firms to discourage shelters.[16]

Clearly, something needs to be done to remedy the situation. But what can be done to alleviate these pressures? Government intervention and professional pressure are two remedies that have been suggested.

The Clinton administration proposed increased disclosure requirements and tougher penalties . . . penalties extended beyond the taxpayer to promoters, advisers, facilitators and others involved in making a shelter work. It recommended writing into law the doctrine of economic substance – a court-developed principle that a transaction must have economic reality beyond its tax consequences to be allowable.

The ABA tax section has proposed that companies be required to disclose any transaction that results in more than $10 million of tax savings, and require a "responsible" corporate officer to sign off on it. Lawyers in the tax section think that would make companies less inclined to buy prepackaged shelters.[17]

But what of the accounting profession? What is their role to be in this tax crisis? The suggestion would be to take the standards seriously and review the policy of profit by any means legally possible. A great deal would be accomplished if there were voluntary compliance with the spirit of the law by the Big Five accounting firms. Nevertheless, there will always be a great deal of pressure exerted on accountants, who consider themselves professionals and take their obligations to the public seriously, to capitulate to the demands of their companies. This raises the age-old problem for a professional who is an employee. Does one have a responsibility to the profession before the responsibility to the company for which one works? As small entrepreneurial practices are absorbed by larger firms, as happens not only in accounting but also in medicine, law, real estate, financial services, and elsewhere, this becomes more and more a crucial problem where the individual's ethics are compromised by the company's policies. We will return to that problem in the last chapter.

We will conclude this chapter by noting other standards that appear in the SSTS.

Standard Statement No. 1. The realistic possibility standard: "In general, a member should have a good-faith belief that the tax return position being recommended has a realistic possibility of being sustained administratively or judicially on its merits if challenged."[18] In a rather Byzantine section of the standards, the preparer is advised to avoid "frivolous positions," which are those advanced in bad faith, but can advise a position that has a realistic possibility of being in conformity with existing law. But the realistic possibility is less stringent than the "substantial authority standard," which is a position defended by recognized authorities. It is also less stringent than the "more likely than not" standard, but more stringent than the "reasonable basis" standard in the Internal Revenue Code.

What is a reasonable basis? According to the IRC Section 1.662–3 (b) (3), "The reasonable basis standard is not satisfied by a return position that is merely arguable or that is merely a colorable claim. If a return position is reasonably based on one or more of the authorities set forth in Section 1.6662–2 (d) (3) iii, the return position will generally satisfy the reasonable basis standard." Authorities include, but are not limited to, things such as applicable provisions of the IRC and other statutory provisions, regulations, proposed or final, rulings, treasury department explanations, court cases, congressional intent, general explanations prepared by the joint committee on taxations, private letter rulings, technical advice memoranda, general counsel memoranda, cases, and revenue rulings. However, conclusions reached in treatises, legal periodicals, legal opinions or opinions rendered by tax professionals are not authority. "There may be substantial authority for a position only if the weight of the authorities supporting the treatment is substantial in relation to the weight of authorities supporting contrary treatment." (Section 1.6662 (d) (3) of IRC).

The realistic possibility standard, set out by the AICPA, lies between the reasonable basis and substantial authority standards. "To meet the realistic possibility standard, a member should have a good-faith belief that the position is warranted by existing law or can be supported by a good-faith argument for an extension, modification or reversal of the existing law through the administrative or judicial process."[19] The long and the short of this means that the professional tax accountant ought to look at the intention of the laws and take only those positions that can be upheld by some authority. It will not do to take a position to save substantial money for the client if there is no reasonable basis on which to base the return, with the anticipation that if detected and fined the penalties will be minimal, and the risk of penalty is well worth the frivolous claim.

Statement No. 2: This statement is non-problematic and prescribes the following: "A member should make a reasonable effort to obtain from the taxpayer the information necessary to provide appropriate answers to all questions on a tax return before signing as preparer."

Statement No. 3. Obligation to examine or verify supporting data: A preparer can rely on the good faith of the client to provide accurate information in preparing a tax return, but "should not ignore the implications of information furnished and should make reasonable inquiries if the information appears to be incorrect, incomplete or inconsistent" (SSTS, p. 21). Here the obligation to the tax system is clear. The preparer will sign the statement attesting that the information contained therein is true, correct, and complete to the best of the preparer's knowledge. Consequently, if the preparer concludes because of an inconsistency that the information can't be correct or complete, the preparer has an obligation not to sign the return.

Statement No. 4. Use of estimates: This is another non-problematic standard. A preparer may use the taxpayer's estimates if it is not practical to obtain the exact data and if the preparer determines the estimates are reasonable, based on the preparer's knowledge.

Statement No. 5. Departure from a previous position: Here again is a rather technical standard. "As provided in SSTS No. 1, *Tax Return Positions*, the member may recommend a tax return position or prepare or sign a tax return that departs from the treatment of an item as concluded in an administrative proceeding or court decision with respect to a prior return of the taxpayer" (SSTS, p. 26).

Statement No. 6. Knowledge of error: What needs to be done when a preparer becomes aware of an error in a taxpayer's previously filed tax return? The member should "inform the taxpayer promptly" and "recommend the corrective measures to be taken" (SSTS, p. 28). If in preparing the current year's return the preparer discovers that the taxpayer has not taken appropriate action to correct an error from a prior year, the preparer needs to decide whether to continue the relationship with the taxpayer. This withdrawal should occur if the taxpayer is unwilling to correct the error, and if the error has a significant effect on the return.

Statement No. 7. Knowledge of error: administrative proceeding: If in the course of an administrative proceeding the preparer detects an error, the preparer should "request the taxpayer's agreement to disclose the error to the taxing authority. Lacking such agreement the member should consider whether to withdraw from representing the taxpayer in the administrative proceeding" (SSTS, pp. 31–2).

Statement No. 8. Form and content of advice to taxpayers: This statement does not prescribe any standard form or content of advice because the range of advice is so extensive and specific to each individual taxpayer's needs. What it does recommend is that the advice reflect professional competence and serve the taxpayer's needs.

That summarizes the standards for tax services that the AICPA expects of its members who are tax preparers. They are standards that ought to be generally applicable to tax accountants in most countries since they appeal to universal principles of proper behavior of professionals within the tax area.

In the light of the standards it becomes fairly clear what our obligations are in the case of the three scenarios[20] that we introduced earlier.

1. *You assured your client that a particular expenditure was deductible only to find out later that it was not. However, it is unlikely the item will be detected by the IRS. Do you tell your client about your mistake and change the form, or do you let it stand as it is?*
    Clearly you need to tell your client of the error and recommend that it be reported to the IRS.

2. *You discover that the client's previous year's return, which someone else prepared, listed a deduction $3000 in excess of the actual expenditure. The mistake was not intentional and the IRS will probably not detect the error. Should you correct the error, costing your client additional liability? What if you prepared the return the previous year so that the mistake was yours?*
    This situation is covered in standard six. You need to advise the taxpayer of the error. It is the taxpayer's responsibility to decide whether to correct it, but if the taxpayer does not choose to correct it, the accountant needs to reconsider whether to continue the relationship with that client. There are laws of privileged communication that affect this situation.

3. *You are preparing a tax return for a very wealthy client, who can provide you with excellent referrals. You have reason to think the client is presenting information that will reduce his tax liability inappropriately. Should you inquire about the veracity of this information or just prepare the tax form with the information as given?*
    Clearly, as pointed out in standard three, the accountant cannot ignore this. The accountant needs to attest to the veracity of the statements. The accountant should encourage his or her client to prepare the form accurately or consider terminating the relationship with the taxpayer.

▲ NOTES ▲

1. Evelyn C. Hume, Ernest R. Larkins, and Govind Iyer, "On Compliance with Ethical Standards in Tax Return Preparation," *Journal of Business Ethics*, 18: 229–38, 1999, p. 237.
2. Ibid., p. 230.

3. See AICPA, *Statements on Responsibilities in Tax Practice: 1991 Revision* (New York: American Institute of Certified Public Accountants).

4. John D. McKinnon and Greg Hitt, "How the Treasury Department Lost a Battle Against a Dubious Security," *Wall Street Journal*, February 4, 2002.

5. *Statements on Standards for Tax Services*, issued by the Tax Executive Committee of the AICPA, 2000, p. 6.

6. Ibid., p. 5.

7. The above three are adapted from Evelyn C. Hume, Ernest R. Larkins, and Govind Iyer, "On Compliance with Ethical Standards in Tax Return Preparation," *Journal of Business Ethics*, 18: 229–38, 1999.

8. Abraham J. Briloff, "The 'Is' and the 'Ought'," *Accounting Today*, September 26, 1999, p. 6.

9. *United States v. Arthur Young and Co. et al.*, 104 S.Ct, 465 US 805, 1984.

10. "The Hustling of Rated Shelters" in *Forbes Magazine*, December 14, 1998.

11. Albert B. Crenshaw, "When Shelters Aren't Aboveboard: IRS, Hill Step Up Efforts as Improper Deals to Help Firms Cut Taxes Rise." *Washington Post*, November 23, 1999, p. E01.

12. A Statement to the House of Representatives Committee on Ways and Means in their hearings on corporate tax shelters, November 10, 1999.

13. Albert B. Crenshaw, "When Shelters Aren't Aboveboard: IRS, Hill Step Up Efforts as Improper Deals to Help Firms Cut Taxes Rise." *Washington Post*, November 23, 1999, p. E01.

14. Crenshaw, ibid.

15. Scott Yetmar, Robert Cooper, and Garry Frank, "Practice and Procedures: Ethical Helps and Challenges," *The Tax Adviser*, February 1999, p. 114.

16. Albert B. Crenshaw, "When Shelters Aren't Aboveboard: IRS, Hill Step Up Efforts as Improper Deals to Help Firms Cut Taxes Rise." *Washington Post*, November 23, 1999, p. E01.

17. Crenshaw, ibid.

18. *Statements on Standards for Tax Services*, issued by the Tax Executive Committee of the AICPA, 2000, p. 12, Interpretation No. 1–1.

19. *Statements on Standards for Tax Services*, ibid., p. 13, Interpretation No. 1–1.

20. These three are adapted from Evelyn C. Hume, Ernest R. Larkins, and Govind Iyer, "On Compliance with Ethical Standards in Tax Return Preparation," *Journal of Business Ethics*, 18: 229–38, 1999.

chapter ten

The Ethics of the Accounting Firm: The Accounting Profession in Crisis

In 1997 the Subcommittee on Reports, Accounting and Managing of the US Senate Committee on Governmental Affairs (The Metcalf Committee) released a report entitled *The Accounting Establishment*, in which it expressed deep concern about "improving the professionalism and independence of auditors."

> The committee is also committed to *fair* [authors' italics] competition as a basic principle of the Nation's economic system. The benefits derived from professional self-regulation carry with them a corresponding responsibility of self-restraint from engaging in activities that detract from professional ideals. The subcommittee firmly believes the important functions of independently auditing publicly owned corporations should be and is financially rewarding and personally satisfying in its own right without any need for engaging in activities that *appear* [authors' italics] to detract from professional responsibilities.[1]

Whether the regulatory scrutiny worked from the 1970s to the 1990s is a matter for dispute. Be that as it may, a series of high-profile corporate accounting "frauds that auditors missed at companies including Cendant, Sunbeam and Livent occurred. Public shareholders lost hundreds of millions of dollars in these cases, and confidence in accountants was shaken."[2]

> Last January, partners and employees at PricewaterhouseCoopers were found by the S.E.C. to have routinely violated rules forbidding their ownership of stock in companies they were auditing. The investigation found 8,064 violations at the firm, which then dismissed five

partners. Pricewaterhouse said at the time that it did not believe that
the integrity of any audit had been compromised by the violations."³

Finally, the role Arthur Andersen played in the Enron collapse led
Business Week to author a special report called "Accounting in
Crisis."⁴ According to the article:

> As shocking as Enron is, it's only the latest in a dizzying succession of
> accounting meltdowns, from Waste Management to Cendant. Lynn
> E. Turner, former chief accountant for the SEC and now a professor
> at Colorado State University, calculates that in the past half-dozen
> years investors have lost close to $200 billion in earnings restatements
> and lost market capitalization following audit failures. And the pace
> seems to be accelerating. Between 1997 and 2000 the number of
> restatements doubled, from 116 to 233.

These stories of inappropriate behavior by accounting firms lead
us to ask what is going on in the accounting establishment today and
whether the general tenor of what is going on in those firms is
ethically acceptable. What seems to be going on, at least from the
point of view of those critical of the direction the accounting
profession is taking today, is that the profession has ceased to be a
profession and succumbed to the pressures endemic to being a
business driven by the profit motive. Some, like John C. Bogle, as
we saw earlier, claim that the accounting profession, rather than
maintaining its status as an honorable profession in which members
looked out for clients and the public, has gotten involved in the
enterprise of business, where its main concerns are not fidelity to its
various trusts, but fidelity to the bottom line. Such critics would
maintain that, just as commercialization is infecting professions like
medicine, teaching, law, and others, profit-motivated business
interests conflict with the accountant's professional responsibilities
and corrupt the behavior of the professional. This tension between
the demands of professionalism and the demands of business has
created an identity crisis in the industry today. We would like to
examine that crisis in this chapter.

▲ ACCOUNTING AS A BUSINESS ▲

There is an old saw one gets tired of hearing: "There's no such thing
as business ethics." There is also a more sophisticated version of the

old saw that asserts, "Business ethics, that's an oxymoron, a contradiction in terms, sort of like military-intelligence or jumbo-shrimp." At times, these quips are the self-righteous condemnation of business offered by anti-business academics or artists who rarely engage in business (or so they think). They would maintain that concerning oneself with business activity is banal. Their attitude reflects a point of view that goes as far back as ancient Greek philosophers, who asserted that to engage in business activities was to do something illiberal. For philosophers such as Plato and Aristotle, business was not a worthy pursuit for a free human being. Academic and artistic elitists adopting that position have a negative attitude toward business and deplore the concern with materialistic goods and the engagement in conspicuous consumption that business brings about.

At other times, these quips are delivered, with a nervous laugh, by business people. The nervousness might be due to the fact that those who utter such maxims are in bad faith – i.e. they are people engaged in unethical business dealings, who may be rationalizing their own unethical behavior, which they would rather not face. Such critics fail to see that the majority of business dealings are done ethically and above board, and that if they weren't, business as we know it would cease to function. Finally, these quips may be delivered by those who realize there is ethical behavior in business, but are bemoaning the fact that their competitors don't necessarily act ethically.

Our contention, even though it is shaken by the sight of the seemingly unchecked greed in the case of Enron, is that a little reflection will show that ethics is essential for the running of business. We claim that without ethics in business, the smooth functioning of trade and commerce would not be possible. Of course, what holds for business in general will hold for accounting in particular. To make the point, consider what would it mean if a businessperson really thought there was no such thing as business ethics. It would mean he or she thinks it's acceptable to be dishonest in their dealings with you. It would mean he or she thinks it's fine to sell you a faulty product to make more money if they thought they could get away with it.

Now ask such a person the following question: "If you really think acting unethically is OK, why would you tell us that?" If someone tells us they cheat all the time, we would be foolish to trust them. A clever cheat keeps that fact to themselves. If someone really thinks there is no ethics in business, he or she is really just an unscrupulous person silly enough to tell you about it. The simple answer is, don't deal with silly and unscrupulous people. The point is, most people doing business don't believe there is no ethics in business and don't act as if they do. What they probably mean, as we've already said, is that there are some, perhaps many, people who behave unethically in business. But to recognize that fact is to implicitly condemn such activity.

The claim that there is no such thing as business ethics is not only indefensible, it is also outmoded and has outworn its usefulness, if it ever had any. Ethics in business is an idea whose time has come. Furthermore, it is often the case that good ethics is good business, and if at times, which occur but rarely, good ethics is not good business, then business interests should capitulate to ethical interests. For example, in a situation where the behavior necessary to do the ethical thing will jeopardize profit, the business persons with integrity would hold that the pursuit of profit should defer to doing what is right.

However, if the claim "business ethics is an oxymoron" is nonsense, it is important to ask why such nonsense arises in the first place; important because, nonsense or not, the attitude has become part of our cultural fiber and is used to justify (rationalize) much unethical behavior. Further, an examination of this question may help us understand the conflict between professionalism and profit that is besetting the accounting industry. Our contention is that the claim arose because of a mistaken but strong consensus about the purpose, nature, and responsibility of business. The consensus is the widely held and taught belief that the primary responsibility of business is to maximize profit or shareholder value.

To the extent that accounting is a business, and such behavior is expected of businesses, the accounting firm will come under the profit-maximizing rubric. When an accounting firm whose primary function is to give adequate attestation begins to look at itself as primarily a business, the necessity to make a profit begins to override that primary function of attesting to the truth and correctness of financial statements. Recent events in the accounting profession – the movement of firms from primarily audit and attest functions to management consulting – have altered the perception of the accounting firm from a view that sees the firm as a group of professionals dedicated to public services to a view of the firm as a business in a competitive marketplace, primarily concerned with maximizing partner or shareholder wealth.

Since adopting as a driving principle the overriding necessity of profit maximization leads to such a tension, it behooves us to ask how such an ideal developed and whether it is defensible.

▲ THE SOCIAL RESPONSIBILITY ▲ OF BUSINESS

The contemporary idea of business as a social institution developed according to a perception that viewed its fundamental concern as making a profit. The perception was most clearly articulated by Milton Friedman in his now classic utterance, "The primary and only responsibility of business is to use its resources and engage in activities designed to increase its profits so long as it stays within the rules of the game, which is to say, engages in open and free competition without deception and fraud."[5] Such a principle refocused business' primary purpose from the generation of products and services (for example, attest and audit in accounting) to monetary accumulation. Profit making was taken to be primary and displaced the generation of products and services as the primary role of business; the generation of products and services was reduced to being merely the instrumental means for making profit. This reversal puts the cart before the horse. Let us see how.

This notion that the primary function of business is profit making has its roots in a reading (we would argue, an incomplete reading) of the eighteenth century classic *The Wealth of Nations* written by Adam Smith.[6] In that book, Smith sets up the model of the self-interested maximizer, the person concerned with increasing his or her own utility. Smith sees humans as motivated by self-interest. He notes: "It is not from the benevolence of the butcher, the brewer, or the baker, that we expect our dinner, but from their regard to their own interest."[7]

Smith's genius was in maintaining that it is the pursuit of self-interest that makes commerce and society flourish. He gave currency to the belief that the entire society will be better off if each businessperson pursues his or her own interest. In arguing this he makes reference to the infamous "invisible hand" – leave the market forces alone and people's pursuit of their individual interests will make the entire society flourish.

As every individual, therefore, endeavors as much as he can both to employ his capital in the support of domestic industry, and so to direct that industry that its produce may be of the greatest value, every individual necessarily labors to render the annual revenue of the society as great as he can. He generally, indeed, neither intends to promote the public interest, nor knows how much he is promoting it. By directing that industry in such a manner as its produce may be of the greatest value, he intends only his own gain, and he is in this, as in many other cases, led by an *invisible hand* to promote an end which was no part of his intention. Nor is it always the worse for society that it was no part of it. By pursuing his own interest he frequently promotes that of the society more effectually than when he really intends to promote it. I have never known much good done by those who affected to trade for the public good. It is an affectation, indeed, not very common among merchants, and very few words need be employed in dissuading them from it.[8]

Friedman and other contemporary followers of Smith claim this has happened. The success of our economic system that governs how business works is attributable to the fact that when we let business worry about nothing but profit, competition is created, more goods are produced and the entire society enjoys a higher standard of living, and hence is better off. The fact that the economic system of capitalism has led to the production of more goods and services than any other economic system in the history of mankind – that it has led to the highest material standard of living, for more people than any other system – is the evidence for the invisible hand argument.

The utilitarian structure of the argument is simple enough to see. The activity or practice of self-interested pursuits is justified because of the good that will accrue to society if such a system, profit-oriented, is adopted. In short, the greatest good for the greatest number will be served if the market, driven by self-interest, is allowed to operate. Look out for your own concerns and society, as a whole, will be better off.

That may be true, most of the time. In fact, that seems to be what such thinkers as Gauthier and McClennen are trying to show.[9] But if we forget the goal of everyone pursuing their own interest is to make the society better off, a problem arises with the position. Societal benefit is the end that justifies the pursuit of profit. The pursuit of profit cannot stand as an end in itself. The unconstrained and exclusive pursuit of self-interest can and does at times hurt others. It is not always the case that following one's self-interest will make the society better off. So, the sticking point is those times when the pursuit of self-interest does not lead to the good of the whole, but is at the expense of others. At that time what is the proper thing to do? Pursue profits or concern oneself with lessening the expense of others? If societal benefit justifies self-interest, what happens when the benefit is not there? At those times there seems to be a need to put constraints on that self-interested pursuit. Indeed, Smith claims the pursuit of self-interest is only justified so long as it does not violate the laws of justice.

However, to determine what justice demands requires us to be clear about the proper end of business. We have said its ideal purpose is primarily the generation of goods and services. Let us make the case for that point of view. If we view business as a practice, we see that it is a conventional practice, i.e. one designed by human beings and not something natural – it is a societal practice, a developed conventional form of life. What does that entail?

If it is a social construction, several things must be true. Since it was constructed by society, we assume it was constructed to benefit society, since no society or group would create a social institution to harm itself. Rather, institutions are created and approved to the extent they promote some good for the society or group. So, the purpose of any societally constructed system or institution has to be an end that is compatible with some social good, which may or may not be compatible with an individual's interest. For example, our society does not sanction the creation of groups to manufacture and distribute heroin, or create pornographic films which exploit children, because they do not see these activities as having any redeeming social value.

Given the above, it follows that society (should have) instituted business and its practices and rules, by which we mean the competitive profit-motivated free-enterprise system, to help itself (society) develop and survive. Business should be created and organized in such a way as to be beneficial to society. Hence, the claim is made, from Adam Smith on down, that such a competitive profit-motivated free-enterprise system is a very efficient *means* of bringing about a laudable goal, namely benefits to society. But if such a system, such an instrumental good, begins to harm society, it should be modified or done away with.

The somewhat regulated capitalist economic system, which our society permits, is permitted because it is seen as a very productive system, if not the most productive economic system in history. While our system of business as it has developed is not the only way to produce goods and services, it is argued that it is the most efficient. This capitalist system centers on rules governing the distribution of profits. Profits are utilized as a way to incentivize or motivate the entrepreneur. But profits cannot be the be all and end all. They are merely the means to achieving the purpose of business, and as the means should not usurp the ultimate goal of business.

What happened in the development of the view that the primary responsibility of business is to maximize profits, was that the self-interested motive and incentive for doing business, profit making, was confused with and turned into the purpose of business. The problem, of course, is that turning the means, self-interested motivation, into a purpose opens a Pandora's box. The legitimization of such a self-interested means unleashes what the theologians call "greed." The "rational maximizer" can become the greedy, grasping, acquisitive, profit-motivated, bottom-line oriented entrepreneur, who feels no responsibility to the public welfare, because of the belief that whatever he or she does leads to the public welfare. The benefits of utilizing the profit motive are obvious, but so are the undesirable externalities.

There is a counter argument to those who adopt a Friedmanian stance. If we maintain that the purpose of business is to provide goods and services, while the motive is making a profit, it becomes clear that the responsibility of the manager or agent of the business is not simply to pursue profits, but to pursue them regulated by the demands of the public interest. Of course, to determine what those demands are is another area beyond the scope of this discussion.

Hence, we have seen, if we confuse the purpose of an activity or practice with the motives for performing that activity or engaging in that practice, and reduce the former (purposes) to the latter (the motives), we make it impossible to give a theoretical ground for legitimate ethical restraints on business, other than those required by a Kantian formalism. Conversely, if we construe business as an artifact created for the sake of society, specifically for the sake of the production of goods and services, we have grounds for constraining it when its operations violate the demands of justice. An ethical business will be one that fulfills its purposes, which aim at the betterment of society through production of goods and services.

Is this a mere semantic quibble between motives and purposes? We think not. The meaning of the word "purpose" involves the "what for?" of an activity. Purposes direct us to the goal of an activity, in this case the goal being creating goods for society. But goals are not motivating forces. Motivating forces refer to the psychological whys for doing things. Such motivating forces are not necessarily self-justifying and they must be constrained by purposes. To confuse a purpose with a motive is like confusing the purpose of a train, to get people from place to place, with what drives the train, the engine. The engine is analogous to the motive, since it moves the train. Keeping the train analogy in mind we see that from a societal point of view, the purpose of business is to promote the production and distribution of goods and/or services, not to benefit the producer. Society certainly needs to incentivize and motivate producers, but that is always for a further purpose. Clarifying the distinction may not amount to much, but it will allow us to call greed "greed" because it does not fulfill, but often frustrates, the purpose of business rather than forcing us to accept it as the ultimate driving force of business.

So we see that a person's motive for doing something is not the same as the purpose of the action. There can be many motives for the same action. For example, the purpose of giving to charity is to help the poor. But an individual may not be in the least bit interested in helping the poor when they give to charity. They may give to charity simply to impress their friends. So there is a social (outside) view of the purpose of charity, and a personal (inside) view of an individual's motive for the charity. If giving to charity not only fulfills my duty, but rewards me as well, I'll be more inclined to give to charity. But whether I am inclined to give to charity or not, there is still the need to give to charity. Similarly, the purpose of business is not to benefit me, primarily. It is not to make a profit. If doing business rewards me with a profit, I will be inclined to get into it, but the purpose of business, why society allowed it to be set up, or allowed it to exist in its profit-oriented form was so that it would provide goods and services.

There are all sorts of ways to make money, and wanting to make money is certainly acceptable as a *motive*, but the purpose of the practice of accounting is not to make money, any more than the purpose of the practice of medicine is to make money. Medicine's purpose is to minister to the sick. Thus, the social practices have their own purposes independent of the motives of the persons engaged in the practices. These examples should help to make it clear that our motives for doing something may or may not accord with the purpose of the activity. Hence, profit maximization cannot be the final goal of business. It must defer to the primary goal of business which is to make society better off by the production of goods and services.

To sum up, one of the recurrent themes of this book is that from an ethical point of view it is important to be clear about the purpose of something, since knowing a thing's purpose gives us a standard by which to judge that thing. Just as we judge a knife by how well it fulfills its purpose to cut, we can judge a business by how well it fulfills its purpose. If a business' purpose is to make a profit, then a business whose bottom line is healthy, which keeps generating healthy profits, is a good business no matter how it helps or hurts people. But if the purpose of business is to provide goods and services, and it is for such a purpose that society allows businesses to exist, then we don't judge a business simply on how much profit it generates. We must take into consideration questions about how good its products are. To conclude, making a profit cannot be the "primary and only" purpose of business as Friedman says. Making a profit may be a necessary condition for business to survive, and while it certainly is a *motive* for doing business, profit making is not business' primary purpose. If, then, the purpose of business is to provide goods and services, a good business will be one which provides acceptable goods and services.

This is a more adequate view of business, one which is becoming increasingly prevalent. Business is now more often viewed as an institution that society has allowed to develop, whose primary purpose is to provide goods and services for society. As we already noted, society bans some businesses precisely because their products are seen as detrimental to society, as in the case of the government banning the production and distribution of heroin or cocaine.

But that leaves us with a problem. How do we motivate justice or ethical behavior? The most recent move encouraged by a shared ethical concern has been to try to conflate the purpose and motives of business. Hence we get the new maxim, "Good ethics is good business." Consider the following:

> Although behaving ethically should be an end in itself, there also are valid business reasons for doing what's right. If you look closely at examples of unethical business behavior, you discover two things: the company derives only short-term advantages from its actions, and over the longer term, skimping on quality or service doesn't pay. It's not good business.
>
> Consider the food company that, a few years ago, came under fire

for selling a sweet-flavored and colored drink labeled as pure apple juice. Whatever short-term profits it gained in passing off the cheaper drink as fruit juice, the damage to a good company's reputation was far more costly in the long run.

Another example is the Lockheed Corporation, whose aircraft have served this country in times of war and peace. Yet, some people remember it for a long-ago bribery scandal, and the company has had to spend years fighting the adverse publicity generated by the case.

On the other hand, Johnson and Johnson immediately took its pain reliever, Tylenol, off the market when faced with claims of product tampering. J&J knew the decision would be costly in dollars, but refused to put a price tag on its integrity. Some thought their sales could never recover, but the company ended up reinforcing its strong market leadership.[10]

Let's now look at how this maxim that good ethics is good business applies to the accounting profession and accounting firms in particular.

To begin, good ethics affects the good name of the company and builds trust. It is obvious that to cut corners for short-term gain will only erode the good name of the company. An accounting firm that cannot be trusted is useless, since people depend on the firm and individual accountants to provide them with accurate pictures of the financial status of other organizations.

Next, if a firm treats its clients or customers well and fairly, not only might sales increase but there will also be positive effects on the employees of the company. As Archie Carroll said,[11] if a company is concerned with profit and success at any cost, then its motive is greed. Employees are aware when a company is greedy, and that greed, that uncaring search for profit must erode the morale and the loyalty of employees who realize that the only thing motivating their company is greed. Such an attitude on the part of the company must be counter-productive, for if the company is seen as putting the customer second, behind profit, where will it put the employees?

Third, being ethical has a more subtle benefit for managers than for the other employers. Kenneth Lux points out that:

From the self-interest doctrine we inherit the picture of the business-man or woman as only greedy. This is exemplified by Dickens' portrayal of Scrooge, which is just one among scores of such portraits. But the real story may be rather different. The book that is the foundation of modern management theory, *The Human Side of Enter-*

prise, by Douglas McGregor (1960), recognized the virtues of the businessperson, as well as the economic value of those virtues. All contemporary business texts (which are distinguished, ironically, from economic texts) of any influence reflect the same humanistic values that McGregor recognized and advocated.[12]

The benefit, then, is that in an ethical company the manager will be allowed to let his or her humanism show. Most of us learned to disapprove of Scrooge. It is regrettable that an emphasis on profit driven by greed would make us dampen our moral sensibilities and become like the Scrooge we despise. However, our society, with its emphasis on business ethics, is telling us that we don't have to sink to that level; that the cynical phrase justifying inhuman behavior, "that's just business," is no longer acceptable. Managers, if ethical behavior can override the greed of business, do not need to live in two worlds, the one of their humanistic ethical life, and the other of their ruthless business life. They do not need to check their ethics at the door when they come into work.

Thus, there seems to be a fourfold motivation for ethical behavior. Ethical behavior leads to: (1) long-term profits for the company; (2) personal integrity and satisfaction for the persons engaged in business; (3) honesty and loyalty from the employees; and (4) confidence and satisfaction from the customer. In effect, the idea whose time has come is the idea that corporations should behave ethically, partly because that will usually have good consequences for the company. The collapse of Arthur Andersen because of its part in the Enron debacle attests to all that.

Still, as David Vogel points out, ethics and profit don't always go hand in hand, and sometimes management will have to make a choice between what's right and what's profitable, but by and large it is more prudent to be ethical than not, and we would hope that at those times when the right choice is the non-profitable one, business would choose the right.

But even if the consequences of behaving ethically aren't always profitable and beneficial, it can be argued that in those cases businesses have responsibilities over and above making a profit. As we saw, this runs counter to the popular belief that the sole purpose of business is to make a profit, the belief that defends some behavior simply on the grounds that "that's business." However, we have just seen the limitations of that view.

In the light of the above, what is the ethical responsibility of business in general and of accounting firms in particular? To answer this question it will be helpful to examine a certain aspect of a corporation. The corporation is an entity empowered by law to do things that affect others. Since that's the case, it is necessary to view businesses as entities, who through their owners and managers enter into relationships with individuals and groups, and relationships carry responsibilities with them. In doing business, a business gets involved in relationships. These relationships become the basis of ethical obligations that the business has toward those stakeholders, and, vice versa, those stakeholders have toward the business.

If we apply the above framework to an accounting firm, what can we say about the responsibilities of such firms? Certainly an accounting firm needs to make some profit or increase the value of the business or partnership, but there are limits on profit making. An accounting firm has other responsibilities besides concern for the bottom line. To be sure, no firm can stay in existence without paying attention to the bottom line, but in the accounting world there are other concerns as well.

To begin, the very existence of accounting came about to provide a service and benefit to its clients and the public. Hence, hurting the public or clients violates the very purpose of the firm. Doing what would harm customers in the name of profit would be contrary to the purpose of being an accountant. As we have shown, accounting firms have specific functions, functions that society has licensed, of providing certain goods and services. Accounting is a service industry. The chief service is to provide information about the financial situation of companies. Another is to attest to the accuracy of that information. Thus, a good accounting firm should provide as clear a picture as possible of an organization's financial situation, and/or attest to the fairness of such pictures. Any practice which violates that purpose contradicts the very essence of the accounting firm.

So, it should be clear that the responsibility of an accounting firm is to provide the kind of services we just described, and there is a limit on the profit it can make if the making of that profit jeopardizes its primary work. However, having said all that, it is important to note that the profit-maximizing pressure is bringing the accounting profession into a crisis today.

▲ ACCOUNTING: A PROFESSION IN ▲
CRISIS TODAY

The Arthur Andersen/Enron debacle has made it abundantly clear that it is naïve to think that contemporary accounting firms are not manipulated by the profit motive. There are troubles in the profession and among the firms. But this was known before Enron imploded. Abraham J. Briloff, the perennial scold of the accounting profession, in an article in *Accounting Today* indicated there was a gap between the "is" of the accounting profession and the "ought" of the accounting profession – what accountants do, and what they ought to do. In an editorial on the same page of that publication, Rick Telberg laments a recent move by KPMG to merge with Cisco Systems, since it jeopardizes the independence of the Peat-Marwick branch of the corporation. In a *Forbes Magazine* article, Deloitte and Touche are reported to be "hustling" tax strategies.[13]

Now, of course, defenders of such practices will argue that these activities are necessary given the competition of the marketplace. But as Telberg suggests, if accountants are willing to go along with such pressures, "then the profession's entire system and philosophy of independence will need re-thinking."

We repeat the pessimistic words of Telberg we quoted earlier.

In fact we are probably past the time when independence mattered. CPA firms long ago became more like insurance companies – complete with their focus on assurances and risk-managed audits – than attesters. Auditors are backed by malpractice insurance in the same way that a re-insurer backs an insurance company, so they have become less like judges of financial statements than underwriters weighing probabilities.

Some in the profession have even argued that auditors should function less like ultimate arbiters of fact and financial reality, and be allowed, instead, to function more like investment bankers, and provide only "due diligence." So that CPAs, who once valued fairness and truthfulness in financial reporting, would then promise little more than nods and winks, all beyond the reach of meaningful oversight.[14]

The danger is that if every auditor or attestor acted in that way, the audits and attestations would be worthless. There would still be a use for accountants as tax preparers, and financial reporters, but the audit function, the heart of the accounting profession, would be cut out of the practice, rendered virtually useless by its misuse. One could, of course, capitulate and envision the function of the accountant as simply to do what is required for a company to flourish monetarily. But that would be to capitulate to the view that profit maximizing is the only purpose of business and we would have no ethics.

So, would that bring about the demise of accounting? Hardly. Telberg fails to take into account the fact that the economic system would still need audited reports which were truthful and accurate for all the financial operations to continue in an effective manner. Even if the delivery of such reports is not profitable and existing accounting firms committed to maximizing their own profit turn away from the audit function, there will still be a large accounting task to be done. Someone will step into the gap and perform the service. New firms will arise, and the people in that firm will then be subject to the same ethical requirements as the professional auditor of today, while the auditor of today will be just another management consultant with accounting expertise. The names may change, but the function, and hence the ethical responsibilities, will remain.

Let's look more specifically at the problems facing the accounting firm today with respect to keeping on an ethical plane. In a remarkable document, the SEC details these dramatic changes occurring in the profession. In the preface to the SEC Independence Regulations we find the following.

> The changes in the accounting profession, combined with increasing pressures on companies, raise questions about auditor independence and investor confidence in the financial statements of public companies that those auditors audit. To respond to some of these questions, we [the SEC] proposed, and are now adopting, new rules relating to the financial and employment relationships independent auditors may have with their audit clients, business and financial relationships between accounting firms and audit clients, and the non-audit services that auditors can provide to audit clients without impairing their independence.
>
> The accounting industry is in the midst of dramatic transformation. Firms have merged, resulting in increased size, both domestically and internationally. They have expanded into international networks, affiliating and marketing under a common name. Increasingly, accounting firms are becoming multi-disciplinary service organizations and are entering into new types of business relationships with their audit clients. Accounting professionals have become more mobile, and

geographic location of firm personnel has become less important due to advances in telecommunications. In addition, there are more dual-career families, and audit clients are increasingly hiring firm partners, professional staff, and their spouses for high-level management positions.

In conjunction with these changes, accounting firms have expanded significantly the menu of services offered to their audit clients, and the list continues to grow. Companies are turning to their auditors to perform their internal audit, pension, financial, administrative, sales, data processing, and marketing functions, among many others.

As we noted in the Proposing Release, U.S. revenues for management advisory and similar services for the five largest public accounting firms (the "Big Five") amounted to more than $15 billion in 1999. Moreover, revenues for these service lines are now estimated to constitute half of the total revenues for these firms. In contrast, these service lines provided only thirteen percent of total revenues in 1981. From 1993 to 1999, the average annual growth rate for revenues from management advisory and similar services has been twenty-six percent; comparable growth rates have been nine percent for audit and thirteen percent for tax services.

For the largest firms, the growth in management advisory and similar services involves both audit clients and non-audit clients. For the largest public accounting firms, MAS fees from SEC audit clients have increased significantly over the past two decades. In 1984, only one percent of SEC audit clients of the eight largest public accounting firms paid MAS fees that exceeded the audit fee. For the Big Five firms, the percentage of SEC audit clients that paid MAS fees in excess of audit fees did not exceed 1.5% until 1997. In 1999, 4.6% of Big Five SEC audit clients paid MAS fees in excess of audit fees, an increase of over 200% in two years. For the Big Five firms, average MAS fees received from SEC audit clients amounted to ten percent of all revenues in 1999. Almost three-fourths of Big Five SEC audit clients purchased no MAS from their auditors in 1999. This means that purchases of MAS services by one-fourth of firms' SEC audit clients account for ten percent of all firm revenues.

Some smaller firms are consolidating their audit practices and seeking public investors in the resulting company. Other firms are entering into agreements to sell all of their assets, except their audit practices, to established financial services companies. As part of these agreements, the financial services companies hire the employees, and in some cases the partners, of the accounting firm, and then lease back the majority or all of the assets and audit personnel to the "shell" audit firm. These lease arrangements allow the financial services firm to pay the professional staff for "nonprofessional" services for the corporate organization as well as professional attest services rendered for the audit firm.

Recently, Ernst & Young sold its management-consulting business to Cap Gemini Group SA, a large and publicly traded computer services company headquartered in France. KPMG has sold an equity interest in KPMG Consulting to Cisco Corporation and is in the process of registering additional shares in its consulting business to sell to the public in an initial public offering. In addition, Pricewaterhouse-Coopers has publicly announced an intention to sell portions of its consulting businesses. Also, Grant Thornton recently sold its e-business consulting practice.

Simultaneous with this metamorphosis of the accounting profession, public companies have come under increasing pressure to meet earnings expectations. Observers suggest that this pressure has intensified in recent years, especially for companies operating in certain sectors of the economy. The extent of the pressure becomes apparent each time a company loses a significant percentage of its market capitalization after failing to meet analysts' expectations. These intense pressures on companies lead to enhanced pressure on auditors to enable their clients to meet expectations.[15]

These are the facts of the accounting profession and accounting firms today. Given those facts, what are the challenges facing the profession today?

The biggest challenge is to be professional, which means set up the interest of clients and public above considerations of self-interest. John C. Bogle of the Independence Standards Board, in a presentation aptly named "Public Accounting: Profession or Business?", gives an account of what he sees as the main factors pushing accounting away from its dedication to its professional goals into the arena of simply a profit maximizing operation.[16] Written in the year 2000, well before the collapse of Enron, it is remarkably prophetic. It is so perceptive, it deserves to be liberally quoted. Bogle indicates there are numerous issues pressuring accountants and accounting firms to be profit maximizers before they are professionals, but he chooses to concentrate on five of the most important ones.

The first issue is the adequacy of the "generally accepted accounting principles." As Bogle puts the issue, accountants need to examine the adequacy and hidden assumptions of the accounting principles they are using, for they all have ethical implications with respect to the accountant's obligation to give true and accurate pictures. Bogle asks,

Can the accounting principles that have served the Old Economy so well over so many years properly be applied to the New Economy? Is what's seen as a narrow accounting model applying to businesses with tangible capital equipment, hard assets, and even so-called "goodwill" applicable to businesses in which human capital is the principal asset, information is the stock in trade, and "first mover" status is the driving force in valuation? Clearly, many, indeed most, New Economy companies are valued at staggering – even infinite – multiples of any earnings that GAAP could possibly uncover. Interestingly, however, during the past seven months, at least the Internet business-to-consumer companies have reconciled that gap, as it were, in favor of GAAP.

So while that seemingly omnipotent master, "the stock market," may be telling the profession that the 1930s-based model of reporting doesn't work any more, please don't write off too hastily the possibility that the *model* may be right and the *market* wrong. And don't forget that no matter what "the market" may say today, its level on future tomorrows well down the road *will* – not *may* – be determined by earnings and dividends. Nonetheless, a re-examination of today's basic accounting principles should be a high priority. And let the chips fall where they may.

One might also mention in this account the general reluctance of accountants to develop principles that adequately predict and internalize externalities, as well as the reluctance to engage in enterprises such as social audits. Of course, the reason is clear: both of those procedures could substantially impact negatively on the bottom line, and what company wants an accountant who costs them profits?

The second issue that Bogle mentions is the question of earnings management, the diplomatic term for the possible cooking of the books. One particularly skeptical accountant was known to tell his students, "You can show anything you want using accounting principles." Whether that is true or not, it is true that one can manage the picture of the earning. Hence Bogle notes,

> . . . we live in a world of managed earnings. The desideratum is steady earnings growth – manage it to at least the 12 percent level if you can – and at all costs avoid falling short of the earnings expectations at which the corporation has hinted, or whispered, or "ball parked" before the year began. If all else fails, obscure the real results by merging, taking big one-time write-off, and relying on pooling-of-interest accounting (although that procedure will soon become unavailable). All of this creative financial engineering apparently

serves to inflate stock prices, enrich corporate managers, and to deliver to institutional investors what they want.

But if the stock market is to be the arbiter of value, it will do its job best, in my judgment, if it sets its valuations based on accurate corporate financial reporting and a focus on the long-term prospects of the corporations it values. The market today seems to be focusing at least a bit more on those verities, but there is still much room for improvement. For while the accounting practices of America's corporations may well be the envy of the world, our nation's financial environment has become permeated with the concept of managed earnings. There is a "numbers game" going on, and *pro forma* operating profits permeate financial statements. *Pro forma* seems to mean, in an Alice-in-Wonderland-world, whatever the Corporation chooses it to mean, excluding such charges as amortization of goodwill, taxes on option exercises, equity losses in investees, in-process R&D, for example, as these costs vanish in the struggle to meet earnings expectations. Since this game is played in press releases, it is not clear where the solution lies. But I hope that the accounting profession will get involved before the coin of the realm – earnings statements with integrity – is further debased. That corporate clients may not be enamored of having the issue of managed earnings raised is – or ought to be – irrelevant.

Bogle then turns to an examination of the issue of accounting for stock options.

. . . as Warren Buffett has long argued, if options *are* compensation, why aren't they charged to earnings? And if options *aren't* compensation, what are they? Surely the profession ought to play a more aggressive role in answering that question and taking a stand on proper stock option accounting. Recent study by a Wall Street firm listed four industry groups in which accounting for stock options would have reduced earnings by an average of 28 percent in 1997, 23 percent in 1998, and another 25 percent in 1999; 21 companies in which 1999 earnings would have been reduced from 50% to 700%(!) (*sic*); and 13 companies with 1999 *pro forma* (there's that word again) pre-tax stock option compensation ranging from $500 million to $1.1 billion. Financial statements place options in a sort-of "no man's land" in which options are not treated as compensation. Quite important enough as an issue now, the question of accounting for stock options will rise to even greater importance as corporations whose stocks have faltered – even plummeted – in the recent market decline re-price their options. I hope that FASB interpretation 44 on re-pricing underwater options will help to deal with this issue.

The fourth issue that Bogle addresses is the one we looked at in the case of the tax accountant, the situation of overly aggressive and potentially illegal tax shelters. Bogle refers to remarks made early in the year 2000 by US Treasury Secretary Lawrence Summers, who according to Bogle "excoriated the proliferation of 'engineered trans-actions that are devoid of economic substance . . . with no goal other than to reduce a corporation's tax liabilities'."

> Such transactions strike a blow at the integrity – here, an especially well-chosen word – of the tax system. He challenges, I assume accurately, the professional conduct of the firms involved in the creation of abusive tax shelters and suggests sanctions on firms – here, the Treasury Secretary pointedly included public accountants – that issue opinions, limits on contingent fees, and excise taxes on such fee income. The Secretary is right: And when companies demand – and receive – "black-box" features in such transactions designed to make them impenetrable to all but those who designed them, something perilously close to fraud is going on. . . .
>
> It is not my place to evaluate the role of the accounting profession in these tax abuses. But it must be clear that any firm that helps develop such schemes or opines on their purported validity wins favor with the client involved, and runs a heavy risk of compromising its independence. Faustian bargains of that nature, to the extent they may exist, could even require the addition of tax services to the list of services that public accounting firms would be barred from offering to their clients. Surely, that's a high price for public accounting firms to pay.

The fifth and final issue that Bogle raises is the issue of how the independence of firms and the future of the profession's indepen-dence will hold up to the conflicts of interest that may be generated by the newly evolving novel forms of firm structure and organiza-tions. Bogle puts the problem in the following way.

> The traditional simple partnership model is being supplanted by alternative business structures. In one model, a group of smaller attest firms are consolidated through the sale of their non-audit prac-tice to a third party (in a private or public offering) with the audit practice retained by the partners. An operational link remains between the two parties. In another – the "roll up" model – firms are united under a single umbrella through combination and then sale of their non-audit businesses to a third party or the public. *Byzantine* is the word that comes to mind as one looks at the organ-

izational charts portraying these relationships. While "Byzantine" isn't necessarily bad, such dual employment surely raises important independence issues. And when CPA firms – whose integrity and independence are their stock in trade – are in fact principally investment advisory firms offering financial products sponsored by their parents, a whole other set of questions about the meaning of *professional responsibility* come to the fore.

We have seen these new mergers and acquisitions and the problems they have caused already for Price-Waterhouse/Coopers & Lybrand, as well as the questioning of the independence of Peat-Marwick because of its merger into KPMG, and its involvement with Cisco Systems.

Bogle concludes with the following remarks.

> How attest firms respond to these independence issues – and indeed whether they do – will shape the future of the profession. Most of them are clearly framed by the over-arching issue of the proper place to draw the line between business and profession. But perhaps my comments are just the ramblings of an aging auditor who wants to bring back a proud age of tradition that will never return. In my own mutual fund industry, I *know* that the age of professional stewardship will return. While I do not understand the field of accounting nearly as well, I am confident that if financial market participants come to understand that the independent oversight of financial figures plays a critical role in our system of disclosure, that independence is at the core of integrity, and that the integrity of our financial markets is essential to their well-being, the age of professional accounting too will shake off today's challenges and return to its roots.

To sum up, the accounting profession and accounting firms are facing sea changes in structure and operations. There is an ever-expanding gap between what *is* the case and what *ought* to be the case. But the fact that accountants everywhere are looking at and evaluating that gap gives hope for the future. Behind each of these assessments lie the assumptions that it is right to be just and fair and ethical, and the struggles over those issues merely confirm that there is agreement about the necessity of being ethical in accounting. It's just that with changing circumstances it is not always easy to figure out how that is to be done.

All of the above was exacerbated by the Enron debacle and Arthur Andersen's role in it. As happens so often, huge scandals give rise to serious reform. The Big Five accounting firms reexamined their consultancy operations, and how these affected their independence. Congress looked more carefully at what regulations would be helpful in making sure that the firms and the professional organization would meet their obligations. Any number of reforms were suggested, including the following: enact self-regulation with teeth; bar consulting to audit clients; mandate rotation of auditors; impose more forensic auditing; limit auditors' moves to companies; reform the internal audit committees; and clean up the accounting rules.[17] To determine which of those proposed reforms are wise, and to what extent, will be left to the legislatures and regulators. It is beyond the purview of this book. But even with the crisis in the accounting profession there is a silver lining to be seen.

In spite of the Enron fiasco, the remarks of Robert Bruce, which preceded the revelations, give reasons for hope.

> The profession is on the move again. Its great strength over the past 35 years or so has been its astonishing ability to adapt. Outsiders never understand this. They see accountants as stolid folk with limited imagination, but an ability to make money. Accountants are invariably characterized as the dullest of people. Yet, in this country, their profession has consistently reinvented itself.
>
> Once they were simply auditors and advisers. Now they are in the van of e-anything. They are consultants. They are tax advisers. They are advisers to the world on the transforming of economies. Their organizations are huge financial services colossi bestriding the globe. None of the professions that you might have expected to do this has done so. Lawyers may well be fabulously rich. But they have had not a tenth of the imagination and business acumen that has carried the accountancy profession so far.
>
> And now it looks as though we are entering a phase in which the profession is about to evolve again. The most obvious sign of this is the turmoil in Pricewaterhouse-Coopers, the world's largest firm. Just under two years ago the constituent parts of Price-Waterhouse and Coopers & Lybrand were insisting that a merger to create a vast leviathan of a partnership was the only way forward. Now, less than two years later, the talk is all of breaking it up and changing the focus of the large accounting firm yet again.
>
> At the time of the merger the firms argued furiously that it was the only way. The story was that only by going hugely global could the firms raise the capital needed properly to service a global range of clients. Vast investments in technology were, it was argued, a matter of survival. Clients were furious. Finance directors and clients were in open revolt. The reduction of the big firms to a mere five would create

huge areas of conflict. Regulators were grudging in their eventual formal approval. But the firm had its way. And in two months' time it will celebrate two years of the merged organization.

But now it all looks very different. The firms no longer want consultancy arms. They no longer want outsourcing firms. They want to realize the value of the different areas of business they transformed. Partly, the firms will argue, this is because of the pressure from regulators. And certainly Pricewaterhouse-Coopers, after its lamentable showing on the ethics front in America, is quite properly being pressed by the main regulator there, the Securities and Exchange Commission (SEC).

The SEC, like many regulators around the world, is unhappy about firms offering both audit and consultancy services. It is unhappy about possible conflicts of interest. The firms say that clients are grown-ups and know what they are buying and will buy from whoever they reckon will do the best job. This is one factor in the drive for the firms to change strategic direction.

They need to retrench. They will define the core as quality advice and quality execution of skills. Partners will be more secure and, after the fright that spiraling costs and plummeting profitability gave them, will become once more canny and wealthy souls. It is an interesting thought. But it does look as though the next evolutionary stage for the accountancy profession is to reinvent itself in the image of the traditional Scottish accountant – revered for integrity, advice and a sly cunning when it comes to money-making.[18]

One might say, the accounting profession is not so much in crisis as in the midst of substantial change. Individual professionals are absorbed into accounting firms. Other accountants are entering into the financial service areas of financial planning and joining in multi-disciplinary firms, associations which bring with them a host of their own problems. All of these issues need to be addressed, but are not within the scope of this work.

What we have tried to do in this book is give a method for evaluating what the accountant ought to do, what responsibilities the accountant has. The general approach is to look at the various functions an accountant performs, the specific responsibilities of those functions, and how those are to be performed well with honesty and integrity. We have not studied all the possible activities and functions of the accountant. We have concentrated on what we take to be the three main functions – auditing, managerial accounting, and tax accounting. For the others, the ethical evaluation scheme is fairly straightforward: look at the purpose of the activity and judge how well that purpose is being fulfilled. Finally, look at the relationships involved in that function and determine what ethical responsibilities those ethical relationships involve.

▲ NOTES ▲

1. As quoted in Abraham J. Briloff, *The Truth About Corporate Accounting* (Harper & Row, 1980), p. 149.
2. Gretchen Morgenson, "S.E.C. Seeks Increased Scrutiny And New Rules for Accountants," *New York Times*, May 11, 2000, Thursday, late edition, section C Business/Financial Desk, p. 1, column 2.
3. Morgenson, ibid.
4. Nanette Byrnes et al., "Accounting In Crisis," *Business Week*, January 28, 2002, pp. 44–8.
5. Milton Friedman, "The Social Responsibility of Business is to Increase Its Profits," *New York Times Magazine*, September 13, 1970.
6. Adam Smith, *The Wealth of Nations*, 1776 (Ed. Edwin Canan. New York: Random House, 1937), I, ii, 2.
7. Ibid.
8. Milton Friedman, "The Social Responsibility of Business is to Increase Its Profits," *New York Times Magazine*, September 13, 1970.
9. Cf. David Gauthier, *Morals By Agreement* (Oxford University Press, 1987).
10. Thomas G. Labrecque's article, "Good Ethics in Good Business," *USA Today Magazine*, May 1990, p. 21. Copyright © by Society for the Advancement of Education.
11. Archie Carroll paints a picture of the immoral manager in his article "In Search of the Moral Manager," *Business Horizons*, March/April 1987, p. 8: "If Management is actively opposed to what is regarded as ethical, the clear implication is that management knows right from wrong. Thus, it is motivated by greed. Its goals are profitability and organizational success at almost any price. Immoral management does not care about others' claims to be treated fairly or justly."
12. Kenneth Lux, quoted in *Business Ethics*, May/June, 1991, p. 30.
13. "The Hustling of Rated Shelters" in *Forbes Magazine*, December 14, 1998.
14. Rick Telberg, editorial, *Accounting Today*, September 26, 1999.
15. Securities and Exchange Commission: Revision of the Commission's Auditor Independence Requirements, 17 CFR, Parts 210 and 240. Available at http://www.sec.gov/rules/final/p27–4504.
16. John C. Bogle, "Public Accounting: Profession or Business?" presentation at NYU, October 16, 2000. Available online at www.cpaindependence.org.

17. Cf. Nanette Byrnes et al., "Accounting in Crisis," *Business Week*, January 28, 2002, pp. 45ff.
18. Robert Bruce, "Evolution Will Bring Salvation," *The Times* (London), Thursday, April 27, 2000.

appendix i

The Code of Professional Conduct of the American Institute of Certified Public Accountants

The Code of Professional Conduct of the American Institute of Certified Public Accountants consists of two sections: (1) the Principles and (2) the Rules. The Principles provide the framework for the Rules, which govern the performance of professional services by members. The Council of the AICPA is authorized to designate bodies to promulgate technical standards under the Rules, and the *bylaws* require adherence to those Rules and standards.

The Code of Professional Conduct was adopted by the membership to provide guidance and rules to all members – those in public practice, in industry, in government, and in education – in the performance of their professional responsibilities.

Compliance with the Code of Professional Conduct, as with all standards in an open society, depends primarily on members' understanding and voluntary actions, secondarily on reinforcement by peers and public opinion, and ultimately on disciplinary proceedings, when necessary, against members who fail to comply with the Rules.

Interpretations of Rules of Conduct consist of interpretations which have been adopted, after exposure to state societies, state boards, practice units and other interested parties, by the professional ethics division's executive committee to provide guidelines as to the scope and application of the Rules but are not intended to limit such scope or application. A member who departs from such guidelines shall have the burden of justifying such departure in any disciplinary hearing. *Interpretations* which existed before the adoption of the Code of Professional Conduct on January 12, 1988, will remain in effect until further action is deemed necessary by the appropriate senior technical committee.

Ethics Rulings consist of formal rulings made by the professional ethics division's executive committee after exposure to state societies, state boards, practice units and other interested parties. These rulings summarize the application of Rules of Conduct and Interpretations to a particular set of factual circumstances. Members who depart from such rulings in similar circumstances will be requested to justify such departures. *Ethics Rulings* which existed before the adoption of the Code of Professional Conduct on January 12, 1988, will remain in effect until further action is deemed necessary by the appropriate senior technical committee.

Publication of an Interpretation or Ethics Ruling in *The Journal of Accountancy* constitutes notice to members. Hence, the effective date of the pronouncement is the last day of the month in which the pronouncement is published in *The Journal of Accountancy*. The professional ethics division will take into consideration the time that would have been reasonable for the member to comply with the pronouncement.

A member should also consult, if applicable, the ethical standards of his state CPA society, state board of accountancy, the Securities and Exchange Commission, and any other governmental agency which may regulate his client's business or use his report to evaluate the client's compliance with applicable laws and related regulations.

▲ Section 50 – Principles of ▲ Professional Conduct

Preamble

.01 Membership in the American Institute of Certified Public Accountants is voluntary. By accepting membership, a certified public accountant assumes an obligation of self-discipline above and beyond the requirements of laws and regulations.

.02 These Principles of the Code of Professional Conduct of the American Institute of Certified Public Accountants express the profession's recognition of its responsibilities to the public, to clients, and to colleagues. They guide members in the performance of their professional responsibilities and express the basic tenets of ethical and professional conduct. The Principles call for an unswerving commitment to honorable behavior, even at the sacrifice of personal advantage.

Section 52 – Article I: Responsibilities
In carrying out their responsibilities as professionals, members should exercise sensitive professional and moral judgments in all their activities.

.01 As professionals, certified public accountants perform an essential role in society. Consistent with that role, members of the American Institute of Certified Public Accountants have responsibilities to all those who use their professional services. Members also have a continuing responsibility to cooperate with each other to improve the art of accounting, maintain the public's confidence, and carry out the profession's special responsibilities for self-governance. The collective efforts of all members are required to maintain and enhance the traditions of the profession.

Section 53 – Article II: The Public Interest
Members should accept the obligation to act in a way that will serve the public interest, honor the public trust, and demonstrate commitment to professionalism.

.01 A distinguishing mark of a profession is acceptance of its responsibility to the public. The accounting profession's public consists of clients, credit grantors, governments, employers, investors, the business and financial community, and others who rely on the objectivity and integrity of certified public accountants to maintain the orderly functioning of commerce. This reliance imposes a public interest responsibility on certified public accountants. The public interest is defined as the collective well-being of the community of people and institutions the profession serves.

.02 In discharging their professional responsibilities, members may encounter conflicting pressures from among each of those groups. In resolving those conflicts, members should act with integrity, guided by the precept that when members fulfill their responsibility to the public, clients' and employers' interests are best served.

.03 Those who rely on certified public accountants expect them to discharge their responsibilities with integrity, objectivity, due professional care, and a genuine interest in serving the public. They are expected to provide quality services, enter into fee arrangements, and offer a range of services – all in a manner that demonstrates a level of professionalism consistent with these Principles of the Code of Professional Conduct.

.04 All who accept membership in the American Institute of Certified Public Accountants commit themselves to honor the public trust. In return for the faith that the public reposes in them, members should seek continually to demonstrate their dedication to professional excellence.

Section 54 – Article III: Integrity

To maintain and broaden public confidence, members should perform all professional responsibilities with the highest sense of integrity.

.01 Integrity is an element of character fundamental to professional recognition. It is the quality from which the public trust derives and the benchmark against which a member must ultimately test all decisions.

.02 Integrity requires a member to be, among other things, honest and candid within the constraints of client confidentiality. Service and the public trust should not be subordinated to personal gain and advantage. Integrity can accommodate the inadvertent error and the honest difference of opinion; it cannot accommodate deceit or subordination of principle.

.03 Integrity is measured in terms of what is right and just. In the absence of specific rules, standards, or guidance, or in the face of conflicting opinions, a member should test decisions and deeds by asking: "Am I doing what a person of integrity would do? Have I retained my integrity?" Integrity requires a member to observe both the form and the spirit of technical and ethical standards; circumvention of those standards constitutes subordination of judgment.

.04 Integrity also requires a member to observe the principles of objectivity and independence and of due care.

Section 55 – Article IV: Objectivity and Independence

A member should maintain objectivity and be free of conflicts of interest in discharging professional responsibilities. A member in public practice should be independent in fact and appearance when providing auditing and other attestation services.

.01 Objectivity is a state of mind, a quality that lends value to a member's services. It is a distinguishing feature of the profession. The principle of objectivity imposes the obligation to be impartial, intellectually honest, and free of conflicts of interest. Independence precludes relationships that may appear to impair a member's objectivity in rendering attestation services.

.02 Members often serve multiple interests in many different capacities and must demonstrate their objectivity in varying circumstances. Members in public practice render attest, tax, and management advisory services. Other members prepare financial statements in the employment of others, perform internal auditing services, and serve in financial and management capacities in industry, education, and government. They also educate and train those who aspire to admission into the profession. Regardless of service or capacity, members should protect the integrity of their work, maintain objectivity, and avoid any subordination of their judgment.

.03 For a member in public practice, the maintenance of objectivity and independence requires a continuing assessment of client relationships and public responsibility. Such a member who provides auditing and other attestation services should be independent in fact and appearance. In providing all other services, a member should maintain objectivity and avoid conflicts of interest.

.04 Although members not in public practice cannot maintain the appearance of independence, they nevertheless have the responsibility to maintain objectivity in rendering professional services. Members employed by others to prepare financial statements or to perform auditing, tax, or consulting services are charged with the same responsibility for objectivity as members in public practice and must be scrupulous in their application of generally accepted accounting principles and candid in all their dealings with members in public practice.

Section 56 – Article V: Due Care

A member should observe the profession's technical and ethical standards, strive continually to improve competence and the quality of services, and discharge professional responsibility to the best of the member's ability.

.01 The quest for excellence is the essence of due care. Due care requires a member to discharge professional responsibilities with competence and diligence. It imposes the obligation to perform professional services to the best of a member's ability with concern for the best interest of those for whom the services are performed and consistent with the profession's responsibility to the public.

.02 Competence is derived from a synthesis of education and experience. It begins with a mastery of the common body of knowledge required for designation as a certified public accountant. The maintenance of competence requires a commitment to learning and professional improvement that must continue throughout a member's professional life. It is a member's individual responsibility. In all engagements and in all responsibilities, each member should undertake to achieve a level of competence that will assure that the quality of the member's services meets the high level of professionalism required by these Principles.

.03 Competence represents the attainment and maintenance of a level of understanding and knowledge that enables a member to render services with facility and acumen. It also establishes the limitations of a member's capabilities by dictating that consultation or referral may be required when a professional engagement exceeds the personal competence of a member or a member's firm. Each member is responsible for assessing his or her own competence – of evaluating whether education, experience, and judgment are adequate for the responsibility to be assumed.

.04 Members should be diligent in discharging responsibilities to clients, employers, and the public. Diligence imposes the responsibility to render services promptly and carefully, to be thorough, and to observe applicable technical and ethical standards.

.05 Due care requires a member to plan and supervise adequately any professional activity for which he or she is responsible.

Section 57 – Article VI: Scope and Nature of Services
A member in public practice should observe the Principles of the Code of Professional Conduct in determining the scope and nature of services to be provided.
.01 The public interest aspect of certified public accountants' services requires that such services be consistent with acceptable professional behavior for certified public accountants. Integrity requires that service and the public trust not be subordinated to personal gain and advantage. Objectivity and independence require that members be free from conflicts of interest in discharging professional responsibilities. Due care requires that services be provided with competence and diligence.

.02 Each of these Principles should be considered by members in determining whether or not to provide specific services in individual circumstances. In some instances, they may represent an overall constraint on the nonaudit services that might be offered to a specific client. No hard-and-fast rules can be developed to help members reach these judgments, but they must be satisfied that they are meeting the spirit of the Principles in this regard.

.03 In order to accomplish this, members should

* Practice in firms that have in place internal quality-control procedures to ensure that services are competently delivered and adequately supervised.
* Determine, in their individual judgments, whether the scope and nature of other services provided to an audit client would create a conflict of interest in the performance of the audit function for that client.
* Assess, in their individual judgments, whether an activity is consistent with their role as professionals (for example, Is such activity a reasonable extension or variation of existing services offered by the member or others in the profession?).

Section 90 – Rules: Applicability and Definitions

Section 91 – Applicability

As adopted January 12, 1988,
unless otherwise indicated

.01 The bylaws of the American Institute of Certified Public Accountants require that members adhere to the Rules of the Code of Professional Conduct. Members must be prepared to justify departures from these Rules.

.02 *Interpretation Addressing the Applicability of the AICPA Code of Professional Conduct.* For purposes of the applicability section of the Code, a "member" is a member or international associate of the American Institute of CPAs.

1. The Rules of Conduct that follow apply to all professional services performed except (*a*) where the wording of the rule indicates otherwise and (*b*) that a member who is practicing outside the United States will not be subject to discipline for departing from any of the rules stated herein as long as the member's conduct is in accord with the rules of the organized accounting profession in the country in which he or she is practicing. However, where a member's name is associated with

financial statements under circumstances that would entitle the reader to assume that United States practices were followed, the member must comply with the requirements of Rules 202 and 203.

2.   A member shall not knowingly permit a person, whom the member has the authority or capacity to control, to carry out on his or her behalf, either with or without compensation, acts which, if carried out by the member, would place the member in violation of the rules. Further, a member may be held responsible for the acts of all persons associated with him or her in the practice of public accounting whom the member has the authority or capacity to control.

3.   A member (as defined in interpretation 101–9) may be considered to have his or her independence impaired, with respect to a client, as the result of the actions or relationships of certain persons or entities, as described in Rule 101 and its interpretations and rulings, whom the member does not have the authority or capacity to control. Therefore, nothing in this section should lead one to conclude that the member's independence is not impaired solely because of his or her inability to control the actions or relationships of such persons or entities.

[Paragraph added, August, 1989, effective November 30, 1989. Revised December, 1998.]

Section 92 – Definitions

As adopted January 12, 1988, unless otherwise indicated

[*Pursuant to its authority under the bylaws (BL § 3.6.2.2) to interpret the Code of Professional Conduct, the Professional Ethics Executive Committee has issued the following definitions of terms appearing in the code effective November 30, 1989.*]

.01 Client. (This replaces the previous definition of "Client" at paragraph .01.) A client is any person or entity, other than the member's employer, that engages a member or a member's firm to perform professional services or a person or entity with respect to which professional services are performed. For purposes of this paragraph, the term "employer" does not include –

A.   Entities engaged in the practice of public accounting; or

B.   Federal, state, and local governments or component units thereof provided the member performing professional services with respect to those entities –

    i. Is directly elected by voters of the government or compo-
nent unit thereof with respect to which professional services
are performed; or
   ii. Is an individual who is (1) appointed by a legislative body
and (2) subject to removal by a legislative body; or
  iii. Is appointed by someone other than the legislative body, so
long as the appointment is confirmed by the legislative
body and removal is subject to oversight or approval by the
legislative body.
[Revised December, 1998.]

.02 Council. The Council of the American Institute of Certified
Public Accountants.

.03 Enterprise. (This replaces the previous definition of "Enterprise" at paragraph .03.) For purposes of the Code, the term
"enterprise" is synonymous with the term "client."

.04 Financial statements. A presentation of financial data, including accompanying notes, if any, intended to communicate an entity's
economic resources and/or obligations at a point in time or the
changes therein for a period of time, in accordance with generally
accepted accounting principles or a comprehensive basis of accounting other than generally accepted accounting principles.

Incidental financial data to support recommendations to a client
or in documents for which the reporting is governed by Statements
on Standards for Attestation Engagements and tax returns and
supporting schedules do not, for this purpose, constitute financial
statements. The statement, affidavit, or signature of preparers
required on tax returns neither constitutes an opinion on financial
statements nor requires a disclaimer of such opinion.
[Revised May, 1996.]

.05 Firm. A form of organization permitted by state law or regulation whose characteristics conform to resolutions of Council that is
engaged in the practice of public accounting, including the individual
owners thereof.
[Revised January, 1992.]

.06 Institute. The American Institute of Certified Public
Accountants.

.07 Interpretations of rules of conduct. Pronouncements issued
by the division of professional ethics to provide guidelines concerning
the scope and application of the rules of conduct.

.08 Member. A member, associate member, or international associate of the American Institute of Certified Public Accountants.

.09 Practice of public accounting. (This replaces the previous definition of "Practice of public accounting" at paragraph .09.) The practice of public accounting consists of the performance for a client, by a member or a member's firm, while holding out as CPA(s), of the professional services of accounting, tax, personal financial planning, litigation support services, and those professional services for which standards are promulgated by bodies designated by Council, such as Statements of Financial Accounting Standards, Statements on Auditing Standards, Statements on Standards for Accounting and Review Services, Statement on Standards for Consulting Services, Statements of Governmental Accounting Standards, and Statements on Standards for Attestation Engagements.

However, a member or a member's firm, while holding out as CPA(s), is not considered to be in the practice of public accounting if the member or the member's firm does not perform, for any client, any of the professional services described in the preceding paragraph. [Revised April, 1992.]

.10 Professional services. (This replaces the previous definition of "Professional services" at paragraph .10.) Professional services include all services performed by a member while holding out as a CPA.

.11 Holding out. In general, any action initiated by a member that informs others of his or her status as a CPA or AICPA-accredited specialist constitutes holding out as a CPA. This would include, for example, any oral or written representation to another regarding CPA status, use of the CPA designation on business cards or letterhead, the display of a certificate evidencing a member's CPA designation, or listing as a CPA in local telephone directories.

Section 100 – Independence, Integrity, and Objectivity

ET Section 101 – Independence

.01 Rule 101 – Independence. A member in public practice shall be independent in the performance of professional services as required by standards promulgated by bodies designated by Council. [As adopted January 12, 1988.]

Interpretations under Rule 101 – Independence

In the performance of professional services requiring independence, a member should consult his or her state board of public accountancy, his or her state CPA society if applicable, the Independence Standards Board if the client is a registrant of the U.S. Securities and Exchange Commission, the U.S. Department of Labor (DOL) if the client or the client's sponsor is required to report to the DOL, and any other regulatory or private organization that issues or enforces standards of independence. Such bodies may have independence interpretations or rulings that significantly differ from and are more restrictive than those of the AICPA.

.02 101–1 – Interpretation of Rule 101. Independence shall be considered to be impaired if, for example, a member had any of the following transactions, interests, or relationships:

A. During the period of a professional engagement or at the time of expressing an opinion, a member or a member's firm

    1. Had or was committed to acquire any direct or material indirect financial interest in the enterprise.

    2. Was a trustee of any trust or executor or administrator of any estate if such trust or estate had or was committed to acquire any direct or material indirect financial interest in the enterprise.

    3. Had any joint, closely held business investment with the enterprise or with any officer, director, or principal stockholders thereof that was material in relation to the member's net worth or to the net worth of the member's firm.

    4. Had any loan to or from the enterprise or any officer, director, or principal stockholder of the enterprise except as specifically permitted in interpretation 101–5.

B. During the period covered by the financial statements, during the period of the professional engagement, or at the time of expressing an opinion, a member or a member's firm

    1. Was connected with the enterprise as a promoter, underwriter or voting trustee, as a director or officer, or in any capacity equivalent to that of a member of management or of an employee.

    2. Was a trustee for any pension or profit-sharing trust of the enterprise.

.01 Rule 102 – Integrity and objectivity. In the performance of any professional service, a member shall maintain objectivity and integrity, shall be free of conflicts of interest, and shall not

knowingly misrepresent facts or subordinate his or her judgment to others.
[As adopted January 12, 1988.]

Interpretations under Rule 102 – Integrity and Objectivity

.02 102–1 – Knowing misrepresentations in the preparation of financial statements or records. A member who knowingly makes, or permits or directs another to make, false and misleading entries in an entity's financial statements or records shall be considered to have knowingly misrepresented facts in violation of Rule 102.

.03 102–2 – Conflicts of interest. A conflict of interest may occur if a member performs a professional service for a client or employer and the member or his or her firm has a relationship with another person, entity, product, or service that could, in the member's professional judgment, be viewed by the client, employer, or other appropriate parties as impairing the member's objectivity. If the member believes that the professional service can be performed with objectivity, and the relationship is disclosed to and consent is obtained from such client, employer, or other appropriate parties, the rule shall not operate to prohibit the performance of the professional service. When making the disclosure, the member should consider Rule 301, *Confidential client information.*

Certain professional engagements, such as audits, reviews, and other attest services, require independence. Independence impairments under Rule 101, its interpretations, and rulings cannot be eliminated by such disclosure and consent.

.01 Rule 201 – General standards. A member shall comply with the following standards and with any interpretations thereof by bodies designated by Council.

A. *Professional Competence.* Undertake only those professional services that the member or the member's firm can reasonably expect to be completed with professional competence.

B. *Due Professional Care.* Exercise due professional care in the performance of professional services.

C. *Planning and Supervision.* Adequately plan and supervise the performance of professional services.

D. *Sufficient Relevant Data.* Obtain sufficient relevant data to afford a reasonable basis for conclusions or recommendations in relation to any professional services performed.

[As adopted January 12, 1988.]

.01 Rule 202 – Compliance with standards. A member who performs auditing, review, compilation, management consulting, tax, or other professional services shall comply with standards promulgated by bodies designated by Council.
[As adopted January 12, 1988.]

.01 Rule 203 – Accounting principles. A member shall not (1) express an opinion or state affirmatively that the financial statements or other financial data of any entity are presented in conformity with generally accepted accounting principles or (2) state that he or she is not aware of any material modifications that should be made to such statements or data in order for them to be in conformity with generally accepted accounting principles, if such statements or data contain any departure from an accounting principle promulgated by bodies designated by Council to establish such principles that has a material effect on the statements or data taken as a whole. If, however, the statements or data contain such a departure and the member can demonstrate that due to unusual circumstances the financial statements or data would otherwise have been misleading, the member can comply with the rule by describing the departure, its approximate effects, if practicable, and the reasons why compliance with the principle would result in a misleading statement.
[As adopted January 12, 1988.]

.01 Rule 301 – Confidential client information. A member in public practice shall not disclose any confidential client information without the specific consent of the client.

This rule shall not be construed (1) to relieve a member of his or her professional obligations under Rules 202 and 203, (2) to affect in any way the member's obligation to comply with a validly issued and enforceable subpoena or summons, or to prohibit a member's compliance with applicable laws and government regulations, (3) to prohibit review of a member's professional practice under AICPA or state CPA society or Board of Accountancy authorization, or (4) to preclude a member from initiating a complaint with, or responding to any inquiry made by, the professional ethics division or trial board of the Institute or a duly constituted investigative or disciplinary body of a state CPA society or Board of Accountancy.

Members of any of the bodies identified in (4) above and members involved with professional practice reviews identified in (3) above

shall not use to their own advantage or disclose any member's confidential client information that comes to their attention in carrying out those activities. This prohibition shall not restrict members' exchange of information in connection with the investigative or disciplinary proceedings described in (4) above or the professional practice reviews described in (3) above.
[As amended January 14, 1992.]

.01 Rule 302 – Contingent fees. A member in public practice shall not

(1) Perform for a contingent fee any professional services for, or receive such a fee from a client for whom the member or the member's firm performs,
(a) an audit or review of a financial statement; or
(b) a compilation of a financial statement when the member expects, or reasonably might expect, that a third party will use the financial statement and the member's compilation report does not disclose a lack of independence; or
(c) an examination of prospective financial information; or
(2) Prepare an original or amended tax return or claim for a tax refund for a contingent fee for any client.

The prohibition in (1) above applies during the period in which the member or the member's firm is engaged to perform any of the services listed above and the period covered by any historical financial statements involved in any such listed services.

Except as stated in the next sentence, a contingent fee is a fee established for the performance of any service pursuant to an arrangement in which no fee will be charged unless a specified finding or result is attained, or in which the amount of the fee is otherwise dependent upon the finding or result of such service. Solely for purposes of this rule, fees are not regarded as being contingent if fixed by courts or other public authorities, or, in tax matters, if determined based on the results of judicial proceedings or the findings of governmental agencies.

A member's fees may vary depending, for example, on the complexity of services rendered.
[As adopted May 20, 1991.]

.01 Rule 501 – Acts discreditable. A member shall not commit an act discreditable to the profession.
[As adopted January 12, 1988.]

appendix ii

Institute of Management Accountants: Ethical Standards

Ethical Behavior for Practitioners of Management Accounting and Financial Management

In today's modern world of business, individuals in management accounting and financial management constantly face ethical dilemmas. For example, if the accountant's immediate superior instructs the accountant to record the physical inventory at its original costs when it is obvious that the inventory has a reduced value due to obsolescence, what should the accountant do? To help make such a decision, here is a brief general discussion of ethics and the standards of conduct for practitioners of management accounting and financial management.

Ethics, in its broader sense, deals with human conduct in relation to what is morally good and bad, right and wrong. To determine whether a decision is good or bad, the decision maker must compare his/her options with some standard of perfection. This standard of perfection is not a statement of static position but requires the decision maker to assess the situation and the values of the parties affected by the decision. The decision maker must then estimate the outcome of the decision and be responsible for its results. Two good questions to ask when faced with an ethical dilemma are, "Will my actions be fair and just to all parties affected?" and "Would I be pleased to have my closest friends learn of my actions?"

Individuals in management accounting and financial management have a unique set of circumstances relating to their employment. To help them assess their situation, the Institute of Management Accountants has developed the following *Standards of Ethical Conduct for Practioners of Management Accounting and Financial Management.*

Practitioners of management accounting and financial management have an obligation to the public, their profession, the organization they serve, and themselves, to maintain the highest standards of ethical conduct. In recognition of this obligation, the Institute of Management Accountants has promulgated the following standards of ethical conduct for practitioners of management accounting and financial management. Adherence to these standards, both domestically and internationally, is integral to achieving the *Objectives of Management Accounting*. Practitioners of management accounting and financial management shall not commit acts contrary to these standards nor shall they condone the commission of such acts by others within their organizations.

Competence

Practitioners of management accounting and financial management have a responsibility to:
- Maintain an appropriate level of professional competence by ongoing development of their knowledge and skills.
- Perform their professional duties in accordance with relevant laws, regulations, and technical standards.
- Prepare complete and clear reports and recommendations after appropriate analyses of relevant and reliable information.

Confidentiality

Practitioners of management accounting and financial management have a responsibility to:
- Refrain from disclosing confidential information acquired in the course of their work except when authorized, unless legally obligated to do so.
- Inform subordinates as appropriate regarding the confidentiality of information acquired in the course of their work and monitor their activities to assure the maintenance of that confidentiality.
- Refrain from using or appearing to use confidential information acquired in the course of their work for unethical or illegal advantage either personally or through third parties.

Integrity

Practitioners of management accounting and financial management have a responsibility to:
- Avoid actual or apparent conflicts of interest and advise all appropriate parties of any potential conflict.
- Refrain from engaging in any activity that would prejudice their ability to carry out their duties ethically.
- Refuse any gift, favor, or hospitality that would influence or would appear to influence their actions.
- Refrain from either actively or passively subverting the attainment of the organization's legitimate and ethical objectives.
- Recognize and communicate professional limitations or other constraints that would preclude responsible judgment or successful performance of an activity.
- Communicate unfavorable as well as favorable information and professional judgments or opinions.
- Refrain from engaging in or supporting any activity that would discredit the profession.

Objectivity

Practitioners of management accounting and financial management have a responsibility to:
- Communicate information fairly and objectively.
- Disclose fully all relevant information that could reasonably be expected to influence an intended user's understanding of the reports, comments, and recommendations presented.

Resolution of ethical conflict

In applying the standards of ethical conduct, practitioners of management accounting and financial management may encounter problems in identifying unethical behavior or in resolving an ethical conflict. When faced with significant ethical issues, practitioners of management accounting and financial management should follow the established policies of the organization bearing on the resolution of such conflict. If these policies do not resolve the ethical conflict, such practitioners should consider the following courses of action.
- Discuss such problems with the immediate superior except when it appears that the superior is involved, in which case the problem

should be presented initially to the next higher managerial level. If a satisfactory resolution cannot be achieved when the problem is initially presented, submit the issues to the next higher managerial level. If the immediate superior is the chief executive officer, or equivalent, the acceptable reviewing authority may be a group such as the audit committee, executive committee, board of directors, board of trustees, or owners. Contact with levels above the immediate superior should be initiated only with the superior's knowledge, assuming the superior is not involved. Except where legally prescribed, communication of such problems to authorities or individuals not employed or engaged by the organization is not considered appropriate.

- Clarify relevant ethical issues by confidential discussion with an objective advisor (e.g. IMA Ethics Counseling Service) to obtain a better understanding of possible courses of action. Consult your own attorney as to legal obligations and rights concerning the ethical conflict.

- If the ethical conflict still exists after exhausting all levels of internal review, there may be no other recourse on significant matters than to resign from the organization and to submit an informative memorandum to an appropriate representative of the organization. After resignation, depending on the nature of the ethical conflict, it may also be appropriate to notify other parties.

Statement on Auditing Standards: A Summary

CONSIDERATION OF FRAUD IN A FINANCIAL STATEMENT AUDIT[1]

February 28, 2002

(Supersedes Statement on Auditing Standards No. 82, Consideration of Fraud in a Financial Statement Audit, AU section 316 (which superseded SAS 53 "The Auditor's Responsibility to Detect Errors and Irregularities" and amends SAS No. 1, Codification of Auditing Standards and Procedures, vol. 1, AU section 230, "Due Professional Care in the Performance of Work").

Prepared by the AICPA Auditing Standards Board for comment from persons interested in auditing and reporting issues.

EFFECTIVE DATE

This Statement is effective for audits of financial statements for periods beginning on or after December 15, 2002. Early application of the provisions of this Statement is permissible.

SUMMARY

Why issued

This proposed Statement on Auditing Standards (SAS) establishes standards and provides guidance to auditors in fulfilling their responsibility as it relates to fraud in an audit of financial statements conducted in accordance with generally accepted auditing standards (GAAS). The exposure draft also includes Appendix B, "A Proposed Amendment to SAS No. 1, Codification of Auditing

Standards and Procedures (AICPA, Professional Standards, vol. 1, AU section 230, 'Due Professional Care in the Performance of Work')." In 1997 the Auditing Standards Board (ASB) issued SAS No. 82, Consideration of Fraud in a Financial Statement Audit (AICPA, Professional Standards, vol.1, AU sections 110, 230, 312, and 316), with an objective of enhancing auditor performance by providing auditors with additional operational guidance on the consideration of material fraud in a financial statement audit.

At the time of issuance of SAS No. 82, the ASB committed to study the impact the standard would have on practice after its implementation and determine whether further enhancements would be appropriate. In response to that commitment, the Fraud Research Steering Task Force was formed and sponsored five academic research projects to obtain information that would be useful in the reexamination. The results of those research projects are briefly summarized in a section entitled "Additional Background Information."

In 1998, at the request of the Securities and Exchange Commission, the Public Oversight Board (POB) appointed a Panel on Audit Effectiveness (the Panel) to examine the current audit model, including the way independent audits are performed regarding the auditor's consideration of fraud. The Panel provided a "Report and Recommendations" on August 31, 2000, including a number of recommendations addressed to the ASB that concerned earnings management and fraud.

Since the issuance of SAS No. 82, the International Auditing Practices Committee (IAPC) of the International Federation of Accountants has examined the auditor's responsibility to consider fraud and error, resulting in the issuance of a revised International Standard on Auditing (ISA 240) in the spring of 2001. That standard incorporated many of the concepts formulated in SAS No. 82 and provided guidance beyond that included in SAS No. 82.

Largely in response to the developments outlined above, the current Fraud Task Force was formed in September 2000. Its objective directed the Task Force to consider the need to revise SAS No. 82 based on the preceding academic research, recommendations from the Panel, and information and recommendations provided by other financial reporting stakeholders. It also instructed the Task Force to be sensitive to international developments and the long-term need to work toward global audit standard-setting solutions.

This important initiative of the ASB and its Fraud Task Force is part of a broader AICPA program to address the growing concerns about fraudulent financial reporting. Although the proposed Statement resulting from this initiative addresses the auditor's effectiveness in detecting material misstatements in financial statements due to fraud, broader efforts are needed focusing not only on the auditor's role, but on that of management, the audit committee, regulators, and others in addressing this important issue, and focusing not only on the *detection* of fraud, but on *prevention* and *deterrence* as well.

What it provides

This proposed Statement does not change the auditor's responsibility to plan and perform the audit to obtain reasonable assurance about whether the financial statements are free of material misstatement, whether caused by error or fraud (as described in AU section 110.01). However, the proposed Statement does establish standards and provide guidance to auditors in fulfilling that responsibility, as it relates to fraud.

The following is an overview of the content of the proposed Statement:

• *Description and characteristics of fraud.* This section of the proposed Statement describes fraud and its characteristics, including the aspects of fraud particularly relevant to an audit of financial statements. (See endnotes 2 and 3.)

• *Discussion among engagement personnel regarding the risks of material misstatement due to fraud.* This section requires, as part of planning the audit, that there be a discussion among the audit team members to consider the susceptibility of the entity to material misstatement due to fraud and to reinforce the importance of adopting an appropriate mindset of professional skepticism.

• *Obtaining the information needed to identify the risks of material misstatement due to fraud.* This section requires the auditor to gather the information necessary to identify the risks of material misstatement due to fraud, by the following:

1. Making inquiries of management and others within the entity;
2. Considering the results of the analytical procedures performed in planning the audit (the proposed Statement also requires that the auditor perform analytical procedures relating to revenue);
3. Considering fraud risk factors;
4. Considering certain other information.

• *Identifying risks that may result in a material misstatement due to fraud.* This section requires the auditor to use the information gathered above to identify risks that may result in a material misstatement due to fraud.

• *Assessing the identified risks after taking into account an evaluation of the entity's programs and controls.* This section requires the auditor to evaluate the entity's programs and controls that address the identified risks of material misstatement due to fraud, and to assess the risks taking into account this evaluation.

• *Responding to the results of the assessment.* This section requires the auditor to respond to the results of the risk assessment. This response may include the following:
1. A response to identified risks that has an overall effect on how the audit is conducted, that is, a response involving more general considerations apart from the specific procedures otherwise planned;
2. A response to identified risks that involves the nature, timing, and extent of the auditing procedures to be performed;
3. A response involving the performance of certain procedures to further address the risk of material misstatement due to fraud involving management override of controls.

• *Evaluating audit test results.* This section requires the auditor's assessment of the risk of material misstatement due to fraud to be ongoing throughout the audit and that the auditor evaluate at the completion of the audit whether the accumulated results of auditing procedures and other observations affect the assessment. It also requires the auditor to consider whether identified misstatements may be indicative of fraud and, if so, directs the auditor to evaluate their implications.

• *Communicating about fraud to management, the audit committee, and others.* This section provides guidance regarding the auditor's communications about fraud to management, the audit committee, and others.[4]

• *Documenting the auditor's consideration of fraud.* This section describes related documentation requirements.

▲ HOW IT AFFECTS PRACTICE ▲

The ASB believes that the requirements and guidance provided in the proposed Statement, if adopted, would result in a substantial change in auditor's performance and thereby improve the likelihood that auditors will detect material misstatements due to fraud in a financial statement audit. The ASB also believes that the proposed Statement's adoption would result in an increased focus on professional skepticism in the consideration of the risk of fraud in a financial statement audit. The following is a more specific discussion of the changes in the auditor's consideration of fraud that would result from the adoption of the proposed Statement as contrasted with presently existing standards. (See SAS No. 82.)

1. *Discussions among engagement personnel.* In response to a recommendation by the POB Panel on Audit Effectiveness that was widely supported in discussions with other stakeholders, the proposed Statement would require, as part of planning the audit, a discussion among the audit team members. The discussion would include the following:
• A sharing of insights and an exchange of ideas about how and where the audit team members believe the entity's financial statements might be susceptible to material misstatement due to fraud.
• Emphasizing the importance of maintaining the proper state of mind throughout the audit regarding the potential for material misstatement due to fraud.

2. *Expanded inquiries of management and others within the entity.* Consistent with input the Task Force received from stakeholders, particularly comments from forensic auditors regarding the effectiveness of appropriate inquiry as an auditing procedure that increases the likelihood of fraud detection, the proposed Statement expands the audit requirement and guidance regarding the inquiries of management and others. The expanded inquiries would include the following:

- Inquiries of management about (a) whether management has knowledge of fraud; (b) whether management is aware of any allegations of fraudulent financial reporting; (c) management's understanding about the risks of fraud in the entity; (d) the programs and controls that management has established to mitigate fraud risks and how management monitors such programs and controls; (e) for an entity with multiple locations, the nature and extent of monitoring of operating locations or business segments, and whether there are particular operating locations or business segments for which a risk of fraud may be more likely to exist; and (f) whether and how management communicates to employees its views on business practices and ethical behavior.

- An understanding of how the audit committee exercises its oversight of the entity's assessment of risks of fraud and the programs and controls the entity has established to mitigate those risks, and an inquiry of the audit committee (or at least its chair) regarding the audit committee's views about the risks of fraud and whether the audit committee has knowledge of any fraud or suspected fraud.

- For those entities with an internal audit function, an inquiry of appropriate internal audit personnel about their views of the risks of fraud, any procedures performed to identify or detect fraud and management's response to resulting findings, and whether they have knowledge of any fraud or suspected fraud.

In addition, the proposed Statement requires that the auditor use professional judgment to determine others within the entity (for example, operating management not directly involved in the financial reporting process and employees with different levels of authority) to whom inquiries should be directed and the extent of those inquiries.

3. *Reorganization and modification of risk factor examples.* The proposed Statement includes a reorganized presentation of fraud risk factor examples, following the three fundamental conditions existing when a fraud has occurred, that is, incentive/pressure, opportunity, and attitude/rationalization. An organization of the risk factors in the context of these three fundamental conditions facilitates the risk assessment. Regarding the risk factor examples themselves, the proposed Statement generally retains the SAS No. 82 factors, with selected additions.[5]

4. *Expanded fraud risk assessment approach.* The proposed Statement would require gathering a broader range of information as a source of input for the fraud risk assessment beyond simply the consideration of risk factors as provided in SAS No. 82. It also provides additional guidance on how this information is considered in the risk assessment. The output of the assessment process is identified risks of material misstatement due to fraud that should be considered in the auditor's response, not simply risk factors.

5. *Expanded guidance on revenue recognition as a likely risk.* Since material misstatements due to fraudulent financial reporting often involve revenue recognition issues, the proposed Statement notes that the auditor will ordinarily determine that there is a risk of material misstatement due to fraud relating to revenue recognition. The proposed Statement also provides additional guidance regarding possible responses by the auditor when revenue recognition has been identified as a risk.

6. *Evaluating the entity's response to identified fraud risks.* The proposed Statement contains expanded guidance dealing with the evaluation of an entity's response to identified fraud risks, and requires the auditor to assess the risks of material misstatement due to fraud after giving effect to the entity's programs and controls that address the risks.

7. *The linkage between identified risks and the auditor's response.* In response to the results of the AICPA-sponsored research and the feedback the Task Force received from practitioners, regarding the linkage of identified risks of material misstatement due to fraud with the auditor's response, the proposed Statement includes more extensive examples of responses to selected risks than contained in SAS No. 82.

8. *Professional skepticism.* In a response to widespread comments gathered in the Task Force's solicitation of input, including comments in the POB Panel's "Report and Recommendations," the proposed Statement increases the focus on professional skepticism, including (a) the discussion of its importance in audit team planning meetings (see point 1 above) and (b) its effect as it relates to the gathering and evaluation of evidential matter when fraud risks are identified.[6]

9. *Responses to further address the risk of management override of*

controls. The POB Panel recommended a requirement for the auditor to perform specified substantive tests, primarily in response to a risk of management override that cannot easily be addressed through reliance on traditional controls. An example of such tests recommended by the POB Panel is the examination of nonstandard journal entries. The proposed Statement implements this recommendation by specifying selected auditing procedures that would be "appropriate for every audit – absent a conclusion by the auditor that, in the particular circumstance, their performance is unnecessary." The proposed Statement provides circumstances involving audits of non-public entities that might overcome the need to perform the procedures, and indicates that in a public entity audit the procedures should always be performed. The auditing procedures proposed to address the risk of management override would be the following:
• Examining journal entries and other adjustments;
• Reviewing accounting estimates for bias, including a retrospective review of significant management estimates;
• Evaluating the business rationale for significant unusual transactions.

10. *Documentation.* Although SAS No. 82 contains specific documentation requirements relating to the auditor's consideration of fraud, this proposed Statement significantly extends those requirements, requiring documentation supporting compliance with substantially all the major requirements of the proposed Statement. This is in response to a view that such documentation requirements will help ensure effective implementation of the requirements of the standard.

11. *Incorporating more of a technology focus into the SAS.* In response to observations from stakeholders, including recommendations from the Computer Auditing Subcommittee of the ASB, the proposed Statement incorporates added commentary and examples specifically recognizing the impact technology has on the risks of fraud, as well as noting the opportunities technology-oriented tools and techniques provide to the auditor in designing auditing procedures.

HOW IT AFFECTS EXISTING STANDARDS

A new SAS on fraud in a financial statement audit would:
• Supersede SAS No. 82.

• Amend SAS No. 1, Codification of Auditing Standards and Procedures (AICPA, Professional Standards, vol. 1, AU section 230, "Due Professional Care in the Performance of Work").

▲ COMMENTATOR GUIDE TO ▲ SIGNIFICANT ISSUES

The ASB and the Fraud Task Force have deliberated extensively on the merits of the proposed changes in auditing standards and have proposed what they believe are sound solutions to the issues they considered. Some of the significant issues that were considered are outlined below. The ASB and Fraud Task Force have an interest in the views and observations of commentators on these issues, as well as observations identifying other issues that may not have been addressed and conclusions in the proposed Statement that may be unclear.

The risk assessment approach

The overall approach to the assessment of material misstatement due to fraud in the proposed Statement includes (a) obtaining information necessary to identify the risks, (b) using that information to identify risks of material misstatement due to fraud, (c) assessing the identified risks after taking into account an evaluation of the entity's programs and controls that address the risks, and (d) responding to the results of the assessments. Is this approach understandable? How may this approach be improved?

Once the information necessary to identify the risks of material misstatement due to fraud has been accumulated, the proposed Statement provides guidance about factors to be considered in subsequently determining whether risks, in fact, exist. Are these factors appropriate? If not, describe how this guidance may be improved.

The classification of the risk factors

The risk factors are classified in the proposed statement by the three conditions present when fraud exists, that is, incentive/pressure, opportunity, and attitude/rationalization. Is there a more appropriate way to classify these factors?

Is the guidance directing the auditor to consider these same three conditions in the identification of the risks of material misstatement due to fraud appropriate and helpful? If not, how may the guidance be improved?

Identification of revenue recognition as a fraud risk

The proposed Statement indicates that the auditor will ordinarily determine that there is a risk of material misstatement due to fraud relating to revenue recognition. Does this guidance provide the appropriate emphasis on the issue of revenue recognition? If not, how may the guidance be improved? Are the examples outlining possible auditing procedures in response to a risk of material misstatement due to fraud relating to revenue recognition sufficient? Describe other examples of possible auditing procedures addressing this risk or other risks that should be included in the guidance on the auditor's response to this risk.

The consideration of the risk of management override of controls

Is the overall approach to how the auditor is required to consider the risk of management override of controls appropriate and sufficiently reconcilable with the existing audit risk model? Describe how this guidance may be improved.

Is the threshold presumption regarding the applicability of the required procedures in response to the risk of override appropriate, including the distinction in application between public and non-public entities? If not, describe how this guidance should be modified.

Are the specific procedures to be performed to further address the risk of management override of controls appropriate? Are they sufficiently defined? In this context, do you have suggestions for additional required procedures?

The inquiry of audit committees about fraud

In order to ensure appropriate sensitivity to and coordination with international standard setters, the Task Force activities were observed by four representatives closely involved with IAPC standard-setting activities. The Task Force also monitored concurrent fraud-related standard-setting activities of the IAPC.

The recommendations of the POB Panel on Audit Effectiveness

The Task Force's deliberations were influenced heavily by the recommendations contained in the August 2000 report of the POB Panel on Audit Effectiveness. The report is available at www.pobauditpanel.org. Chapter 3 of that report contains the Panel's findings on the effectiveness of audits in detecting fraud and a number of thoughtful recommendations directed to the ASB, audit firms, audit committees, and others aimed at improving the conduct of audits. In addition, a member of the Panel staff attended many Task Force meetings and two POB Board members attended a number of board deliberations on this subject, in both cases providing very helpful insights and suggestions.

The Panel's overriding directive to the ASB was "to develop stronger and more definitive auditing standards to effect a substantial change in auditors' performance and thereby improve the likelihood that auditors will detect fraudulent financial reporting." The substance of a great majority of the Panel's specific recommendations have been incorporated into the proposed Statement, and the ASB and Task Force believe that adoption of the proposed Statement will result in achieving the Panel's overriding directive.

The results of AICPA-sponsored academic research

As noted earlier in this summary, responsive to an AICPA commitment made at the time SAS No. 82 was issued, the AICPA sponsored five academic research projects that focused on the impact SAS No. 82 has had on practice.

On an overall basis, the research indicated that auditors are more responsive to fraud risk now than they were prior to the issuance of SAS No. 82. After SAS No. 82, research participants indicated a greater understanding of the need to revise audit programs in response to the presence of fraud risk factors than did pre-SAS No. 82 research participants. Once fraud risk factors have been identified, the research indicated that auditors were effective in reacting to increased risk by expanding tests and using more experienced staff on the engagement, but results were mixed on whether auditors effectively changed the nature of the auditing procedures performed. This is generally consistent with the feedback the Task Force received from practitioners indicating that responding effectively to identified fraud risks is more challenging than the identification of fraud risks.

The research observed that practitioners and forensic experts weight those fraud risk factors described in the SAS No. 82 "management characteristics" category as significantly more important than those in the other two SAS No. 82 categories, but the Task Force concluded that there was insufficient support for commenting on the relative weight of the risk factors in the proposed Statement. Risk factors identified as relevant in the research beyond those existing in SAS No. 82 were considered by the Task Force and, in some cases included in the proposed Statement.

⚜ IMPLEMENTATION GUIDANCE ⚜

In order to help with the implementation process of the proposed Statement, the AICPA plans to (a) develop appropriate continuing education material; (b) update the existing implementation guidance, "Considering Fraud in a Financial Statement Audit: Practical Guidance for Applying SAS No. 82"; and (c) work with other stakeholders to prepare guidance for financial statement preparers, audit committees, and auditors on management anti-fraud programs and controls, focusing not only on detection of fraud, but on prevention and deterrence as well.

⚜ Authors' Addendum ⚜
Paragraph 67
EVALUATING AUDIT TEST RESULTS

67. Assessing risks of material misstatement due to fraud throughout the audit. The auditor's assessment of the risks of material misstatement due to fraud should be ongoing throughout the audit. Conditions may be identified during fieldwork that change or support a judgment regarding the assessment of the risks, such as the following:
• Discrepancies in the accounting records, including:
  – Transactions that are not recorded in a complete or timely manner or are improperly recorded as to amount, accounting period, classification, or entity policy;
  – Unsupported or unauthorized balances or transactions;

- Last-minute adjustments that significantly affect financial results;
- Evidence of employees' access to systems and records inconsistent with that necessary to perform their authorized duties.
• Conflicting or missing evidential matter, including:
  - Missing documents;
  - Unavailability of other than photocopied or electronically transmitted documents when documents in original form are expected to exist;
  - Significant unexplained items on reconciliations;
  - Inconsistent, vague, or implausible responses from management or employees arising from inquiries or analytical procedures;
  - Unusual discrepancies between the entity's records and confirmation replies;
  - Missing inventory or physical assets of significant magnitude;
  - Unavailable or missing electronic evidence, inconsistent with the entity's record retention practices or policies;
  - Inability to produce evidence of key systems development and program change testing and implementation activities for current-year system changes and deployments.
• Problematic or unusual relationships between the auditor and client, including:
  - Denial of access to records, facilities, certain employees, customers, vendors, or others from whom audit evidence might be sought;
  - Undue time pressures imposed by management to resolve complex or contentious issues;
  - Complaints by management about the conduct of the audit or management intimidation of audit team members, particularly in connection with the auditor's critical assessment of audit evidence or in the resolution of potential disagreements with management;
  - Unusual delays by the entity in providing requested information;
  - Tips or complaints to the auditor about alleged fraud;
  - Unwillingness to facilitate auditor access to key electronic files for testing through the use of computer-assisted audit techniques;
  - Denial of access to key IT operations staff and facilities, including security, operations, and systems development personnel.

▲ NOTES ▲

1. Copyright © 2002 by American Institute of Certified Public Accountants, Inc. Permission is granted to make copies of this work provided that such copies are for personal, intraorganizational, or educational use only and are not sold or disseminated and provided further that each copy bears the following credit line: "Copyright © 2002 by American Institute of Certified Public Accountants, Inc. Used with permission."

2. Paragraph 5. Fraud is a broad legal concept and auditors do not make legal determinations of whether fraud has occurred. Rather, the auditor's interest specifically relates to acts that result in a material misstatement of the financial statements. The primary factor that distinguishes fraud from error is whether the underlying action that results in the misstatement of the financial statements is intentional or unintentional. Unlike error, fraud is intentional and usually involves deliberate concealment of the facts. It may involve one or more members of management, employees, or third parties.

3. Paragraph 6. Two types of misstatements are relevant to the auditor's consideration of fraud – misstatements arising from fraudulent financial reporting and misstatements arising from misappropriation of assets.

   • *Misstatements arising from fraudulent financial reporting* are intentional misstatements or omissions of amounts or disclosures in financial statements designed to deceive financial statement users where the effect causes the financial statements not to be presented, in all material respects, in conformity with generally accepted accounting principles (GAAP). Fraudulent financial reporting may be accomplished by the following:
     – Manipulation, falsification, or alteration of accounting records or supporting documents from which financial statements are prepared;
     – Misrepresentation in or intentional omission from the financial statements of events, transactions, or other significant information;
     – Intentional misapplication of accounting principles relating to amounts, classification, manner of presentation, or disclosure.

   • *Misstatements arising from misappropriation of assets* (sometimes referred to as theft or defalcation) involve the theft of an entity's assets where the effect of the theft causes the financial statements not to be presented, in all material respects, in conformity with GAAP. Misappropriation of assets can be accomplished in various ways, including embezzling receipts, stealing assets, or causing an entity to pay for goods or services that have not been received. Misappropriation of assets may be accompanied by false or misleading records or documents, possibly created by circumventing controls. The scope of this

Statement includes only those misappropriations of assets for which the effect of the misappropriation causes the financial statements not to be presented, in all material respects, in conformity with GAAP.
4. With reference to the question of confidentiality, the following paragraphs are important.

Communicating about possible fraud to management, the audit committee, and others

Paragraph 78. Whenever the auditor has determined that there is evidence that fraud may exist, that matter should be brought to the attention of an appropriate level of management. This is appropriate even if the matter might be considered inconsequential, such as a minor defalcation by an employee at a low level in the entity's organization. Fraud involving senior management and fraud (whether caused by senior management or other employees) that causes a material misstatement of the financial statements should be reported directly to the audit committee. In addition, the auditor should reach an understanding with the audit committee regarding the nature and extent of communications about misappropriations perpetrated by lower-level employees.

Paragraph 79. If the auditor, as a result of the assessment of the risks of material misstatement, has identified risks of material misstatement due to fraud that have continuing control implications (whether or not transactions or adjustments that could be the result of fraud have been detected), the auditor should consider whether these risks represent reportable conditions relating to the entity's internal control that should be communicated to senior management and the audit committee. (See SAS No. 60, "Communication of Internal Control Related Matters Noted in an Audit" [AICPA, Professional Standards, vol. 1, AU section 623.04].) The auditor also should consider whether the absence of or deficiencies in programs and controls to mitigate specific risks of fraud or to otherwise help prevent, deter, and detect fraud represent reportable conditions that should be communicated to senior management and the audit committee.

Paragraph 80. The auditor also may wish to communicate other risks of fraud identified as a result of the assessment of the risks of material misstatements due to fraud. Such a communication may be a part of an overall communication to the audit committee of business and financial statement risks affecting the entity and/or in conjunction with the auditor communication about the quality of the entity's accounting principles (see SAS No. 61, AU section 380.11).

Paragraph 81. The disclosure of possible fraud to parties other than the client's senior management and its audit committee ordinarily is not part of the auditor's responsibility and ordinarily would be precluded by the auditor's ethical or legal obligations of confidentiality unless the matter is reflected in the auditor's report. The auditor should recognize, however, that in the following circumstances a duty to disclose to parties outside the entity may exist:

a. To comply with certain legal and regulatory requirements;
b. To a successor auditor when the successor makes inquiries in accordance with SAS No. 84, "Communications Between Predecessor and Successor Auditors 38" (AICPA, Professional Standards, vol. 1, AU section 315);
c. In response to a subpoena;
d. To a funding agency or other specified agency in accordance with requirements for the audits of entities that receive governmental financial assistance. Because potential conflicts with the auditor's ethical and legal obligations for confidentiality may be complex, the auditor may wish to consult with legal counsel before discussing matters covered by paragraphs 78 through 81 with parties outside the client.

Documenting the auditor's consideration of fraud

Paragraph 82. The auditor should document the following:

- The discussion among engagement personnel in planning the audit regarding the susceptibility of the entity's financial statements to material misstatement due to fraud, including how and when the discussion occurred, the audit team members who participated, and the subject matter discussed.
- The procedures performed to obtain information necessary to identify and assess the risks of material misstatement due to fraud.
- Specific risks of material misstatement due to fraud that were identified, and a description of the auditor's response to those risks.
- If the auditor concludes that the performance of some or all of the additional procedures to further address the risk of management override of controls was unnecessary in a particular circumstance, the reasons supporting the auditor's conclusion.
- Other conditions that caused the auditor to believe that additional auditing procedures or other responses were required and any further responses the auditor concluded were appropriate, to address such risks or other conditions.
- The nature of the communications about fraud made to management, the audit committee, and others.

5. Paragraph 7. Three conditions generally are present when fraud occurs. First, management or other employees have an *incentive* or are under *pressure*, which provides a reason to commit fraud. Second, circumstances exist – for example, the absence of controls, ineffective controls, or the ability of management to override controls – that provide an *opportunity* for a fraud to be perpetrated. Third, those involved are able to *rationalize* a fraudulent act as being consistent with their personal code of ethics. Some individuals possess an *attitude*, character, or set of ethical

values that allow them to knowingly and intentionally commit a dishonest act. However, even otherwise honest individuals can commit fraud in an environment that imposes sufficient pressure on them. The greater the incentive or pressure, the more likely an individual will be able to rationalize the acceptability of committing fraud. Identifying individuals with the requisite attitude to commit fraud, or recognizing the likelihood that management or other employees will rationalize to justify committing the fraud, is difficult.

6. Paragraph 16. Due professional care requires the auditor to exercise professional skepticism. See SAS No. 1, "Codification of Auditing Standards and Procedures" (AICPA, Professional Standards, vol. 1, AU sections 230.07–.09, "Due Professional Care in the Performance of Work"). Professional skepticism is an attitude that includes a questioning mind and a critical assessment of audit evidence. The auditor should conduct the engagement with a questioning mind that recognizes the possibility that a material misstatement due to fraud could be present, regardless of any past experience with the entity and regardless of the auditor's belief about management's honesty and integrity. The discussion described in paragraph 7 (see note 5 above) and 15 should emphasize the need to maintain this questioning mind throughout the engagement and should lead the audit team members continually to be alert for information or other conditions (such as those presented in paragraph 67 – see addendum) that indicate that a material misstatement due to fraud may have occurred. Furthermore, the discussion should emphasize that in exercising professional skepticism in gathering and evaluating evidence, the members of the audit team should not be satisfied with less than persuasive evidence because of a belief that management is honest.

appendix iv

Revision of the Securities and Exchange Commission's Auditor Independence Requirements

AGENCY: Securities and Exchange Commission.

ACTION: Final rule.

SUMMARY: The Securities and Exchange Commission ("SEC" or "Commission") is adopting rule amendments regarding auditor independence. The amendments modernize the Commission's rules for determining whether an auditor is independent in light of investments by auditors or their family members in audit clients, employment relationships between auditors or their family members and audit clients, and the scope of services provided by audit firms to their audit clients. The amendments, among other things, significantly reduce the number of audit firm employees and their family members whose investments in audit clients are attributed to the auditor for purposes of determining the auditor's independence. The amendments shrink the circle of family and former firm personnel whose employment impairs an auditor's independence. They also identify certain non-audit services that, if provided by an auditor to public company audit clients, impair the auditor's independence. The scope of services provisions do not extend to services provided to non-audit clients. The final rules provide accounting firms with a limited exception from being deemed not independent for certain inadvertent independence impairments if they have quality controls and satisfy other conditions. Finally, the amendments require most public companies to disclose in their annual proxy statements certain information related to, among other things, the non-audit services provided by their auditor during the most recent fiscal year.

Effective Date: February 5, 2001.

Transition Dates: Until August 5, 2002, providing to an audit client the non-audit services set forth in § 210.2–01(c)(4)(iii) (appraisal or valuation services or fairness opinions) and § 210.2–01(c)(4)(v) (internal audit services) will not impair an accountant's independence with respect to the audit client if performing those services did not impair the accountant's independence under pre-existing requirements of the SEC, the Independence Standards Board, or the accounting profession in the United States. Until May 7, 2001, having the financial interests set forth in § 210.2–01(c)(1)(ii) or the employment relationships set forth in § 210.2–01(c)(2) will not impair an accountant's independence with respect to the audit client if having those financial interests or employment relationships did not impair the accountant's independence under pre-existing requirements of the SEC, the Independence Standards Board, or the accounting profession in the United States. Until December 31, 2002, § 210.2–01(d)(4) shall not apply to offices of the accounting firm located outside of the United States. Registrants must comply with the new proxy and information statement disclosure requirements for all proxy and information statements filed with the Commission after the effective date.

For further information contact: John M. Morrissey, Deputy Chief Accountant, or Sam Burke, Assistant Chief Accountant, Office of the Chief Accountant, at (202) 942–4400, or with respect to questions about investment companies, John S. Capone, Chief Accountant, Division of Investment Management, at (202) 942–0590, Securities and Exchange Commission, 450 Fifth Street, N.W., Washington, D.C. 20549.

Supplementary information: The Commission today is adopting amendments to Rule 2–01 of Regulation S-X[1] and Item 9 of Schedule 14A[2] under the Securities Exchange Act of 1934 (the "Exchange Act").[3]

▲ I. EXECUTIVE SUMMARY ▲

We are adopting amendments to our current rules regarding auditor independence.[4] The final rules advance our important policy goal of protecting the millions of people who invest their savings in our securities markets in reliance on financial statements that are prepared by public companies and other issuers and that, as required by Congress, are audited by independent auditors.[5] We believe the final rules strike a reasonable balance among commenters' differing views about the proposals while achieving our important public policy goals.[6]

Independent auditors have an important public trust.[7] Investors must be able to rely on issuers' financial statements.[8] It is the auditor's opinion that furnishes investors with critical assurance that the financial statements have been subjected to a rigorous examination by an objective, impartial, and skilled professional, and that investors, therefore, can rely on them. If investors do not believe that an auditor is independent of a company, they will derive little confidence from the auditor's opinion and will be far less likely to invest in that public company's securities.[9]

One of our missions is to protect the reliability and integrity of the financial statements of public companies. To do so, and to promote investor confidence, we must ensure that our auditor independence requirements remain relevant, effective, and fair in light of significant changes in the profession, structural reorganizations of accounting firms, and demographic changes in society.[10] There have been important developments in each of these areas since we last amended our auditor independence requirements in 1983.[11]

More and more individual investors participate in our markets, either directly or through mutual funds, pension plans, and retirement plans. Nearly half of all American households are invested in the stock market.[12] As technology has advanced, investors increasingly have direct access to financial information, and they act decisively upon relatively small changes in an issuer's financial results. These and other market changes highlight the importance to the market and to investor confidence of financial information that has been audited by an auditor whose only master is the investing public.[13]

As discussed in the Proposing Release and below, the accounting industry has been transformed by significant changes in the structure of the largest firms. Accounting firms have woven an increasingly complex web of business and financial relationships with their audit clients. The nature of the non-audit services that accounting firms provide to their audit clients has changed, and the revenues from these services have dramatically increased. In addition, there is more mobility of employees and an increase in dual-career families.

We proposed changes to our auditor independence requirements in response to these developments. As more fully discussed below, we are adopting rules, modified in response to almost 3,000 comment letters we received on our proposal, written and oral testimony from four days of public hearings (about 35 hours of testimony from almost 100 witnesses), academic studies, surveys and other professional literature.

The Independence Standard. Independence generally is understood to refer to a mental state of objectivity and lack of bias.[14] The amendments retain this understanding of independence and provide a standard for ascertaining whether the auditor has the requisite state of mind. The first prong of the standard is direct evidence of the auditor's mental state: independence "in fact." The second prong recognizes that generally mental states can be assessed only through observation of external facts; it thus provides that an auditor is not independent if a reasonable investor, with knowledge of all relevant facts and circumstances, would conclude that the auditor is not capable of exercising objective and impartial judgment. The proposed amendments to Rule 2–01 included in the rule four principles for determining whether an accountant is independent of its audit client. While some commenters supported our inclusion of the four principles in the rule,[15] others expressed concerns about the generality of these principles and raised questions concerning their application to particular circumstances.[16] In response, we have included the four principles instead in a Preliminary Note to Rule 2–01 as factors that the Commission will consider, in the first instance, when making independence determinations in accordance with the general independence standard in Rule 2–01(b).

The amendments identify certain relationships that render an accountant not independent of an audit client under the standard in Rule 2–01(b). The relationships addressed include, among others, financial, employment, and business relationships between auditors and audit clients, and relationships between auditors and audit clients where the auditors provide certain non-audit services to their audit clients.

Financial and Employment Relationships. Current requirements attribute to an auditor ownership of shares held by every partner in the auditor's firm, certain managerial employees, and their families. We believe that independence will be protected and the rules will be more workable by focusing on those persons who can influence the audit, instead of all partners in an accounting firm. Accordingly, we proposed to narrow significantly the application of these rules.

Commenters generally supported our efforts to modernize the current rules because they restrict investment and employment opportunities available to firm personnel and their families in ways that may no longer be relevant or necessary for safeguarding auditor independence and investor confidence.[17] Not all commenters agreed with all aspects of the proposals.[18] We have modified the proposal in some respects, but the final rule, like the proposal, shrinks significantly the circle of firm personnel whose investments are imputed to the auditor. The rule also shrinks the circle of family members of auditors and former firm personnel whose employment with an audit client impairs the auditor's independence.

Non-Audit Services. As we discuss below,[19] there has been growing concern on the part of the Commission and users of financial statements about the effects on independence when auditors provide both audit and non-audit services to their audit clients. Dramatic changes in the accounting profession and the types of services that auditors are providing to their audit clients, as well as increases in the absolute and relative size of the fees charged for non-audit services, have exacerbated these concerns. As the Panel on Audit Effectiveness (the "O'Malley Panel") recently recognized, "The potential effect of non-audit services on auditor objectivity has long been an area of concern. That concern has been compounded in recent years by significant increases in the amounts of non-audit services provided by audit firms."[20]

We considered a full range of alternatives to address these concerns. Our proposed amendments identified certain non-audit services that, when rendered to an audit client, impair auditor independence. The proposed restrictions on non-audit services generated more comments than any other aspect of the proposals. Some commenters agreed with our proposals.[21] Others believed that the proposals were not restrictive enough and recommended a total ban on all non-audit services provided by auditors to their audit clients.[22] Still other commenters opposed any Commission rule on non-audit services.[23] After careful consideration of the arguments on all sides, and for the reasons discussed below, we have determined not to adopt a total ban on non-audit services, despite the recommendations of some, and instead to identify certain non-audit services that, if provided to an audit client, render the auditor not independent of the audit client.

In response to public comments,[24] in several instances we have conformed the restrictions to the formulations set forth in the professional literature or otherwise modified the final rule to better describe, and in some cases narrow, the types of services restricted. For example, the final rule does not ban all valuation and appraisal services; its restrictions apply only where it is reasonably likely that the results of any valuation or appraisal, individually or in the aggregate, would be material to the financial statements, or where the results will be audited by the accountant. The rule also provides several exceptions from the restrictions, such as when the valuation is performed in the context of certain tax services, or the valuation is for non-financial purposes and the results of the valuation do not affect the financial statements. These changes are consistent with our approach to adopt only those regulations that we believe are necessary to preserve investor confidence in the independence of auditors and the financial statements they audit.

We recognize that not all non-audit services pose the same risk to independence. Accordingly, under the final rule, accountants will continue to be able to provide a wide variety of non-audit services to their audit clients. In addition, they of course will be able to provide any non-audit service to non-audit clients.

Quality Controls. The quality controls of accounting firms play a significant role in helping to detect and prevent auditor independence problems. The final rule recognizes this role by providing accounting firms a limited exception from being deemed not independent for certain independence impairments that are cured promptly after discovery, provided that the firm has certain quality controls in place.

Disclosure of Non-Audit Services. Finally, we continue to believe that disclosures that shed light on the independence of public companies' auditors assist investors in making investment and voting decisions. Accordingly, we proposed and are adopting requirements for disclosures that we believe will be useful to investors.[25] In response to commenters' concerns about the breadth of the proposed disclosure requirements,[26] however, we have modified them in the final rule.

▲ NOTES ▲

1. 17 CFR 210.2–01.
2. 17 CFR 240.14a-101.

3. 15 U.S.C. § 78a et seq.

4. The amendments were proposed in Securities Act Release No. 7870 (June 30, 2000) (the "Proposing Release") [65 FR 43148].

5. This release uses the terms "independent auditor," "auditor," "independent public accountant," "accountant," and "independent accountant" interchangeably to refer to any independent certified or independent public accountant who performs an audit of or reviews a public company's financial statements or whose report or opinion is filed with the Commission in accordance with the federal securities laws or the Commission's regulations.

6. In addition to soliciting comments in the Proposing Release, we held four days of public hearings (July 26, Sept. 13, Sept. 20, and Sept. 21). The public comments we received can be reviewed in our Public Reference Room at 450 Fifth Street, N.W., Washington, D.C., 20549, in File No. S7-13-00. Public comments submitted by electronic mail are on our website, www.sec.gov. The written testimony and transcripts from each of our public hearings (July 26, Sept. 13, Sept. 20, and Sept. 21) are available on our website. For purposes of this release, date references following the names of participants at our public hearings indicate the hearing date for which the participant submitted written testimony and/or appeared as a witness.

7. The profession's principles of professional conduct state, "Members should accept the obligation to act in a way that will serve the public interest, honor the public trust, and demonstrate commitment to professionalism." American Institute of Certified Public Accountants ("AICPA") Professional Standards: Code of Professional Conduct ("AICPA Code of Professional Conduct"), ET § 53.

8. Public companies and other public issuers and entities registered with us must have their annual financial statements audited by independent public accountants. See, e.g., Items 25 and 26 of Schedule A to the Securities Act of 1933 (the "1933 Act"), 15 U.S.C. § 77aa(25) and (26), that expressly require that financial statements be audited by independent public or certified accountants. See also infra note 34.

9. See, e.g., Testimony of John Whitehead, retired Chairman, Goldman Sachs & Co. (Sept. 13, 2000) ("Financial statements are at the very heart of our capital markets. They're the basis for analyzing investments. Investors have every right to be able to depend absolutely on the integrity of the financial statements that are available to them, and if that integrity in any way falls under suspicion, then the capital markets will surely suffer if investors feel they cannot rely absolutely on the integrity of those financial statements.").

10. As stated by Baxter Rice, President of the California Board of Accountancy, "[I]n this ever-revolving economy and business environment, it's important that we go back and take a look at these regulations and see

whether they are really applicable, and whether or not what we do is going to in any way interfere with or is going to enhance auditor independence, including the public perception of auditor independence." Testimony of Baxter Rice (Sept. 13, 2000).

11. Financial Reporting Release ("FRR") No. 10 (Feb. 25, 1983).

12. In 1999, an estimated 48.2%, or 49.2 million, U.S. households owned equities either in mutual funds or individually, up from 19% in 1983. Investment Company Institute and Securities Industry Association, "Bull Market, Other Developments Fuel Growth in Equity Ownership" (available at www.sia.com/html/pr834.html.).

13. See, e.g., Testimony of Senator Howard Metzenbaum (Ret.), Chairman, Consumer Federation of America (Sept. 20, 2000) ("Our nation's current prosperity and future financial security are tied up as never before in our financial markets. For that reason, whether they know it or not, Americans are enormously dependent on independent auditors, both to . . . ensure the reliability of the information they use to make individual investment decisions and to ensure the efficiency of the marketplace in assigning value to stocks."); Testimony of Ralph Whitworth, Managing Member, Relational Investors LLC (Sept. 13, 2000) ("[A]uditor independence goes to the very essence of our capital markets, and it's linked inextricably to the efficiencies of our capitalist system.").

14. See discussion in Proposing Release, Section II.B.

15. See, e.g., Written Testimony of Dennis Paul Spackman, Chairman, National Association of State Boards of Accountancy (Sept. 13, 2000) (The four principles "set a sensible baseline that is simply stated, easy to understand, useable, and square on the mark. They also serve as an exceptional foundation to the other elements of the proposed revision. . . . [T]hey can serve as a bright beacon giving much needed guidance to members of the profession. . . ."); Written Testimony of Robert L. Ryan, Chief Financial Officer, Medtronic, Inc. (Sept. 20, 2000); Written Testimony of John C. Bogle, Member, Independence Standards Board (July 26, 2000).

16. See, e.g., Letter of Arthur Andersen LLP (Sept. 25, 2000) ("Arthur Andersen Letter"); Written Testimony of the New York Society of Certified Public Accountants (Sept. 13, 2000).

17. See, e.g., Letter of Ernst & Young LLP (Sept. 25, 2000) ("Ernst & Young Letter"); Written Testimony of James J. Schiro, Chief Executive Officer PricewaterhouseCoopers (Sept. 20, 2000); Written Testimony of the New York State Society of Certified Public Accountants (Sept. 13, 2000); Written Testimony of James E. Copeland, Chief Executive Officer, Deloitte & Touche LLP (Sept. 20, 2000); Arthur Andersen Letter.

18. Some commenters, for example, believed that the amendments went

too far. See, e.g., Written Testimony of J. Michael Cook, former Chairman and Chief Executive Officer, Deloitte & Touche (July 26, 2000) (supporting proposed rule changes in this area but stating that no partner in an accounting firm should have a financial interest in any of the firm's audit clients); Written Testimony of Ray J. Groves, former Chairman and CEO, Ernst & Young (July 26, 2000) (agreeing with proposals but stating preference to retain current proscription of direct investment in an audit client by all partners, principals, and shareholders of an accounting firm); Testimony of Paul B.W. Miller, Professor, University of Colorado at Colorado Springs (July 26, 2000) ("I want to direct my attention . . . to the ownership [provisions], and my language is plain. It simply says don't do it"); Written Testimony of Ronald Nielsen and Kathleen Chapman, Iowa Accountancy Examining Board (Sept. 20, 2000). While supporting the goals of the modernization, others provided suggestions to address their concerns about possible unintended consequences. See, e.g., Ernst & Young Letter; Letter of PricewaterhouseCoopers LLP (Sept. 25, 2000) ("Pricewaterhouse-Coopers Letter").

19. See infra Section III.C; see also Proposing Release, Section II.C.

20. The Panel on Audit Effectiveness: Report and Recommendations (the "O'Malley Panel Report"), at ¶ 5.6 (Aug. 31, 2000). The Chairman of the Public Oversight Board ("POB") similarly warned about the "uncontrolled expansion" of management advisory services to audit clients. Letter from John J. McCloy, Chairman, POB (former Chairman of the Board of Chase Manhattan Bank and former President of The World Bank), to Walter E. Hanson, Chairman, Executive Committee, SEC Practice Section ("SECPS") (Mar. 9, 1979).

21. See, e.g., Testimony of Robert E. Denham, Member, Independence Standards Board ("ISB") (July 26, 2000) ("I think [the proposals] represent a very thoughtful, rational, coherent set of proposals."); Letter of Michael McDaniel (Aug. 14, 2000) (supporting SEC proposal and disagreeing with a Form Letter from the AICPA to its members ("AICPA Form Letter") urging them to write to the SEC to oppose the scope of services proposal); Letter of Randie Burrell, CPA (Aug. 14, 2000) (same); Letter of Leland D. O'Neal, CPA (Aug. 15, 2000) (same); Letter of David A. Storhaug, CPA (Aug. 21, 2000) (same); Letter of Arthur Gross (Sept. 10, 2000); Letter of Kristian Holvoet (Sept. 8, 2000); Letter of Bettina B. Menzel (Sept. 9, 2000); Letter of Robert Hanseman (Sept. 10, 2000); Written Testimony of Thomas S. Goodkind, CPA (Sept. 13, 2000); Testimony of Senator Howard Metzenbaum (Ret.), Chairman, Consumer Federation of America (Sept. 20, 2000); Written Testimony of Bill Patterson, Director, Office of Investments, AFL-CIO (Sept. 20, 2000); Written Testimony of Frank Torres, Consumers Union (Sept. 20, 2000); Testimony of

Nimish Patel, Attorney, Pollet & Richardson (July 26, 2000). See also Senator George J. Mitchell (Ret.), "How to Keep Investor Confidence," Editorial, Boston Globe, pg. A15 (Oct. 28, 2000) ("The commission's proposal is well-reasoned and appropriate. . . . [T]he commission should adopt this rule to protect investor confidence and strengthen the most vibrant financial market system in the world.").

22. See, e.g., Written Testimony of Kayla J. Gillan, General Counsel, California Public Employees' Retirement System ("CalPERS"), which is the largest public retirement system in the United States with over 1.2 million participants (Sept. 13, 2000) ("The SEC should consider simplifying its Proposal and drawing a bright-line test: no non-audit services to an audit client."); Written Testimony of John H. Biggs, Chairman and CEO of TIAA-CREF, which has 2.2 million participants (July 26, 2000) ("[I]ndependent public audit firms should not be the auditors of any company for which they simultaneously provide other services. It's that simple,"); Written Testimony of Alan P. Cleveland, the New Hampshire Retirement System, with 52,000 members (Sept. 13, 2000) ("We regard the concurrent performance by the company's external auditor of non-auditor services at the direction and under the control of management to be inherently corrosive and fundamentally incompatible with that duty of independence and fidelity owed by the auditor to the investing public"); Testimony of Jack Ciesielski, accounting analyst (July 26, 2000) ("I think the single best way to improve auditor independence and the appearance of auditor independence is to call for an exclusionary ban on non-audit services to audit clients."); Letter of Carson L. Eddy, CPA, (Aug. 22, 2000) ("It is my opinion that the general public would be better served if Certified Public Accountants providing the attest function for a client were unable to do any other consulting work for that client, with the exception for the ability to prepare tax returns."); Letter of William V. Allen, Jr., CPA (Aug. 22, 2000); Letter of Terry Guckes (Sept. 9, 2000); Letter of Art Koolwine (Sept. 8, 2000); Letter of Elliot M. Simon (Sept. 9, 2000); Letter of Melvin Schupack (Sept. 9, 2000); Letter of William Odendahl (Sept. 5, 2000).

23. See, e.g., Letter of the AICPA (Sept. 25, 2000) ("AICPA Letter"); Letter of KPMG (Sept. 25, 2000) ("KPMG Letter"); Letters of Robert Roy Ward, Chairman and Chief Executive Officer, Horne CPA Group (Sept. 20, 2000), Douglas R. Ream, CPA (undated), Jack W. Palmer (Sept. 9, 2000), Sherry Wilson, CPA (Aug. 28, 2000), and Nathaniel Boyle, CPA (Aug. 16, 2000) (each reiterating concerns expressed in the AICPA's Form Letter).

24. See, e.g., Ernst & Young Letter; PricewaterhouseCoopers Letter.

25. Commenters generally agreed that disclosure would be useful to investors. See, e.g., Written Testimony of James W. Barge, Vice President

and Controller, Time Warner (Sept. 20, 2000); Letter of The Institute of Internal Auditors (Sept. 5, 2000); Written Testimony of Dennis Paul Spackman, Chairman of the National Association of State Boards of Accountancy (Sept. 13, 2000); Letter of Marsha Payne, President, Association of College & University Auditors (Sept. 25, 2000); Letter of Keith Johnson, Chief Legal Counsel, State of Wisconsin Board (Sept. 20, 2000); Letter of Peter C. Clapman, Senior Vice President and Chief Counsel, Investments, TIAA-CREF (Sept. 21, 2000).

26. See, e.g., Written Testimony of Clarence E. Lockett, Vice President and Corporate Controller, Johnson & Johnson (Sept. 20, 2000); Written Testimony of Philip A. Laskawy, Chairman, Ernst & Young LLP (Sept. 20, 2000).

appendix v

Statements on Standards for Tax Services Nos 1–8

PREFACE

1. Practice standards are the hallmark of calling one's self a professional. Members should fulfill their responsibilities as professionals by instituting and maintaining standards against which their professional performance can be measured. Compliance with professional standards of tax practice also confirms the public's awareness of the professionalism that is associated with CPAs as well as the AICPA.

2. This publication sets forth ethical tax practice standards for members of the AICPA: Statements on **Standards for Tax Services** (SSTSs or Statements). Although other standards of tax practice exist, most notably Treasury Department Circular No. 230 and penalty provisions of the Internal Revenue Code (IRC), those standards are limited in that (1) Circular No. 230 does not provide the depth of guidance contained in these Statements, (2) the IRC penalty provisions apply only to income-tax return preparation, and (3) both Circular No. 230 and the penalty provisions apply only to federal tax practice.

3. The SSTSs have been written in as simple and objective a manner as possible. However, by their nature, ethical standards provide for an appropriate range of behavior that recognizes the need for interpretations to meet a broad range of personal and professional situations. The SSTSs recognize this need by, in some sections, providing relatively subjective rules and by leaving certain terms undefined. These terms and concepts are generally rooted in tax concepts, and therefore should be readily understood by tax practitioners. It is, therefore, recognized that the enforcement of these rules, as part of the AICPA's Code of Professional Conduct Rule 201, General Standards, and Rule 202, Compliance With Standards, will be undertaken with flexibility in mind and handled on a case-by-case basis. Members are expected to comply with them.

HISTORY

4. The SSTSs have their origin in the Statements on Responsibilities in Tax Practice (SRTPs), which provided a body of advisory opinions on good tax practice. The guidelines as originally set forth in the SRTPs had come to play a much more important role than most members realized. The courts, Internal Revenue Service, state accountancy boards, and other professional organizations recognized and relied on the SRTPs as the appropriate articulation of professional conduct in a CPA's tax practice. The SRTPs, in and of themselves, had become de facto enforceable standards of professional practice, because state disciplinary organizations and malpractice cases in effect regularly held CPAs accountable for failure to follow the SRTPs when their professional practice conduct failed to meet the prescribed guidelines of conduct.

5. The AICPA's Tax Executive Committee concluded that appropriate action entailed issuance of tax practice standards that would become a part of the Institute's Code of Professional Conduct. At its July 1999 meeting, the AICPA Board of Directors approved support of the executive committee's initiative and placed the matter on the agenda of the October 1999 meeting of the Institute's governing Council. On October 19, 1999, Council approved designating the Tax Executive Committee as a standard-setting body, thus authorizing that committee to promulgate standards of tax practice. These SSTSs, largely mirroring the SRTPs, are the result.

6. The SRTPs were originally issued between 1964 and 1977. The first nine SRTPs and the Introduction were codified in 1976; the tenth SRTP was issued in 1977. The original SRTPs concerning the CPA's responsibility to sign the return (SRTPs No. 1, Signature of Preparers, and No. 2, Signature of Reviewer: Assumption of Preparer's Responsibility) were withdrawn in 1982 after Treasury Department regulations were issued adopting substantially the same standards for all tax return preparers. The sixth and seventh SRTPs, concerning the responsibility of a CPA who becomes aware of an error, were revised in 1991. The first Interpretation of the SRTPs, Interpretation 1-1, "Realistic Possibility Standard," was approved in December 1990. The SSTSs and Interpretation supersede and replace the SRTPs and their Interpretation 1-1 effective October 31, 2000. Although the number and names of the SSTSs, and the substance of the rules contained in each of them, remain the same as in the SRTPs, the language has been edited to both clarify and reflect the enforceable nature of the SSTSs. In addition, because the applicability of these standards is not limited to federal income-tax practice, the language has been changed to mirror the broader scope.

ONGOING PROCESS

7. The following Statements on **Standards for Tax Services** and Interpretation 1–1 to Statement No. 1, "Realistic Possibility Standard," reflect the AICPA's standards of tax practice and delineate members' responsibilities to taxpayers, the public, the government, and the profession. The Statements are intended to be part of an ongoing process that may require changes to and interpretations of current SSTSs in recognition of the accelerating rate of change in tax laws and the continued importance of tax practice to members.
8. The Tax Executive Committee promulgates SSTSs. Even though the 1999–2000 Tax Executive Committee approved this version, acknowledgment is also due to the many members whose efforts over the years went into the development of the original statements.

Statement on Standards for Tax Services No. 1, Tax Return Positions

INTRODUCTION

1. This Statement sets forth the applicable standards for members when recommending tax return positions and preparing or signing tax returns (including amended returns, claims for refund, and information returns) filed with any taxing authority. For purposes of these standards, a tax return position is (a) a position reflected on the tax return as to which the taxpayer has been specifically advised by a member or (b) a position about which a member has knowledge of all material facts and, on the basis of those facts, has concluded whether the position is appropriate. For purposes of these standards, a taxpayer is a client, a member's employer, or any other third-party recipient of tax services.

STATEMENT

2. The following standards apply to a member when providing professional services that involve tax return positions:
a. A member should not recommend that a tax return position be taken with respect to any item unless the member has a good-faith

belief that the position has a realistic possibility of being sustained administratively or judicially on its merits if challenged.

b. A member should not prepare or sign a return that the member is aware takes a position that the member may not recommend under the standard expressed in paragraph 2a.

c. Notwithstanding paragraph 2a, a member may recommend a tax return position that the member concludes is not frivolous as long as the member advises the taxpayer to appropriately disclose. Notwithstanding paragraph 2b, the member may prepare or sign a return that reflects a position that the member concludes is not frivolous as long as the position is appropriately disclosed.

d. When recommending tax return positions and when preparing or signing a return on which a tax return position is taken, a member should, when relevant, advise the taxpayer regarding potential penalty consequences of such tax return position and the opportunity, if any, to avoid such penalties through disclosure.

3. A member should not recommend a tax return position or prepare or sign a return reflecting a position that the member knows –

a. Exploits the audit selection process of a taxing authority.

b. Serves as a mere arguing position advanced solely to obtain leverage in the bargaining process of settlement negotiation with a taxing authority.

4. When recommending a tax return position, a member has both the right and responsibility to be an advocate for the taxpayer with respect to any position satisfying the aforementioned standards.

EXPLANATION

5. Our self-assessment tax system can function effectively only if taxpayers file tax returns that are true, correct, and complete. A tax return is primarily a taxpayer's representation of facts, and the taxpayer has the final responsibility for positions taken on the return.

6. In addition to a duty to the taxpayer, a member has a duty to the tax system. However, it is well established that the taxpayer has no obligation to pay more taxes than are legally owed, and a member has a duty to the taxpayer to assist in achieving that result. The standards contained in paragraphs 2, 3, and 4 recognize the members' responsibilities to both taxpayers and to the tax system.

7. In order to meet the standards contained in paragraph 2, a member should in good faith believe that the tax return position is warranted in existing law or can be supported by a good-faith argument for an extension, modification, or reversal of existing law. For example, in reaching such a conclusion, a member may consider a well-reasoned construction of the applicable statute, well-reasoned articles or treatises, or pronouncements issued by the applicable taxing authority, regardless of whether such sources would be treated as authority under Internal Revenue Code section 6662 and the regulations thereunder. A position would not fail to meet these standards merely because it is later abandoned for practical or procedural considerations during an administrative hearing or in the litigation process.

8. If a member has a good-faith belief that more than one tax return position meets the standards set forth in paragraph 2, a member's advice concerning alternative acceptable positions may include a discussion of the likelihood that each such position might or might not cause the taxpayer's tax return to be examined and whether the position would be challenged in an examination. In such circumstances, such advice is not a violation of paragraph 3a.

9. In some cases, a member may conclude that a tax return position is not warranted under the standard set forth in paragraph 2a. A taxpayer may, however, still wish to take such a position. Under such circumstances, the taxpayer should have the opportunity to take such a position, and the member may prepare and sign the return provided the position is appropriately disclosed on the return or claim for refund and the position is not frivolous. A frivolous position is one that is knowingly advanced in bad faith and is patently improper.

10. A member's determination of whether information is appropriately disclosed by the taxpayer should be based on the facts and circumstances of the particular case and the authorities regarding disclosure in the applicable taxing jurisdiction. If a member recommending a position, but not engaged to prepare or sign the related tax return, advises the taxpayer concerning appropriate disclosure of the position, then the member shall be deemed to meet these standards.

11. If particular facts and circumstances lead a member to believe that a taxpayer penalty might be asserted, the member should so advise the taxpayer and should discuss with the taxpayer the opportunity to avoid such penalty by disclosing the position on the tax return. Although a member should advise the taxpayer with respect to disclosure, it is the taxpayer's responsibility to decide whether and how to disclose.

12. For purposes of this Statement, preparation of a tax return includes giving advice on events that have occurred at the time the advice is given if the advice is directly relevant to determining the existence, character, or amount of a schedule, entry, or other portion of a tax return.

Interpretation No. 1–1, "Realistic Possibility Standard" of Statement on Standards for Tax Services No. 1, Tax Return Positions

BACKGROUND

1. Statement on **Standards for Tax Services** (SSTS) No. 1, Tax Return Positions, contains the standards a member should follow in recommending tax return positions and in preparing or signing tax returns. In general, a member should have a good-faith belief that the tax return position being recommended has a realistic possibility of being sustained administratively or judicially on its merits, if challenged. The standard contained in SSTS No. 1, paragraph 2a, is referred to here as the realistic possibility standard. If a member concludes that a tax return position does not meet the realistic possibility standard:

a. The member may still recommend the position to the taxpayer if the position is not frivolous, and the member recommends appropriate disclosure of the position; or

b. The member may still prepare or sign a tax return containing the position, if the position is not frivolous, and the position is appropriately disclosed.

2. A frivolous position is one that is knowingly advanced in bad faith and is patently improper (see SSTS No. 1, paragraph 9). A member's determination of whether information is appropriately disclosed on a tax return or claim for refund is based on the facts and circumstances of the particular case and the authorities regarding disclosure in the applicable jurisdiction (see SSTS No. 1, paragraph 10).

3. If a member believes there is a possibility that a tax return position might result in penalties being asserted against a taxpayer, the member should so advise the taxpayer and should discuss with the taxpayer the opportunity, if any, of avoiding such penalties through disclosure (see SSTS No. 1, paragraph 11). Such advice may be given orally.

GENERAL INTERPRETATION

4. To meet the realistic possibility standard, a member should have a good-faith belief that the position is warranted by existing law or can be supported by a good-faith argument for an extension, modification, or reversal of the existing law through the administrative or judicial process. Such a belief should be based on reasonable interpretations of the tax law. A member should not take into account the likelihood of audit or detection when determining whether this standard has been met (see SSTS No. 1, paragraphs 3a and 8).

5. The realistic possibility standard is less stringent than the substantial authority standard and the more likely than not standard that apply under the Internal Revenue Code (IRC) to substantial understatements of liability by taxpayers. The realistic possibility standard is stricter than the reasonable basis standard that is in the IRC.

6. In determining whether a tax return position meets the realistic possibility standard, a member may rely on authorities in addition to those evaluated when determining whether substantial authority exists under IRC section 6662. Accordingly, a member may rely on well-reasoned treatises, articles in recognized professional tax publications, and other reference tools and sources of tax analyses commonly used by tax advisers and preparers of returns.

7. In determining whether a realistic possibility exists, a member should do all of the following:

- Establish relevant background facts.
- Distill the appropriate questions from those facts.
- Search for authoritative answers to those questions.
- Resolve the questions by weighing the authorities uncovered by that search.
- Arrive at a conclusion supported by the authorities.

8. A member should consider the weight of each authority to conclude whether a position meets the realistic possibility standard. In determining the weight of an authority, a member should consider its persuasiveness, relevance, and source. Thus, the type of authority is a significant factor. Other important factors include whether the facts stated by the authority are distinguishable from those of the taxpayer and whether the authority contains an analysis of the issue or merely states a conclusion.

9. The realistic possibility standard may be met despite the absence of certain types of authority. For example, a member may conclude that the realistic possibility standard has been met when the position is supported only by a well-reasoned construction of the applicable statutory provision.

10. In determining whether the realistic possibility standard has been met, the extent of research required is left to the professional judgment of the member with respect to all the facts and circumstances known to the member. A member may conclude that more than one position meets the realistic possibility standard.

SPECIFIC ILLUSTRATIONS

11. The following illustrations deal with general fact patterns. Accordingly, the application of the guidance discussed in the General Interpretation section to variations in such general facts or to particular facts or circumstances may lead to different conclusions. In each illustration there is no authority other than that indicated.

12. Illustration 1. A taxpayer has engaged in a transaction that is adversely affected by a new statutory provision. Prior law supports a position favorable to the taxpayer. The taxpayer believes, and the member concurs, that the new statute is inequitable as applied to the taxpayer's situation. The statute is constitutional, clearly drafted, and unambiguous. The legislative history discussing the new statute contains general comments that do not specifically address the taxpayer's situation.

13. Conclusion. The member should recommend the return position supported by the new statute. A position contrary to a constitutional, clear, and unambiguous statute would ordinarily be considered a frivolous position.

14. Illustration 2. The facts are the same as in illustration 1 except that the legislative history discussing the new statute specifically addresses the taxpayer's situation and supports a position favorable to the taxpayer.

15. Conclusion. In a case where the statute is clearly and unambiguously against the taxpayer's position but a contrary position exists based on legislative history specifically addressing the taxpayer's situation, a return position based either on the statutory language or on the legislative history satisfies the realistic possibility standard.

16. Illustration 3. The facts are the same as in illustration 1 except that the legislative history can be interpreted to provide some evidence or authority in support of the taxpayer's position; however, the legislative history does not specifically address the situation.

17. Conclusion. In a case where the statute is clear and unambiguous, a contrary position based on an interpretation of the legislative

history that does not explicitly address the taxpayer's situation does not meet the realistic possibility standard. However, because the legislative history provides some support or evidence for the taxpayer's position, such a return position is not frivolous. A member may recommend the position to the taxpayer if the member also recommends appropriate disclosure.

18. Illustration 4. A taxpayer is faced with an issue involving the interpretation of a new statute. Following its passage, the statute was widely recognized to contain a drafting error, and a technical correction proposal has been introduced. The taxing authority issues a pronouncement indicating how it will administer the provision. The pronouncement interprets the statute in accordance with the proposed technical correction.

19. Conclusion. Return positions based on either the existing statutory language or the taxing authority pronouncement satisfy the realistic possibility standard.

20. Illustration 5. The facts are the same as in illustration 4 except that no taxing authority pronouncement has been issued.

21. Conclusion. In the absence of a taxing authority pronouncement interpreting the statute in accordance with the technical correction, only a return position based on the existing statutory language will meet the realistic possibility standard. A return position based on the proposed technical correction may be recommended if it is appropriately disclosed, since it is not frivolous.

22. Illustration 6. A taxpayer is seeking advice from a member regarding a recently amended statute. The member has reviewed the statute, the legislative history that specifically addresses the issue, and a recently published notice issued by the taxing authority. The member has concluded in good faith that, based on the statute and the legislative history, the taxing authority's position as stated in the notice does not reflect legislative intent.

23. Conclusion. The member may recommend the position supported by the statute and the legislative history because it meets the realistic possibility standard.

24. Illustration 7. The facts are the same as in illustration 6 except that the taxing authority pronouncement is a temporary regulation.

25. Conclusion. In determining whether the position meets the realistic possibility standard, a member should determine the weight to be given the regulation by analyzing factors such as whether the regulation is legislative or interpretative, or if it is inconsistent with the statute. If a member concludes that the position does not meet the realistic possibility standard, because it is not frivolous, the position may nevertheless be recommended if the member also recommends appropriate disclosure.

26. Illustration 8. A tax form published by a taxing authority is incorrect, but completion of the form as published provides a benefit to the taxpayer. The member knows that the taxing authority has published an announcement acknowledging the error.

27. Conclusion. In these circumstances, a return position in accordance with the published form is a frivolous position.

28. Illustration 9. A taxpayer wants to take a position that a member has concluded is frivolous. The taxpayer maintains that even if the taxing authority examines the return, the issue will not be raised.

29. Conclusion. The member should not consider the likelihood of audit or detection when determining whether the realistic possibility standard has been met. The member should not prepare or sign a return that contains a frivolous position even if it is disclosed.

30. Illustration 10. A statute is passed requiring the capitalization of certain expenditures. The taxpayer believes, and the member concurs, that to comply fully, the taxpayer will need to acquire new computer hardware and software and implement a number of new accounting procedures. The taxpayer and member agree that the costs of full compliance will be significantly greater than the resulting increase in tax due under the new provision. Because of these cost considerations, the taxpayer makes no effort to comply. The taxpayer wants the member to prepare and sign a return on which the new requirement is simply ignored.

31. Conclusion. The return position desired by the taxpayer is frivolous, and the member should neither prepare nor sign the return.

32. Illustration 11. The facts are the same as in illustration 10 except that a taxpayer has made a good-faith effort to comply with the law by calculating an estimate of expenditures to be capitalized under the new provision.

33. Conclusion. In this situation, the realistic possibility standard has been met. When using estimates in the preparation of a return, a member should refer to SSTS No. 4, Use of Estimates.

34. Illustration 12. On a given issue, a member has located and weighed two authorities concerning the treatment of a particular expenditure. A taxing authority has issued an administrative ruling that required the expenditure to be capitalized and amortized over several years. On the other hand, a court opinion permitted the current deduction of the expenditure. The member has concluded that these are the relevant authorities, considered the source of both authorities, and concluded that both are persuasive and relevant.

35. Conclusion. The realistic possibility standard is met by either position.

36. Illustration 13. A tax statute is silent on the treatment of an item under the statute. However, the legislative history explaining the statute directs the taxing authority to issue regulations that will require a specific treatment of the item. No regulations have been issued at the time the member must recommend a position on the tax treatment of the item.

37. Conclusion. The member may recommend the position supported by the legislative history because it meets the realistic possibility standard.

38. Illustration 14. A taxpayer wants to take a position that a member concludes meets the realistic possibility standard based on an assumption regarding an underlying non-tax legal issue. The member recommends that the taxpayer seek advice from its legal counsel, and the taxpayer's attorney gives an opinion on the non-tax legal issue.

39. Conclusion. A member may in general rely on a legal opinion on a non-tax legal issue. A member should, however, use professional judgment when relying on a legal opinion. If, on its face, the opinion of the taxpayer's attorney appears to be unreasonable, unsubstantiated, or unwarranted, a member should consult his or her attorney before relying on the opinion.

40. Illustration 15. A taxpayer has obtained from its attorney an opinion on the tax treatment of an item and requests that a member rely on the opinion.

41. Conclusion. The authorities on which a member may rely include well-reasoned sources of tax analysis. If a member is satisfied about the source, relevance, and persuasiveness of the legal opinion, a member may rely on that opinion when determining whether the realistic possibility standard has been met.

Statement on Standards for Tax Services No. 2, Answers to Questions on Returns

INTRODUCTION

1. This Statement sets forth the applicable standards for members when signing the preparer's declaration on a tax return if one or more questions on the return have not been answered. The term questions includes requests for information on the return, in the instructions, or in the regulations, whether or not stated in the form of a question.

STATEMENT

2. A member should make a reasonable effort to obtain from the taxpayer the information necessary to provide appropriate answers to all questions on a tax return before signing as preparer.

EXPLANATION

3. It is recognized that the questions on tax returns are not of uniform importance, and often they are not applicable to the particular taxpayer. Nevertheless, there are at least two reasons why a member should be satisfied that a reasonable effort has been made to obtain information to provide appropriate answers to the questions on the return that are applicable to a taxpayer.

a. A question may be of importance in determining taxable income or loss, or the tax liability shown on the return, in which circumstance an omission may detract from the quality of the return.

b. A member often must sign a preparer's declaration stating that the return is true, correct, and complete.

4. Reasonable grounds may exist for omitting an answer to a question applicable to a taxpayer. For example, reasonable grounds may include the following:

a. The information is not readily available and the answer is not significant in terms of taxable income or loss, or the tax liability shown on the return.

b. Genuine uncertainty exists regarding the meaning of the question in relation to the particular return.

c. The answer to the question is voluminous; in such cases, a statement should be made on the return that the data will be supplied upon examination.

5. A member should not omit an answer merely because it might prove disadvantageous to a taxpayer.

6. If reasonable grounds exist for omission of an answer to an applicable question, a taxpayer is not required to provide on the return an explanation of the reason for the omission. In this connection, a member should consider whether the omission of an answer to a question may cause the return to be deemed incomplete.

Statement on Standards for Tax Services No. 3, Certain Procedural Aspects of Preparing Returns

INTRODUCTION

1. This Statement sets forth the applicable standards for members concerning the obligation to examine or verify certain supporting data or to consider information related to another taxpayer when preparing a taxpayer's tax return.

STATEMENT

2. In preparing or signing a return, a member may in good faith rely, without verification, on information furnished by the taxpayer or by third parties. However, a member should not ignore the implications of information furnished and should make reasonable inquiries if the information furnished appears to be incorrect, incomplete, or inconsistent either on its face or on the basis of other facts known to a member. Further, a member should refer to the taxpayer's returns for one or more prior years whenever feasible.

3. If the tax law or regulations impose a condition with respect to deductibility or other tax treatment of an item, such as taxpayer maintenance of books and records or substantiating documentation to support the reported deduction or tax treatment, a member should make appropriate inquiries to determine to the member's satisfaction whether such condition has been met.

4. When preparing a tax return, a member should consider information actually known to that member from the tax return of another taxpayer if the information is relevant to that tax return and its consideration is necessary to properly prepare that tax return. In using such information, a member should consider any limitations imposed by any law or rule relating to confidentiality.

EXPLANATION

5. The preparer's declaration on a tax return often states that the information contained therein is true, correct, and complete to the best of the preparer's knowledge and belief based on all information known by the preparer. This type of reference should be understood to include information furnished by the taxpayer or by third parties to a member in connection with the preparation of the return.

6. The preparer's declaration does not require a member to examine or verify supporting data. However, a distinction should be made between (a) the need either to determine by inquiry that a specifically

required condition, such as maintaining books and records or sub-stantiating documentation, has been satisfied or to obtain infor-mation when the material furnished appears to be incorrect or incomplete and (b) the need for a member to examine underlying information. In fulfilling his or her obligation to exercise due dili-gence in preparing a return, a member may rely on information furnished by the taxpayer unless it appears to be incorrect, incom-plete, or inconsistent. Although a member has certain responsibilities in exercising due diligence in preparing a return, the taxpayer has the ultimate responsibility for the contents of the return. Thus, if the taxpayer presents unsupported data in the form of lists of tax information, such as dividends and interest received, charitable contributions, and medical expenses, such information may be used in the preparation of a tax return without verification unless it appears to be incorrect, incomplete, or inconsistent either on its face or on the basis of other facts known to a member.

7. Even though there is no requirement to examine underlying documentation, a member should encourage the taxpayer to provide supporting data where appropriate. For example, a member should encourage the taxpayer to submit underlying documents for use in tax return preparation to permit full consideration of income and deductions arising from security transactions and from pass-through entities, such as estates, trusts, partnerships, and S corporations.

8. The source of information provided to a member by a taxpayer for use in preparing the return is often a pass-through entity, such as a limited partnership, in which the taxpayer has an interest but is not involved in management. A member may accept the information provided by the pass-through entity without further inquiry, unless there is reason to believe it is incorrect, incomplete, or inconsistent, either on its face or on the basis of other facts known to the member. In some instances, it may be appropriate for a member to advise the taxpayer to ascertain the nature and amount of possible exposure to tax deficiencies, interest, and penalties, by contact with management of the pass-through entity.

9. A member should make use of a taxpayer's returns for one or more prior years in preparing the current return whenever feasible. Reference to prior returns and discussion of prior-year tax determi-nations with the taxpayer should provide information to determine the taxpayer's general tax status, avoid the omission or duplication of items, and afford a basis for the treatment of similar or related transactions. As with the examination of information supplied for

the current year's return, the extent of comparison of the details of income and deduction between years depends on the particular circumstances.

Statement on Standards for Tax Services No. 4, Use of Estimates

INTRODUCTION

1. This Statement sets forth the applicable standards for members when using the taxpayer's estimates in the preparation of a tax return. A member may advise on estimates used in the preparation of a tax return, but the taxpayer has the responsibility to provide the estimated data. Appraisals or valuations are not considered estimates for purposes of this Statement.

STATEMENT

2. Unless prohibited by statute or by rule, a member may use the taxpayer's estimates in the preparation of a tax return if it is not practical to obtain exact data and if the member determines that the estimates are reasonable based on the facts and circumstances known to the member. If the taxpayer's estimates are used, they should be presented in a manner that does not imply greater accuracy than exists.

EXPLANATION

3. Accounting requires the exercise of professional judgment and, in many instances, the use of approximations based on judgment. The application of such accounting judgments, as long as not in conflict with methods set forth by a taxing authority, is acceptable. These judgments are not estimates within the purview of this Statement. For example, a federal income tax regulation provides that if all other conditions for accrual are met, the exact amount of income or expense need not be known or ascertained at year end if the amount can be determined with reasonable accuracy.

4. When the taxpayer's records do not accurately reflect information related to small expenditures, accuracy in recording some data may be difficult to achieve. Therefore, the use of estimates by a taxpayer in determining the amount to be deducted for such items may be appropriate.

5. When records are missing or precise information about a transaction is not available at the time the return must be filed, a member

may prepare a tax return using a taxpayer's estimates of the missing data.

6. Estimated amounts should not be presented in a manner that provides a misleading impression about the degree of factual accuracy.

7. Specific disclosure that an estimate is used for an item in the return is not generally required; however, such disclosure should be made in unusual circumstances where nondisclosure might mislead the taxing authority regarding the degree of accuracy of the return as a whole. Some examples of unusual circumstances include the following:

a. A taxpayer has died or is ill at the time the return must be filed.

b. A taxpayer has not received a Schedule K-1 for a pass-through entity at the time the tax return is to be filed.

c. There is litigation pending (for example, a bankruptcy proceeding) that bears on the return.

d. Fire or computer failure has destroyed the relevant records.

Statement on Standards for Tax Services No. 5,
Departure From a Position Previously Concluded in an
Administrative Proceeding or Court Decision

INTRODUCTION

1. This Statement sets forth the applicable standards for members in recommending a tax return position that departs from the position determined in an administrative proceeding or in a court decision with respect to the taxpayer's prior return.

2. For purposes of this Statement, administrative proceeding also includes an examination by a taxing authority or an appeals conference relating to a return or a claim for refund.

3. For purposes of this Statement, court decision means a decision by any court having jurisdiction over tax matters.

STATEMENT

4. The tax return position with respect to an item as determined in an administrative proceeding or court decision does not restrict a member from recommending a different tax position in a later year's return, unless the taxpayer is bound to a specified treatment in the later year, such as by a formal closing agreement. Therefore, as provided in Statement on **Standards for Tax Services** (SSTS) No. 1, Tax Return Positions, the member may recommend a tax return position or prepare or sign a tax return that departs from the treatment of an item as concluded in an administrative proceeding or court decision with respect to a prior return of the taxpayer.

EXPLANATION

5. If an administrative proceeding or court decision has resulted in a determination concerning a specific tax treatment of an item in a prior year's return, a member will usually recommend this same tax treatment in subsequent years. However, departures from consistent treatment may be justified under such circumstances as the following:

a. Taxing authorities tend to act consistently in the disposition of an item that was the subject of a prior administrative proceeding but generally are not bound to do so. Similarly, a taxpayer is not bound to follow the tax treatment of an item as consented to in an earlier administrative proceeding.

b. The determination in the administrative proceeding or the court's decision may have been caused by a lack of documentation. Supporting data for the later year may be appropriate.

c. A taxpayer may have yielded in the administrative proceeding for settlement purposes or not appealed the court decision, even though the position met the standards in SSTS No. 1.

d. Court decisions, rulings, or other authorities that are more favorable to a taxpayer's current position may have developed since the prior administrative proceeding was concluded or the prior court decision was rendered.

6. The consent in an earlier administrative proceeding and the existence of an unfavorable court decision are factors that the member should consider in evaluating whether the standards in SSTS No. 1 are met.

Statement on Standards for Tax Services No. 6, Knowledge of Error: Return Preparation

INTRODUCTION

1. This Statement sets forth the applicable standards for a member who becomes aware of an error in a taxpayer's previously filed tax return or of a taxpayer's failure to file a required tax return. As used herein, the term error includes any position, omission, or method of accounting that, at the time the return is filed, fails to meet the standards set out in Statement on **Standards for Tax Services**

(SSTS) No. 1, Tax Return Positions. The term error also includes a position taken on a prior year's return that no longer meets these standards due to legislation, judicial decisions, or administrative pronouncements having retroactive effect. However, an error does not include an item that has an insignificant effect on the taxpayer's tax liability.

2. This Statement applies whether or not the member prepared or signed the return that contains the error.

STATEMENT

3. A member should inform the taxpayer promptly upon becoming aware of an error in a previously filed return or upon becoming aware of a taxpayer's failure to file a required return. A member should recommend the corrective measures to be taken. Such recommendation may be given orally. The member is not obligated to inform the taxing authority, and a member may not do so without the taxpayer's permission, except when required by law.

4. If a member is requested to prepare the current year's return and the taxpayer has not taken appropriate action to correct an error in a prior year's return, the member should consider whether to withdraw from preparing the return and whether to continue a professional or employment relationship with the taxpayer. If the member does prepare such current year's return, the member should take reasonable steps to ensure that the error is not repeated.

EXPLANATION

5. While performing services for a taxpayer, a member may become aware of an error in a previously filed return or may become aware that the taxpayer failed to file a required return. The member should advise the taxpayer of the error and the measures to be taken. Such recommendation may be given orally. If the member believes that the taxpayer could be charged with fraud or other criminal misconduct, the taxpayer should be advised to consult legal counsel before taking any action.

6. It is the taxpayer's responsibility to decide whether to correct the error. If the taxpayer does not correct an error, a member should consider whether to continue a professional or employment relationship with the taxpayer. While recognizing that the taxpayer may not be required by statute to correct an error by filing an amended return, a member should consider whether a taxpayer's decision not to file an amended return may predict future behavior that might require termination of the relationship. The potential for violating Code of Professional Conduct Rule 301 (relating to the member's confidential client relationship), the tax law and regulations, or laws on privileged communications, and other considerations may create a conflict between the member's interests and those of the taxpayer. Therefore, a member should consider consulting with his or her own legal counsel before deciding upon recommendations to the taxpayer and whether to continue a professional or employment relationship with the taxpayer.

7. If a member decides to continue a professional or employment relationship with the taxpayer and is requested to prepare a tax return for a year subsequent to that in which the error occurred, the member should take reasonable steps to ensure that the error is not repeated. If the subsequent year's tax return cannot be prepared without perpetuating the error, the member should consider withdrawal from the return preparation. If a member learns that the taxpayer is using an erroneous method of accounting and it is past the due date to request permission to change to a method meeting the standards of SSTS No. 1, the member may sign a tax return for the current year, providing the tax return includes appropriate disclosure of the use of the erroneous method.

8. Whether an error has no more than an insignificant effect on the taxpayer's tax liability is left to the professional judgment of the member based on all the facts and circumstances known to the member. In judging whether an erroneous method of accounting has more than an insignificant effect, a member should consider the method's cumulative effect and its effect on the current year's tax return.

9. If a member becomes aware of the error while performing services for a taxpayer that do not involve tax return preparation, the member's responsibility is to advise the taxpayer of the existence of the error and to recommend that the error be discussed with the taxpayer's tax return preparer. Such recommendation may be given orally.

Statement on Standards for Tax Services No. 7, Knowledge of Error: Administrative Proceedings

INTRODUCTION

1. This Statement sets forth the applicable standards for a member who becomes aware of an error in a return that is the subject of an

administrative proceeding, such as an examination by a taxing authority or an appeals conference. The term administrative proceeding does not include a criminal proceeding. As used herein, the term error includes any position, omission, or method of accounting that, at the time the return is filed, fails to meet the standards set out in Statement on **Standards for Tax Services** (SSTS) No. 1, Tax Return Positions. The term error also includes a position taken on a prior year's return that no longer meets these standards due to legislation, judicial decisions, or administrative pronouncements having retroactive effect. However, an error does not include an item that has an insignificant effect on the taxpayer's tax liability.

2. This Statement applies whether or not the member prepared or signed the return that contains the error. Special considerations may apply when a member has been engaged by legal counsel to provide assistance in a matter relating to the counsel's client.

STATEMENT

3. If a member is representing a taxpayer in an administrative proceeding with respect to a return that contains an error of which the member is aware, the member should inform the taxpayer promptly upon becoming aware of the error. The member should recommend the corrective measures to be taken. Such recommendation may be given orally. A member is neither obligated to inform the taxing authority nor allowed to do so without the taxpayer's permission, except where required by law.

4. A member should request the taxpayer's agreement to disclose the error to the taxing authority. Lacking such agreement, the member should consider whether to withdraw from representing the taxpayer in the administrative proceeding and whether to continue a professional or employment relationship with the taxpayer.

EXPLANATION

5. When the member is engaged to represent the taxpayer before a taxing authority in an administrative proceeding with respect to a return containing an error of which the member is aware, the member should advise the taxpayer to disclose the error to the taxing authority. Such recommendation may be given orally. If the member believes that the taxpayer could be charged with fraud or other criminal misconduct, the taxpayer should be advised to consult legal counsel before taking any action.

6. It is the taxpayer's responsibility to decide whether to correct the

error. If the taxpayer does not correct an error, a member should consider whether to withdraw from representing the taxpayer in the administrative proceeding and whether to continue a professional or employment relationship with the taxpayer. While recognizing that the taxpayer may not be required by statute to correct an error by filing an amended return, a member should consider whether a taxpayer's decision not to file an amended return may predict future behavior that might require termination of the relationship. Moreover, a member should consider consulting with his or her own legal counsel before deciding on recommendations to the taxpayer and whether to continue a professional or employment relationship with the taxpayer. The potential for violating Code of Professional Conduct Rule 301 (relating to the member's confidential client relationship), the tax law and regulations, laws on privileged communications, potential adverse impact on a taxpayer of a member's withdrawal, and other considerations may create a conflict between the member's interests and those of the taxpayer.

7. Once disclosure is agreed on, it should not be delayed to such a degree that the taxpayer or member might be considered to have failed to act in good faith or to have, in effect, provided misleading information. In any event, disclosure should be made before the conclusion of the administrative proceeding.

8. Whether an error has an insignificant effect on the taxpayer's tax liability is left to the professional judgment of the member based on all the facts and circumstances known to the member. In judging whether an erroneous method of accounting has more than an insignificant effect, a member should consider the method's cumulative effect and its effect on the return that is the subject of the administrative proceeding.

Statement on Standards for Tax Services No. 8, Form and Content of Advice to Taxpayers

INTRODUCTION

1. This Statement sets forth the applicable standards for members concerning certain aspects of providing advice to a taxpayer and considers the circumstances in which a member has a responsibility to communicate with a taxpayer when subsequent developments affect advice previously provided. The Statement does not, however, cover a member's responsibilities when the expectation is that the advice rendered is likely to be relied on by parties other than the taxpayer.

STATEMENT

2. A member should use judgment to ensure that tax advice provided to a taxpayer reflects professional competence and appropriately serves the taxpayer's needs. A member is not required to follow a standard format or guidelines in communicating written or oral advice to a taxpayer.

3. A member should assume that tax advice provided to a taxpayer will affect the manner in which the matters or transactions considered would be reported on the taxpayer's tax returns. Thus, for all tax advice given to a taxpayer, a member should follow the standards in Statement on **Standards for Tax Services** (SSTS) No. 1, Tax Return Positions.

4. A member has no obligation to communicate with a taxpayer when subsequent developments affect advice previously provided with respect to significant matters, except while assisting a taxpayer in implementing procedures or plans associated with the advice provided or when a member undertakes this obligation by specific agreement.

EXPLANATION

5. Tax advice is recognized as a valuable service provided by members. The form of advice may be oral or written and the subject matter may range from routine to complex. Because the range of advice is so extensive and because advice should meet the specific needs of a taxpayer, neither a standard format nor guidelines for communicating or documenting advice to the taxpayer can be established to cover all situations.

6. Although oral advice may serve a taxpayer's needs appropriately in routine matters or in well-defined areas, written communications are recommended in important, unusual, or complicated transactions. The member may use professional judgment about whether, subsequently, to document oral advice in writing.

7. In deciding on the form of advice provided to a taxpayer, a member should exercise professional judgment and should consider such factors as the following:

a. The importance of the transaction and amounts involved.

b. The specific or general nature of the taxpayer's inquiry.

c. The time available for development and submission of the advice.

d. The technical complications presented.

e. The existence of authorities and precedents.

f. The tax sophistication of the taxpayer.

g. The need to seek other professional advice.

8. A member may assist a taxpayer in implementing procedures or plans associated with the advice offered. When providing such assistance, the member should review and revise such advice as warranted by new developments and factors affecting the transaction.

9. Sometimes a member is requested to provide tax advice but does not assist in implementing the plans adopted. Although such developments as legislative or administrative changes or future judicial interpretations may affect the advice previously provided, a member cannot be expected to communicate subsequent developments that affect such advice unless the member undertakes this obligation by specific agreement with the taxpayer.

10. Taxpayers should be informed that advice reflects professional judgment based on an existing situation and that subsequent developments could affect previous professional advice. Members may use precautionary language to the effect that their advice is based on facts as stated and authorities that are subject to change.

11. In providing tax advice, a member should be cognizant of applicable confidentiality privileges.

These Statements on **Standards for Tax Services** and Interpretation were unanimously adopted by the assenting votes of the twenty voting members of the twenty-one-member Tax Executive Committee.

Tax Executive Committee (1999–2000)
David A. Lifson (Chair); Pamela J. Pecarich (Vice Chair); Ward M. Bukofsky; Joseph Cammarata; Stephen R. Corrick; Anna C. Fowler; Jill Gansler; Diane P. Herndon; Ronald S. Katch; Allan I. Kruger; Susan W. Martin; Jeffrey A. Porter; Thomas J. Purcell, III; Jeffrey L. Raymon; Frederick H. Rothman; Barry D. Roy; Jane T. Rubin; Douglas P. Stives; Philip J. Wiesner; Claude R. Wilson, Jr.; Robert A. Zarzar.

SRTP Enforceability Task Force
J. Edwards Swails (Chair); Alan R. Einhorn; John C. Gardner, Ronald S. Katch; Michael E. Mares; Dan L. Mandelson; Daniel A. Noakes; William C. Potter.

AICPA Staff
Gerald W. Padwe (Vice President, Taxation); Edward S. Karl (Director, Taxation).

The AICPA gratefully acknowledges the contributions of William A. Tate, Jean L. Rothbarth, and Leonard Podolin, former chairs of the Responsibilities in Tax Practice Committee; A. M. (Tony) Komlyn and Wilber Van Scoik, former members of the Committee; and Carol B. Ferguson, AICPA Technical Manager.

Note: Statements on **Standards for Tax Services** are issued by the Tax Executive Committee, the senior technical body of the Institute designated to promulgate standards of tax practice. Rules 201 and 202 of the Institute's Code of Professional Conduct require compliance with these standards.

Index